OPPORTUNITY
AND THE FAMILY

OPPORTUNITY

AND THE FAMILY

by John H. Scanzoni

THE FREE PRESS · NEW YORK

COLLIER-MACMILLAN LIMITED · LONDON

Collier-Macmillan Canada Ltd., Toronto, Ontario

Library of Congress Catalog Card Number: 70-84935

printing number
1   2   3   4   5   6   7   8   9   10

CONTENTS

Contents

OPPORTUNITY
AND THE FAMILY

PREFACE

THE FOLLOWING PAGES REPRESENT AN ATTEMPT TO FULFILL SEVERAL related objectives. First and foremost, the book seeks to contribute to the development of systematic sociological theory. To avoid what has been called the "curious ambiguity surrounding the word *theory*," we shall define it in the following terms and seek to follow this definition.

Theory [is] a set of assumptions or postulates with which one approaches some part of the empirical world, a set of concepts in terms of which this part of the world is described, and a set of propositions emerging from the assumptions and relating to concepts about the way this part of the world "works" which are checked against observations of that world.[1]

Although there is considerable data in the chapters that follow, they are ordered on the basis of what is hoped to be a consistent theoretical framework. From this framework hypotheses are derived and tested, conclusions are drawn, and propositions are available for verification in later research.

The substantive area under investigation here is the conjugal family in modern society. But the theoretical questions posed in this study (see Chapter One) have wider significance than simply this area alone. Critics have charged that this field of sociology has been particularly remiss in the development of systematic theory. It is likely that this indictment applies with equal force to most areas of sociological endeavor. In any event, a further objective of this book is to describe and to analyze the conjugal family in meaningful theoretical fashion. No claim is made that what follows is the only way to apprehend the structure and process of this complex social unit. But it is *a* way that draws on varied sociological perspectives in an effort to tap the major strengths of each.

For example, we draw heavily on the structural-functional school at several points. Specifically, it is argued that the main structural tie of the conjugal family to the larger society is through the economic system, in

[1] Sheldon Stryker, "The Interactional and Situational Approaches," in Harold T. Christensen, ed., *Handbook of Marriage and the Family*, Chicago: Rand McNally and Co., 1964, p. 127.

1

particular through the occupation of the husband-father. The point is made repeatedly that the status of all family members is dependent on his occupation, and that the nature of the husband's occupation has important consequences for all members of the conjugal unit. Moreover, from this perspective, stress is laid on the conjugal unit qua unit—as a social system in transaction with several subsystems of the larger society, in this case, the economic system in particular.

Yet one of our objectives is to deal with process as well as structure, and so we draw on the interactionist tradition as well. In fact, in Chapter One, we make explicit our effort to try to synthesize some elements of the functionalist and interactionist schools—at least within the sphere of the conjugal family. From the interactionist tradition, notions are employed such as definition of the situation, significant other, self-esteem, and perception of and evaluation of primary relations. The effort at synthesis is based on the assumption that linkages to the larger society significantly influence interaction between members of the conjugal unit. Still another sociological perspective we shall utilize to help explain this linkage has been variously called *exchange theory* or *reciprocity theory*. In addition, we shall try to consider a classic matter in sociological thought, viz., the question of order-disorder, of cohesion and solidarity. This issue is one of the two or three central questions of sociology, and we shall address ourselves both to its pertinence within the conjugal family and to some of its broader implications as well.

The several perspectives just noted, plus the matter of cohesion, are interrelated within the context of a certain dominant cultural theme of our society, viz., the great stress placed on achievement and success. The argument is made that these all-pervasive "ascetic Protestant" orientations play a central role in both structure and process within the conjugal unit, and are thus essential to our analysis. It has often been noted that the conjugal family is a basic unit of consumption in our society, but the theoretical implications of this assumption have been only minimally explored. To consume, there must be resources. Resources imply some effort at their production. Therefore, consumption ultimately depends on "success" in these production efforts. In other words, it is not merely that the family is a consumption unit, it is also inextricably linked to the production sphere, the sphere of occupational achievements and attainments. Our underlying thesis is that there are important linkages between the "achievement-success syndrome" of our society and the conjugal family; and a major objective, therefore, is to identify some of these linkages and to spell out their implications.

Detailed description of the theoretical schema, plus an extensive rationale for it, are presented in Chapter One. That chapter also sets forth the overall plan of the book and some of the methodological details connected with the study. Additional methodological information and data are to be found in Appendixes A and B.

Grateful acknowledgment is made to the Institute of Social Research at Indiana University under whose auspices the study was carried out. Financial aid to support the project came from the Institute, Indiana University, and the National Science Foundation. In an extensive project of this sort, one finds himself deeply indebted to many people. To single out some is inevitably to leave out others. But the study could never have been completed without the generous cooperation of Michael Schwartz, Acting Director of the Institute during the period of this study. Many thanks are due to the research assistants who participated in preparation of the interview schedule, in data collection and in coding: Marlene Simon, Veronica Elias, Paul Planchon, Ann Boone. Thanks are also in order to those graduate students who participated in the interviewing process. The work of James Landy was invaluable during the stage of data-processing and analysis. The writer is especially grateful to Sheldon Stryker for his careful scrutiny of the total manuscript prior to publication. His criticisms and suggestions for changes contributed significantly to whatever merit the final product contains. Finally, the writer is indebted to his wife Letha for manuscript editing, typing, and useful suggestions to enhance clarity and readability. Nevertheless, in spite of all this generous assistance in preparing the volume, the writer accepts full responsibility for whatever flaws and shortcomings yet remain.

J.S.

CHAPTER

ONE

•

The
Theoretical
Overview

INVESTIGATIONS OF THE FAMILY REPRESENT A LONG-STANDING TRADITION
in social science. The beginnings can be traced to the nineteenth-century
British anthropologists and their voluminous studies of the kinship systems
of primitive societies. If one wishes to venture outside the bounds of social
science and into social philosophy, he can discover a continuous thread of
concern with family structure all the way back to Plato and even beyond.
In this century, sociologists have examined the family in the context not
so much of primitive but of industrial society.

The earliest conclusions regarding relationships of these kinds were
grim indeed. "Industrialism brought with it the factory system of production . . . it drew women into industry, destroyed the unity of the home,
and brought the family to a rapid ruin." [1] What men like Calverton and
others perceived was the contrast between what seemed to them the idyllic
existence of the rural American family system and the illegitimacy, divorce,
and delinquency of the city slums. Cowper's phrase, "God made the
country, but man made the city," expressed the contempt that many held
for what they thought industrial society was doing to the family.

By way of contrast, the current emphasis in modern sociology is to

[1] W. F. Calverton, *The Bankruptcy of Marriage*, New York: The Macaulay
Company, 1928, p. 34.

4

shy away from a priori assumptions pertaining to the family or to any other social structure. On the contrary, much theory and research is devoted to the proposition that although the structure of the family has changed considerably during the last eight or nine decades, these changes or adaptations have in fact enabled it to survive more adequately in the midst of great upheavals in other parts of society. There is general consensus that one of the most evident of these changes has to do with the relationships between the family and the economic system. In the days when our society was predominantly agricultural and rural, there existed intimate and powerful bonds between family and farming pursuits. Thinking in terms of the ideal-type, every member of the family had some meaningful chore to perform—meaningful in that what he did contributed in a very real sense to family survival and well-being. This was especially true, of course, of the father, who cultivated, planted, and harvested on land immediately adjacent to his domicile. But it was equally true of the mother, who fed the father three or often four times per day, maintained a family vegetable garden, and sometimes assisted him in his labor. Likewise, the numerous offspring performed their essential tasks under the direction of or else in direct interaction with one or both parents.

The extensiveness of behavioral interdependence among family members in an economic situation of this kind is evident and striking. There was great need for one another, and there were adequate rewards—both material and affectional—for conformity to expected behavior patterns. With the rise of the modern industrial and business complex, however, and the corresponding growth of the large metropolis, fewer and fewer families remained locked in this type of economic interdependence. Today, in the majority of American families, the father works away from the household, and mother and children rarely contribute economically in direct association with him. When they do contribute, they usually do so through separate activities that are distinct from the household and from other family members. Thus, at the level of shared production behaviors, economic interdependence within the family has been replaced by economic independence.

Looking at the same situation from the perspective of the larger society, it has often been said that the family has "lost" its function of economic production for society. No longer is one of its chief tasks the production of agricultural assets for itself as well as for surplus to be sold. It simply does not do this any more. Instead, its individual members are diffused throughout nonagricultural production units. Previously, there existed a "simple" social structure—a family-based, agricultural-economic unit. With the advent of modernization, differentiation has occurred, the result now being two distinct and complex subsystems emerging from what was formerly more unitary and "simple" in structure. The degree, if any, to which the economic-occupational structure and the conjugal family system are believed to relate to or influence one another varies among sociologists. There are perhaps two broad identifiable perspectives, although several variations are to be found within each major grouping.

Bell and Vogel describe the first perspective in these terms, somewhat overdrawn:

> This approach minimized the importance of social structure by its concentration on the attitudes of individual members, and obscured the organic unity of the family as a group . . . unity was recognized only at the psychological level . . . these studies were usually approached from the older standpoint of the adjustment and happiness of individual family members, or of individual families . . . there was no attempt to treat systematically the relationship between the family and external social systems.[2]

In other words, this perspective puts only minimal stress on systematic linkages between the emergent economic and family subsystems. Instead, the focus is chiefly on interpersonal relations within the conjugal family per se.

Bell and Vogel describe the second perspective as one in which "there has been an increasing interest in . . . trying to develop new and more general conceptualizations of the family . . . there have been a number of studies that have attempted to treat the family as a social system, and that are concerned with the relationships between the family's structure and functioning and external systems. . . ."[3] In terms of Hill and Hansen's classification of approaches to family research, the first may generally be described as the "interactionist approach," the second as the "structural-functional."[4] Researchers in the second tradition see a particularly significant linkage between the two emergent subsystems, viz., the economic and the kinship. In all fairness, however, it must be observed that many researchers currently working within the interactionist school clearly recognize the theoretical problems raised by Bell and Vogel and are also searching for "new and more general conceptualizations of the family." Many of those most active in the development of systematic social theory with respect to contemporary kinship patterns would in fact be found chiefly within the interactionist framework.[5]

2 Norman W. Bell and Ezra F. Vogel, "Toward a Framework for Functional Analysis of Family Behavior," in Norman W. Bell and Ezra F. Vogel, eds., *A Modern Introduction to the Family,* New York: The Free Press, 1960, p. 5.
3 *Ibid.*
4 Reuben Hill and Donald A. Hansen, "The Identification of Conceptual Frameworks Utilized in Family Study," *Marriage and Family Living,* 22 (November 1960), pp. 299–311.
5 For example, see Reuben Hill, "Contemporary Developments in Family Theory," *Journal of Marriage and the Family,* 28 (February 1966), pp. 10–25; John Mogey, "Contemporary Developments in Family Theory: A Discussion," *ibid.,* pp. 26–28; Sheldon Stryker, "The Interactional and Situational Approaches," in

In short, it is futile to argue for the greater validity of one approach as against the other. A case can be made in fact that what Bell and Vogel call *transaction* between the economic and family systems is theoretically inseparable from interaction between family members. In the remainder of their book, this sometimes inevitably comes through. And in a subsequently published study that Vogel did in Japan, in which the data is organized in terms of his earlier model, the transaction-interaction bridge is even more apparent. For instance, in describing why husband-wife companionship has little significance to the modern Japanese, he argues that loyalty to work group and work mates supersedes this particular type of conjugal interaction.[6] In short, if we cut away common-sense notions of "adjustment," "happiness," and so on, and focus instead on "problems of general theory," there is good reason to argue for a synthesis of the structure-function (transaction) and the interaction approaches.

To begin with, Greenfield, drawing on R. T. Smith, describes the functionalist position quite succinctly:

Occupational roles are generally performed by men, with women and children essentially outside, or marginal to, the system. The family ties the women and children to the larger society because the male provides it with money earned in the occupational system. The family then is a subsystem that is articulated with the larger society because the adult males are members of both the family and the occupational system simultaneously. . . . Thus the role of the adult male is vital to the family. To comply with this role expectation he must obtain a position in the occupational system that provides both prestige and sufficient income for the family.[7]

The key idea here is Greenfield's notion of "articulation" of the family with the economic system. There is an overlap or linkage between the economic and conjugal systems mediated through the husband's occupation. Conditions surrounding this structural overlap have consequences (functions) for intraconjugal interaction. Greenfield's idea of articulation goes beyond Bell and Vogel's idea of mere transactions. It makes clear that there is a definite structural interdependence between the two subsystems. The resultant intraconjugal interaction that interested both Smith and Greenfield was the development of the matrifocal family—for Smith in British Guiana, for Greenfield in Barbados. What they conclude is obviously pertinent to the American Negro lower-class matrifocal situation as well. "Matrifocality develops within the family as a result of the male's inability to obtain a position in the occupational system that will provide him with

Harold T. Christensen, ed., *Handbook of Marriage and the Family*, Chicago: Rand McNally and Co., 1964, pp. 125–170.

[6] Ezra F. Vogel, *Japan's New Middle Class*, Berkeley, Calif.: University of California Press, 1963, pp. 102 ff.

[7] Sidney M. Greenfield, *English Rustics in Black Skin*, New Haven, Conn.: College and University Press, 1966, p. 24.

the prestige and adequate income which are his prime obligations to his family." [8] Second, Smith himself concludes: "We further argue that there is a correlation between the nature of the husband-father role and the role of men in the economic system and in the system of social stratification in the total Guianese society. Men, in their role of husband-father, are placed in a position where neither their social status nor their access to, and command of economic resources are of major importance in the functioning of the household group. . . ." [9]

The theoretical implications of their conclusions, particularly Smith's regarding the "correlation" of the male's economic and familial roles, carry beyond the emergence of the matrifocal pattern per se. For example, there is much evidence (from census data and sample surveys) that divorce and class position within the society as a whole are inversely related.[10] Furthermore, even among those currently married, "satisfaction," "happiness," "adjustment," and so on, are known to relate directly to class position.[11]

Over a decade ago, Goode offered a tentative explanation for the direct linkage of class position and marital stability. In a recent statement of his earlier position he writes:

. . . most families feel that their income is insufficient. The responsibility for satisfying these desires rests primarily with the husband, and any failure is his failure. At the same time, almost every study of job satisfaction shows that men in jobs with greater responsibility and prestige enjoy those jobs more than men in lower-ranking jobs enjoy theirs. Thus, both job satisfaction and economic reward point to a similar possibility: that there is more socioeconomic dissatisfaction in the lower strata, and thus possibly more marital tension from this source. Just as personality problems can be displaced onto economic factors within a marriage, so too may economic strains be displaced onto noneconomic relationships, such as sex and marital adjustment.[12]

Whether intended or not, the use of the term "displacement" carries psychoanalytic implications. It often refers, for example, to the transfer of an emotion from the object about which it was originally experienced

8 *Ibid.*, p. 25.

9 Quoted in *ibid.*, p. 25. Originally from Raymond T. Smith, *The Negro Family in British Guiana,* London: Routledge and Kegan Paul, 1956.

10 George Levinger, "Marital Cohesiveness and Dissolution: An Integrative Review," *Journal of Marriage and the Family,* 27 (February 1965), pp. 19–28.

11 See Robert F. Winch, *The Modern Family,* New York: Holt, Rinehart and Winston, Inc., 1963 (rev.), p. 713. The argument we develop in this chapter and throughout the book is quite similar to that advanced by Winch. He argues that increased economic and status resources infused into the family increase *both* its *stability* and the *happiness* of its members.

12 William J. Goode, "Family Disorganization," in Robert K. Merton and Robert A. Nisbet, eds., *Contemporary Social Problems,* New York: Harcourt, Brace and World, Inc., 1966 (rev.), p. 510. His earlier statement appeared in *After Divorce,* New York: The Free Press, 1956, p. 63.

to another object or person. The notion of displacement has apparently not been followed up in the sociological literature with reference to husband-wife relations. Although Murdock has argued that "marriage exists only when the economic and the sexual are united into one relationship," [13] there seems to have been little effort since Goode to investigate potential "displacement" of feelings or attitudes between these two dimensions of conjugal relationships.

A significant exception to this state of affairs appears in a discussion by Winch of marital "happiness" and stability. He suggests that the positive correlations of both types of variables with greater social status are due to the rewards and resources inherent in higher status.[14] Winch, in short, seems to perceive the linkage of economic and expressive conjugal elements as explicable at the level of interlocking reward elements. We shall have much more to say about this notion in the remainder of the book. For now, suffice it to note that Winch's formulation is an attempt to link theoretically these dimensions of conjugal relationships.

Edwards, on the other hand, indicates that some sociologists do not want to see any overlap. He notes that some take a value position that particularism *should* pervade the conjugal family—that universalistic criteria based on achievement and success should not, that they do harm to interpersonal relations. Nevertheless, in spite of their value position, Edwards claims that an overlap—a displacement—does in fact take place.

The point is, rather, that the prospect of quantified rewards has become so pervasive in our society that it permeates virtually all social relationships including those between husband and wife and the progeny . . . we are conditioned, primarily as a result of the pervasiveness of our economic institutions, to react to situations in a manner designed to elicit rewards. When the potential of tangible rewards is absent, interaction tends to be halting and random . . . the prominence of affective behavior in familial relationships as an ideal appears to be a central support for the continuance of these relationships. Still, just how important affective behavior will remain for individuals and how well these needs will be met in the family stand as primary issues in family research . . . given the current preeminence of economic orientations in our value system, *the marital union and family are becoming more highly interdependent with the economic sphere* [italics supplied].[15]

Parsons states that *universalistic* role expectations are "derived from the validity of a set of existential ideas, or the generality of a normative

[13] George Peter Murdock, *Social Structure*, New York: The Free Press, 1949, p. 8.
[14] Robert F. Winch, *loc. cit.*
[15] John N. Edwards, "The Future of the Family Revisited," *Journal of Marriage and the Family*, 29 (August 1967), pp. 508–11.

rule." *Particularistic* role expectations are based on the "cathectic significance of an object or of the status of the object in a relational system." [16] In the family, for example, it is held by many that primary relations are supposed to be cultivated simply because actors stand in a particular group relationship to each other, viz., husband, wife, parent, child, sibling. Edwards, however, is suggesting that primary relations may also come to be influenced by certain universalistic standards, *i.e.*, criteria or "normative rules" that apply equally to all members of the society—in this case, universalistic criteria based on achievement and success.

There are at least two historical threads that help explain why some social scientists and laymen might be prone to take an ideological position regarding the "evils" of pervasive and "creeping universalism" in the family. First and perhaps most pervasive is the mysterious "romantic love complex." Although composed of numerous elements, its central theme is the power of "love." "Love" (undefined) in romantic thought is the supposed supreme independent variable that has the potential to bind husbands and wives together in spite of every conceivable threat to solidarity. Whoever heard of a popular song praising a love object for his capabilities for achievement and success? If anything, these sorts of universalistic notions are downgraded in popular lore as being unworthy of "true love."

Yet, as Waller so shrewdly pointed out many years ago, there are definite elements of "rating" involved in courtship that are based on other than particularistic person-oriented characteristics. Why should not some of these universalistic criteria carry over into marriage and perhaps play an even more important role over the years as romantic passions tend to lessen? Why should it be assumed that marriage suddenly marks the end of universalistic-type evaluations, and *ipso facto* signals the onset solely of particularistic type interaction?

A second tradition is based solidly in Judaeo-Christian-Humanist thought, viz., the preeminence of person qua person, apart from ascribed characteristics over which he has no control, and apart from achievements and material objects. Many observers of the social scene note the lack of "personhood" in modern society, and hold up the family as the one remaining structure where impersonality and manipulation are replaced by personal acceptance and "humanness." Geiger, for example, contends "that modern society makes people lonely, and the family, especially companionate marriage, reduces this painful-experience." [17]

Setting aside for the time being the difficulties engendered by these orientations, let us continue to elaborate the earlier point that the articula-

[16] Talcott Parsons, *The Social System,* New York: The Free Press, 1951, p. 62.
[17] H. Kent Geiger, ed., *Comparative Perspectives on Marriage and the Family,* Boston: Little, Brown and Company, 1968, p. xxv.

tion idea has significance beyond explanation of the matrifocal family form. Thinking of our earlier discussion, we may say that the matrifocal family is the result of the husband's being almost totally blocked from the *opportunity structure*. This important construct appears often in this study and was probably used initially by Cloward and Ohlin, although they in turn drew heavily on Merton for its derivation.[18] Cloward and Ohlin used this suggestive term to describe access or opportunity to the means to learn how to perform in the economic system—for example, education. They also used it to refer to access or opportunity to actual performance of valued occupational roles, with the end in view that this performance would enable one to gain access or have opportunity to display material symbols of success.

It is in this last sense of opportunity or access to visible success that Mizruchi has enlarged the notion considerably.[19] Basically, therefore, the term *opportunity structure*—or more broadly, *economic opportunity structure*—is a means-ends construct. The ends or goals are symbols of success and status; the symbols are often material or physical, but they may be based on prestige and power as well. The means to these valued ends include education, plus attainment of and achievement within occupations that will make the ends more readily accessible. Analytically, it is possible to distinguish these several notions from one another, but in the "real world" they are all of a package. Nonetheless, we will continue to make the basic distinction, and to think of the economic opportunity structure as a complex system of means and achievement, plus an equally intricate system of goals, ends, and success.

Now in contrast to the matrifocal family form where the husband is only rarely employed, in most conjugal families in the United States the husband is employed on a regular basis. There are, however, different degrees of articulation or integration or interdependence of the family with the opportunity structure. If we follow Greenfield's notion that articulation takes place through the occupation of the husband, we may say that all husbands have either more or less access than some others to the opportunity structure—to valued means and to valued ends. Another way to put the same thing is to conceptualize the opportunity structure as a system of highly valued rewards. In this more general sense, both means and ends are valued and sought-after rewards that are parceled out by the society, but not equally to all members. Levels of achievement and success—levels of rewards—vary systematically in our society.

The greater the level of achievement and/or success, the more rewards

[18] Richard A. Cloward and Lloyd E. Ohlin, *Delinquency and Opportunity*, New York: The Free Press, 1960, pp. 148 ff.

[19] Ephraim H. Mizruchi, *Success and Opportunity*, New York: The Free Press, 1964.

one is reaping from the opportunity structure, and the more one may be said to be a part of this system—which is to say, to be articulated or integrated with it. The chronically unemployed male possesses little or no achievement or success—he is not reaping any of the rewards of the opportunity structure, hence may be said to have little or no articulation with it. But just "above" this level, certain husbands have gained greater achievement and success—more rewards from the opportunity system— and thus may be described as having greater articulation with it than those "below" them. And so on for increased levels of achievement and success. Furthermore, as Durkheim noted years ago, there is no ceiling in modern society on reward aspirations.[20] There is no point at which one may be said to possess the maximum possible level of achievement and success. The potentials and possible rewards of the opportunity structure are in this sense "boundless."

Achievement and success (the difference between these notions will be elaborated shortly) in our society are measured in this study in an objective fashion by three "standard measures": occupational status, education, and income. These are objective in the sense that they involve attainments and / or associated behaviors, the meanings of which are defined in more or less common and widely held fashion. For example, a corporation executive with an M.A., making $100,000 per annum, is commonly held to be more successful than a janitor with six years of grade school earning $3,600. It is these kinds of indicators that have been commonly associated inversely with the expressive dimension of husband-wife interaction.

But achievement and success can also be conceived of in a subjective sense, specifically in terms of the twin notions of *alienation* and *anomie*. The definitions and measurements of these constructs appears in Chapter Two. The point here is that achievement and success are "mental states and feelings," as well as being objectively "out there." For instance, it is theoretically possible that our executive does not feel he has achieved well, does not feel he has actually succeeded. We may say, in other words, that he feels alienated from the opportunity structure, or that he feels anomic regarding it.

Likewise, our janitor could theoretically feel that he has achieved very well, that he is eminently successful—he does not feel alienated at all. We would expect, however, that both such occurrences would be "deviant" cases, that for most people there is a correlation of objective conditions and subjective feeling states. The point is that integration into or articulation with the opportunity structure can be viewed both "objectively" and "subjectively." We propose using the three "standard measures" as measures of objective integration into the opportunity structure, and alienation and anomie as indicants of subjective integration or articulation. And the

[20] Cited in Cloward and Ohlin, *op. cit.,* p. 82.

significance of the actual level of integration can be ascertained from the following proposition: the greater is the degree of articulation or integration (objective and subjective) of the conjugal family into the opportunity structure, the greater is the probability of the cohesion of the conjugal family.

Levinger argues that "marital cohesiveness is analogous to group cohesiveness and can be defined accordingly. Group cohesiveness is 'the total field of forces which act on members to remain in the group.' . . . Thus the strength of the marital relationship would be a direct function of the attractions within and barriers around the marriage, and an inverse function of such attractions and barriers from other relationships." [21] Cohesion then is made up of feelings of solidarity and integration resulting from a finite number of relevant forces. In this volume we will necessarily concentrate on only a segment of these forces. While certain psychological variables are included in the analysis, our framework consists chiefly of sociological and social psychological factors. It must be left to a later study to "plug in" additional needed psychological variables, as well as other pertinent social forces.

Cohesion will be viewed as a construct and will have as its prime indicants satisfaction with and evaluation of expressive interaction and also authority relations between husbands and wives. A question that naturally arises here is why look at evaluations of married partners? Are we then not reverting back to notions of "marital adjustment"? The answer to the second question is *no*, because of the answer to the first. And that has to do with Levinger's description of group cohesion in general, which he draws from the work of Festinger and his colleagues.

For whether we approve or not, the modern conjugal family is characterized by freedom and individualism. People marry in order to gain and maintain certain satisfactions from this kind of social situation. But like any other social situation, if it fails to remain attractive, there is a tendency for cohesion to wither, for solidarity to decrease. This can be true in relative degrees even if the group per se does not formally dissolve. Cohesion may thus vary among those currently married because they define (and thus to them it is real) their situations as either *more* or *less* attractive or satis-

---

[21] Levinger, *op. cit.*, p. 19. It is obvious that there must be a "balance" between these external and internal factors, *a balance defined by the couple itself.* In terms of the above hypothesis, for example, a husband could be so highly articulated into the economic opportunity system (as, for instance, a corporation executive) that the job attractions are so great, the family attractions become minimal. Thus, cohesion could be threatened. Sect clergy provide an example of husbands so highly involved with their occupation that the family holds little attraction—yet their wives are not resentful. See John Scanzoni, "Resolution of Occupational-Conjugal Role Conflict in Clergy Marriages," *Journal of Marriage and the Family,* 27 (August 1965), pp. 396–402.

factory. In effect, we are raising the theoretical issue regarding some of the conditions under which marital cohesion is either reinforced or else decreased. And we are attempting to explore this issue through means of a synthesis of structural and social-psychological factors.

The next question that arises pertains to the rationale for the proposition offered above. Why should we expect it to be valid? We know already, of course, that in terms of "objective" indicators, it has some proved validity.[22] But why should this be so? This, of course, takes us back to Goode's notion of displacement. The less "success" one possesses—whether objective or subjective—the more negative one feels about this, and the more these negative feelings tend to be "transferred" on to the expressive components of the conjugal unit, or primary interaction between husbands and wives.

It could be argued that "the 'stable personality' will not be affected by . . . economic strains . . . or by any others . . . while the immature will complain of economic factors in the marriage when the 'real trouble' is emotional." [23] What the role of personality is in the functioning of *any* social system is not totally clear, and this applies to the conjugal family system as well. Though personality factors are obviously important, it would be patently inaccurate to trace the functioning of social systems to those factors alone. In this study, the focus is on *structural* and *interactional* factors that impinge on the family, irrespective of individual personalities.[24] Furthermore, we are also concerned with what is very likely the dominant cultural theme of our society, viz., orientations toward achievement and success. This too pervades the modern conjugal family. Recourse solely to personality factors overlooks in particular the pervasiveness of this theme. That achievement and success are a dominant theme in the culture of Western society has long characterized the theory of many influential sociologists from Max Weber to the present. Therefore, in adddition to our focus on structural and interactional factors, we must consider this central cultural orientation as well.

To begin to examine its effect on the conjugal family, we need to look carefully at one aspect of Weber's conception of *ascetic Protestantism.* Weber argued that the thrust of the Lutheran branch of the Reformation stressed the doctrine of *sola fide,* or salvation by faith without any necessary works or evidence of salvation. The Calvinist-Pietist branch, on the other hand (the branch that most influenced the English and American value system, according to Weber), stressed the *"certitudo saludis* in the sense of

22 Levinger, *op. cit.*

23 Goode, *op. cit.,* 1956, pp. 62–63.

24 Winch, *op. cit.,* p. 712, remarks that "very little has been found in the way of personality traits that are consistent predictors of marital felicity or stabiliy. . . . [Yet, to conclude] that personality makes no difference in the marital relationship . . . seems contrary to common sense."

the recognizability of the state of grace [which] necessarily became of absolutely dominant importance." [25] He continues that this "recognizability" was used to judge whether or not a person could be admitted to communion and full fellowship in the church. In short, his spiritual "worthiness" and "respectability" were judged by significant others within his religious group.

And by what means might others judge him as "worthy"? Weber argues that this occurred chiefly through "worldly activity"—works of piety and devotion. Eventually over a long period of time, economic success came to be viewed as an important sign of God's calling and blessing. This was mutually recognized by those "so blessed," as well as by others within his particular reference group or circle of significant others. Weber quotes John Wesley himself as saying that "religion must necessarily produce both industry and frugality, and these cannot but produce riches." Weber then comments that "a specifically bourgeois economic ethic had grown up. With the consciousness of standing in the fullness of God's grace and being *visibly blessed by* Him, the . . . business man . . . could follow his pecuniary interests . . . [italics supplied]." [26]

Wilensky rightly points out that it was not "ascetic Protestantism" alone that made work central to the evaluation of persons in modern society. As Western society became increasingly secularized, the notion that economic activity was related to transcendental factors diminished significantly.[27] But the linkage of economic activity and personal worth remained. It persisted and indeed was accentuated because, as Wilensky says, "The Protestant Ethic merged with a melange of doctrines . . . *e.g.*, mercantilist abomination of 'idle and unprofitable persons,' the rationalism of the Enlightenment, the 'survival of the fittest' notions of social Darwinists . . . , the laissez-faire liberalism of American captains of industry." [28] He goes on to say, "Since the Greeks expressed their scorn for toil, the doctrines have shifted drastically. Anchored in religious orthodoxy, work became a duty or an expiation for sin; freed from religion it became important for its own sake, the nucleus of the Renaissance image of man as creator, and by the nineteenth century almost a secular religion." [29]

He further argues that "despite talk of the leisure-oriented society, and in the face of affluence for the majority, modern populations remain busy— with some groups becoming busier." His extensive cross-national data on

25 Max Weber, *The Protestant Ethic and the Spirit of Capitalism*, New York: Charles Scribner's Sons, 1958 edition, pp. 110 ff. Translated by Talcott Parsons in 1931, first published in 1905.

26 *Op. cit.*, pp. 175–77.

27 Harold L. Wilensky, "Work As a Social Problem," in Howard S. Becker, ed., *Social Problems: A Modern Approach*, New York: John Wiley & Sons, Inc., 1966, pp. 121–22. Taken from Wilensky's forthcoming book, *Work, Leisure, and Freedom*.

28 *Ibid.*, pp. 122–23.

29 *Ibid.*, p. 125.

several Western countries including the United States, call into serious question the so-called "decline of the Protestant ethic." "The average man's gain in leisure has been exaggerated by selective comparison of gross daily or weekly averages in working hours with those of the 'take-off' period of rapid economic growth in England, France, and America—a time of blood-curdling schedules and conditions." [30] His data show a "growing minority of the urban labor force who usually work 55 hours a week or more." [31] Over the long haul, with more and more people (including women) going to college and becoming a part of the upper strata, there could be less rather than more leisure time available to many Americans. In fact, the one substantial segment of the population that has maximum volition regarding work—women—are working in ever-increasing numbers. This cuts their leisure considerably, because they still find themselves performing many traditional household tasks. In short, Wilensky contends the traditional (Protestant) work ethic is still with us and, what is more, it promises to remain viable for a long time to come.

As Robin Williams puts it, "American culture is marked by a central stress on personal achievement, especially secular occupational achievement. . . . The comparatively striking feature of American culture is its tendency to identify standards of personal excellence with competitive occupational achievement. In the pure type, the value attached to achievement does not comprehend the person as a whole, but only his accomplishments, emphasizing the objective results of his activity." [32] The "striking feature" of identifying "personal excellence" with achievement and success derives from an ascetic Protestant heritage and tradition. Husbands and wives, as members of the conjugal unit, do not escape the impact of the pervasive universalistic criteria surrounding definitions of "personal excellence." The question is how and why, and the displacement hypothesis provides us with a start, because it suggests that positive feelings associated with greater achievement and success in the task-oriented dimension "lap over," or are transferred on to, or help account for, positive feelings in the expressive dimension of the conjugal family. Although the displacement hypothesis describes something of the interpersonal processes involved here, it is admittedly vague. Fortunately, it is possible to go beyond it through utilizing a notion that has received increased attention by sociologists in recent years.

Rodman notes that "Heer has introduced exchange theory into the discussion of marital decision-making." [33] The basic idea (a refinement of

30 *Ibid.*

31 *Ibid.*

32 Robin M. Williams, Jr., *American Society,* New York: Alfred A. Knopf, Inc., 1960 (rev.), pp. 417–18.

33 Hyman Rodman, "Marital Power in France, Greece, Yugoslavia, and the United States," *Journal of Marriage and the Family,* 29 (May 1967), p. 322.

Blood and Wolfe's earlier notions) is the comparison of resources that the wife might earn within as opposed to outside the marriage. The more her husband provides within the marriage, therefore, the more likely he is to exercise greater power. Heer himself notes that the implicit bargaining and exchange involved might "seem to violate some of the tenets of the romantic love complex." [34] He is obviously being sensitive to the kinds of critics Edwards is responding to, *i.e.*, those who believe the universalistic and particularistic spheres should be kept separate within the conjugal unit.

The point is that some sociologists see exchange theory as a way of explaining certain aspects of husband-wife interaction. In this case, how the husband performs in the economic system is exchanged for a measure of power within the conjugal unit. Sussman has argued that exchange theory is also useful in understanding the maintenance of the kin network.

Numerous studies . . . [indicate] . . . that individuals engage in reciprocal acts because they expect to be rewarded; *i.e.*, receive some payoff. In the family field, in contrast, there pervades a certain alarm and fearfulness about talking so blatantly, because it is hard to believe that marital partners engage in activities that result in payoffs for themselves. Rather, we like to believe that individuals in a marriage relationship act according to some moral code which requires each partner to be completely "other" oriented. It becomes obvious to the serious student of social behavior that the kinds of interaction and reasons for such interaction which exist in one societal system must exist in all others.[35]

Sussman's cogent argument is quite adequate for those who might argue on ideological grounds per se that exchange theory is not appropriate for study of our family system. But his chief hypothesis is that reciprocity among the kin promotes maintenance of the kin network. What about maintenance of the conjugal unit itself? Gouldner states that the concept of reciprocity "provides new leverage for analysis of the central problems of sociological theory, namely, accounting for stability and instability in social systems." [36] Inasmuch as we are dealing with precisely this issue in terms of the conjugal unit, exchange theory and the notion of reciprocity could conceivably have theoretical application and thus explanatory power for this social system. Gouldner argues that

[34] David M. Heer, "The Measurement and Bases of Family Power: An Overview," *Marriage and Family Living*, 25 (May 1963), p. 138.

[35] Marvin B. Sussman, "Theoretical Bases for an Urban Kinship Network System," unpublished paper read at a meeting of the theory section, National Council on Family Relations, Oct. 29, 1966, Minneapolis, Minn. See also Winch, *op. cit.*, for what is essentially an application of exchange theory to the conjugal family.

[36] Alvin W. Gouldner, "The Norm of Reciprocity: A Preliminary Statement," *American Sociological Review*, 25 (April 1960), p. 162.

Reciprocity . . . connotes that *each* party has rights *and* duties . . . it would seem that there can be stable patterns of reciprocity *qua* exchange only insofar as *each* party has both rights and duties. In effect, then, reciprocity has its significance for *role systems* in that it tends to structure *each* role so as to include both rights and duties.[37]

Gouldner's application of reciprocity to stability of social systems goes beyond Parsons' stress that stability is based merely on role conformity, and asks why conformity persists. It persists because processes of reciprocity

. . . mobilize egoistic motivations and channel them into the maintenance of the social system . . . egoism can motivate one party to satisfy the expectations of the other, since by doing so he induces the latter to reciprocate and to satisfy his own. . . . The motivation for reciprocity stems not only from the sheer gratification which Alter receives from Ego but also from Alter's internalization of a specific norm of reciprocity which morally obliges him to give benefits to those from whom he has received them. In this respect, the *norm* of reciprocity is a concrete and special mechanism involved in the maintenance of any stable social system. . . . When one party benefits another, an obligation is generated. The recipient (Y) is now *indebted* to the donor (X) and remains so until he repays.[38]

But as soon as Y pays X the cycle commences all over again, and the reciprocal process goes on indefinitely. What is more, there are "mechanisms which induce people to *remain* socially indebted to each other and which *inhibit* their complete repayment."[39] There exists a "certain amount of ambiguity as to whether indebtedness has been repaid and, over time, generates uncertainty about who is in whose debt."[40] Reciprocity, furthermore, need not be equal either in amount or kind. Reciprocity engenders stability because it sets up a chain of enduring obligations and repayments within a system of roles in which *each* role contains both rights and duties.

The principle of reciprocity as exchange has long been observed within the kinship system in terms of the related issues of incest, illegitimacy, and mate selection. The names of Malinowski, Goode, Lévi-Strauss, Parsons, Kingsley Davis, and Merton are attached to this kind of work. Without attempting to summarize this literature in detail, we can nonetheless make two points: one, the norms governing incest, illegitimacy, and mate selection are essentially rules or expectations pertaining to forms of social exchange; two, as Merton remarks:

37 *Ibid.*, p. 169.
38 *Ibid.*, p. 173.
39 *Ibid.*, p. 175.
40 *Ibid.*

This does not at all imply that the exchange is necessarily the result of an explicit utilitarian calculus in which the contractants deliberately weigh the economic and social returns to be gained from the marriage. The event may be experienced by them as simply an affectional relationship, but this *psychic reaction is manifestly structured by the social organization* [italics supplied].[41]

We wish to go one step further and suggest that the exchange principle does not mysteriously vanish upon consummation of the marriage. It may very well continue to be a part of processes within the conjugal unit itself. The application of reciprocity as exchange to the conjugal family is presented graphically in Figure 1. Recalling that it is the husband's occupational role that is articulated with the economic system, and that the status and prestige of the wife and children are dependent on him, we must therefore start the chain of reasoning at Wd. Following the arrows we read:

1. The more positively the husband performs his economic *duties,* the more positively the wife defines her economic *rights* (status, prestige, income [Xr]) as being met.
2. The more (1) is true, the more positively she performs her instrumental household duties ([Xd], washing clothes, preparing meals, and so on, either doing them or seeing they are done), and the more positively the husband defines his instrumental household rights (Wr) being met.
3. The more positively the wife defines her economic rights (Xr) as being met, the more positively she performs her expressive duties (primary relations [Zd]).
4. The more (3) is true, the more the husband defines his expressive rights (Yr) as being met, and the more positively he performs his expressive duties (Yd).
5. *a.* The more (4) is true, the more the wife defines her expressive rights (Zr) being met.
   b. The more (5a) is true, the more motivated the wife is to perform her expressive duties (Zd).
6. The more each spouse defines his expressive and instrumental rights as being met, the more likely each is to experience feelings of gratification ("the sentiment of gratitude joins forces with the sentiment of rectitude and adds a safety-margin in the motivation to conformity" [42]) with each other and with the system or situation in which they find themselves.
7. *a.* The more (6) is true, the more the husband is motivated to continue performance of his economic duties (Wd).

[41] Robert K. Merton, "Intermarriage and the Social Structure: Fact and Theory," in Ruth L. Coser, ed., *The Family: Its Structure and Functions,* New York: St. Martin's Press, 1964, p. 149. Reprinted from *Psychiatry,* August 1941.
[42] Gouldner, *op. cit.,* p. 176.

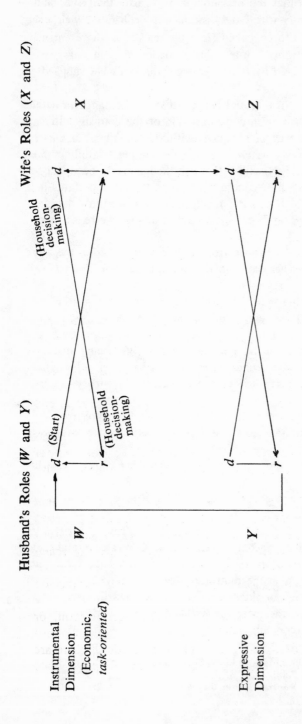

FIGURE 1. Husband-Wife Role Reciprocity.

b. The more (6) is true, the more the shared feelings of solidarity and cohesion, and the greater the motivation to maintain the system, and the greater the stability of the system.

Ultimately, therefore, this chain of propositions rests on the degree to which the husband performs his economic role obligations. In simplified form, we may suggest that the husband in modern society exchanges his status for conjugal solidarity. If we accept as given that expressive satisfactions are the major manifest goals of modern marriage, and the major latent goal is status and economic well-being, then we may say that the latent goal influences the attainment of the manifest goal. Specifically, the greater the degree of the husband's articulation with the economic opportunity system, the more fully and extensively is the interlocking network of conjugal rights and duties performed in reciprocal fashion. The economic rewards he provides induce motivation in the wife to respond positively to him, and her response in turn gives rise to a continuing cycle of rectitude and gratitude. There are obviously numerous questions that emerge in connection with a model of this sort, and the remaining chapters will attempt to deal with many of them.

One point that should be raised here pertains to secondary husband-wife relations, or what is generally called authority or power relations, or the processes of decision-making. *Wr* and *Xd* refer specifically to secondary-type behaviors necessary to every household. These involve decisions regarding who will do what chores, what goods and services and how much of same the family needs, how to discipline the children, and so on. Most studies, for example, including this one (see Chapter Six) find that money is the major source of husband-wife disagreement.[43] Sometimes the decision-making process does focus on primary-type behaviors, but for analytical purposes it seems best to keep the instrumental and expressive dimensions distinct.

We can fit Heer's analysis into Figure 1 by agreeing with him that the husband exchanges his status with his wife for power in these processes of decision-making. The more she perceives *Xr* (status and prestige) being met, *the more she is willing to allow her husband to shape the role definitions of Xd.* The more this is true, the greater are the mutual gratifications on the instrumental level, and the more ongoing is the web of reciprocity; hence, the more cohesive is the system.

Moreover, Goode's general notion of psychological displacement, or transfer, is made more specific by its incorporation into the more rigorous and sociological notion of exchange theory. In other words, if there are indeed negative feelings about limited status, these are displaced onto

---

[43] Levinger, *op. cit.*

expressive elements because certain duties and rights are not being fulfilled, and because the exchange principle that is inherently part of the norm of reciprocity is being improperly met. In summary, the proposition that marital cohesion increases relative to articulation with the economic opportunity system, is based on the rationale that with increased articulation comes increased fulfillment of reciprocal duties and rights, and that on the basis of this exchange system comes increased gratification and thus cohesion. The processes of reciprocity include not only instrumental rights and duties, as suggested by other sociologists, but expressive rights and duties as well.

Smith and also Greenfield have shown what happens when the husband is unable to gain any meaningful economic articulation of his own, and the wife does. In our society, a theoretically related long-range trend may be toward educated women pursuing individualistic careers to the degree that their status is recognized independently of their husband's. What the actual consequences of this might be for the conjugal family system as we now know it is unclear because the pervasiveness of this trend is speculative at best.

Some clue, however, to shore up our speculation, might be gleaned from the entertainment industry. There wives' careers are often totally distinct from husbands' careers, and when hers is more "successful" than his, divorce is a common occurrence. This is, of course, the extreme illustration of the point to which Parsons speaks regarding husband-wife rivalry in the occupational sector. At present, it seems safe to assume that the vast majority of career women (even the most educated) do not view their pursuits in extreme individualistic terms. If the trend becomes such that they do, it is obvious that a model like that in Figure 1 will have to be substantially modified.

Williams makes an important distinction between "achievement"— which refers to "valued accomplishments" particularly in the occupational realm—and "success"—which places primary stress on the rewards of achievement.[44] Achievement refers to the means, to hard work and diligent effort; success to the ends, *i.e.*, conspicuous consumption behavior. Achievement is carried out in the market place, success is displayed in the community.

> . . . The success pattern is still linked to achievement, achievement is still associated with work, and work is still invested with an almost organic complex of ethical values. . . . Achievement is difficult to index, in a highly complex society of diverse occupations . . . money comes to be valued not

---

[44] Williams, *op. cit.*, p. 419. This is the same kind of distinction made by Cloward and Ohlin, *loc. cit.*

only for itself and for the goods it will buy, but as symbolic evidence of success and, thereby, of personal worth.[45]

Thus, personal worth or personal excellence depends ultimately on occupational achievement, but achievement is symbolized in certain visible objects and behaviors. This cluster of visible symbols is part of the success syndrome of our society. For most elements of the population, achievement and success are strongly interconnected. But, as we shall see in the remaining chapters, it is vital to maintain their distinction in terms of their relative consequences for marital interaction.

We are now coming to the conclusion of this introductory chapter. Several key points have been made. The conjugal family is best understood from a perspective that links structural with interactional variables. The basic structure to which the conjugal family is attached is the economic opportunity system—a linkage mediated through the husband's occupation. So-called "objective" variables such as occupational status, education, and income have been known for some time to be related to conjugal interaction, but there has been little systematic effort to account for these linkages theoretically. Furthermore, almost no work has been done with respect to the linkage of subjective feelings of achievement and success (alienation and anomie) and conjugal interaction.[46]

Combining exchange theory and the norm of reciprocity with the implications of "personal excellence" inherent in the dominant orientations of achievement-success, it is suggested that as articulation or integration with the economic opportunity structure increases, so does marital cohesion. Cohesion refers to the levels of attractiveness of or satisfaction with the marital situation. Cohesion is obviously subject to a wide range of psychological and sociological variables, not all of which are considered in this study (need complementarity, or certain personality characteristics, or community networks, for instance). Yet, within the range of variables in the model, it is felt that some contribution toward a systematic theory of marital cohesion can be made. In Chapter Two, considerable attention is given to the definitions and measurement techniques for the independent and dependent variables, as well as for several intervening factors that have an important place in the overall conceptual framework, both from the standpoint of the economic system and of the conjugal family.

To gather data for this study, those census tracts in the greater Indiana-

---

45 Williams, *op. cit.*, pp. 419–21.

46 Some exceptions to this generalization are Dwight G. Dean, "Alienation and Marital Adjustment," unpublished paper read at the annual meeting of the Ohio Valley Sociological Society, Lexington, Ky., May 7, 1965; also Irving Tallman, "Residential Differences in Marital Interaction and Anomia among Working Class Families," unpublished paper read at annual meetings, National Council on Family Relations, 1967.

polis metropolitan area with median household incomes of $4,000 or less were excluded from the sampling frame (see Appendix A for detailed sampling procedures).[47] Thus our multistage cluster sample is presumably a cross section of households stretching roughly from the lower-working class through the lower-upper class. Households were screened for married couples currently living together. Only one of the spouses in each household was interviewed, the sex being predesignated to the interviewer. The resulting sample size was 916, consisting of 497 wives and 419 husbands. Four hundred of the interviews were collected by a professional survey research organization (NORC), the remainder by trained graduate students. The students were collecting the information as a segment of their participation in the Indianapolis Area Project. This ongoing annual effort is conducted by the Institute of Social Research at Indiana University, patterned after the highly successful Detroit Area Project.

In short, this study focuses on "stable" married couples from strata other than the most disadvantaged. A certain proportion of Negro households is included, but because of our sampling requirements, they represent the stable working-class and middle-class Negro population.[48] In fact, when

---

[47] The rationale for this exclusion is as follows: *Methodological*—The tracts excluded were almost exclusively populated by lower-class Negroes. (See Appendix A for exact proportions.) All our interviewers were middle class, almost all were white. In addition to the problems of communication and mutual suspicion that such differences tend to engender, there is the added practical problem of trying to find households in lower-class Negro neighborhoods where both spouses are currently living together. As in many urban areas, between a quarter and a third of such households in Indianapolis simply do not have both spouses present. Therefore, in terms of costs, why expend limited funds to discover what seems clear already, viz., that many households in these areas would obviously not fit our sampling requirements? A block quota sample could have "tracked down" stable households in these areas, but this was not the sampling design used. *Theoretical*—The impact of limited economic resources on the families of the black poor has been ably demonstrated by many researchers. What is not quite so clear is the impact of varying levels of economic resources on the families of those above the poverty line. Had we included stable households from among the poor (though difficult to obtain), the empirical findings of the following chapters would likely be substantially strengthened. Nevertheless, the fact that certain empirical relationships emerge in spite of the absence of the most deprived would only seem to undergird the theoretical connection between economic and expressive elements.

[48] Nonwhites constituted 20.7 percent of the population in the Indianapolis area, according to 1960 census figures. The Indianapolis Commission on Civil Rights, on the basis of its surveys and studies, set the figure at 24.2 percent in 1965. This is the latest figure available, and is considered reliable by organizations—both public and private—that must plan their programs on the basis of it. The proportion of Negroes in our sample is 17 percent (early 1967), showing they are somewhat underrepresented. This underrepresentation is undoubtedly caused by the exclusion of the lowest income census tracts. But since we know nonwhites in the sample do not differ from whites on important variables, we may assume that the 17 percent figure is probably fairly representative of the "stable" Negro population. In short, those Negro families that *should* be represented in the sample *are*—the seven or so percent that should not be are not represented.

controlling for husband's occupation, no statistically significant differences were found between Negroes and whites on any of the variables used in the following chapters. This is highly important and tends to support Goode where, after analysis of census data on Negro marriage and divorce, he concludes that "as the Negro population has become more assimilated into the dominant white culture, both their marriage and divorce behavior has become much like that of whites." [49] And we would add, at *the same class level.*

The three basic forms of marital primary relations are considered in Chapters Two, Three, and Four. Chapter Five is a brief test of one of the further implications of exchange theory, i.e., that expected reciprocal rewards that are not forthcoming generate feelings of hostility and resentment. Chapters Six and Seven take up authority relations, and child-training values, respectively, to determine ways in which these vital elements are also linked to marital cohesion. Chapter Eight is an attempt to pull together the conclusions of the first seven chapters to try to work toward a theory of marital cohesion. This chapter also points up problem areas for further research and contains brief commentary on some practical implications of the findings. Finally, the reader should keep in mind that the chief objective of the book is not to report empirical findings, but to gain theoretical leverage on the conjugal family in modern society. Consequently, sometimes woven into the interpretations of data are arguments that are not conclusively demonstrable here, but which are open to future test, and thereby can further the goal of theory development.

[49] Goode, *op. cit.,* 1966, p. 513.

CHAPTER

TWO

•

Companionship

THE TERM "COMPANIONSHIP" HAS OFTEN BEEN USED TO INCLUDE THE WHOLE gamut of expressive behavior within the conjugal family. For example, Burgess, *et al.,* talk about the transition from institution to "companionate" family, by which they mean that the modern conjugal family places great stress on expressive relations in general between family members.[1] Throughout this book, however, we shall use the general construct *primary relations* to refer to the total expressive realm of husband-wife interaction. The more specific concept *companionship* is reserved for a particular type of primary or expressive behavior.

We shall assume that there are at least three core elements to husband-wife primary relations. Reduced to their simplest, perhaps even colloquial form, modern Americans seek from marriage (not always in this order) someone to do things with, someone to love, someone to talk to. The first element is dealt with in this chapter, and is an extension and expansion of premarital "dating" activities. Because the prime stress here is on action, or doing together, or association, we may label this as the affiliative dimension of primary interaction. The secondary dimension may be described as affective primary interaction, because the major stress there is on the emotional involvement surrounding all aspects of love and physical affection—from the most innocent to the most intimate. Finally, the last may be described as the cognitive dimension of primary interaction, because the emphasis there is on the verbal and intellectual elements inherent in overt symbols of communication and understanding.

[1] Ernest W. Burgess, Harvey J. Locke and Mary Margaret Thomes, *The Family,* New York: American Book Company, 1963 (third edition), p. 3.

26

Obviously, in the "real world," there is overlap between affiliative, affective, and cognitive primary behaviors. But they are sufficiently distinct both substantively and theoretically to be handled separately. For example, there is no necessary correlation of the three. A married person could experience great satisfaction in one or two of these areas, but less in the second and/or third. Therefore, to avoid the conceptual confusion that has often attended examination of the expressive dimension of family relations in the past, as well as to grasp the "real world" in as lucid a fashion as possible, we shall treat these distinct primary relations in this threefold fashion.

First, let us focus solely on *affiliative* primary interaction, *i.e.*, companionship. The operational measure of companionship was got by asking the respondent how he felt about the companionship he had in doing things together with his or her spouse. The key phrase is "doing things together," for in American society the belief is strongly institutionalized that one's mate is someone to do something with (movies, parties, picnics, and so on)— particularly during leisure time.[2]

[2] The exact item, borrowed from Robert O. Blood, Jr., and Donald M. Wolfe, *Husbands and Wives,* New York: The Free Press, 1960, was modified to read as follows:

Which statement best describes how you feel about the companionship that you and your (husband–wife) have in doing things together?
Pretty disappointed—I'm really missing out. (3.4 percent)
It would be nice to have more. (12.3 percent)
It's all right—I really can't complain. (19.9 percent)
Very satisfied—I'm fortunate. (50.9 percent)
Enthusiastic—it couldn't be better. (13.1 percent)

The figures, in parentheses represent the proportion of responses in each category. Assigned weights were 0 through 4, respectively. For all husbands, the mean score was 2.69, standard deviation=.878. For all wives $\bar{x}=2.48$, SD=1.05. There is an obvious upward skewing effect. Had we sampled those families with lowest status, the mean scores would probably have been lower. In spite of their absence, significant differences appear in the tables.

Another important issue here pertains to the reliance on respondent evaluation of primary relations as a valid indicator of same. There are two reasons for our use of this technique. One is pragmatic—it is the simplest way to obtain the desired information. The other, and more significant, reason is theoretical. Thibaut and Kelley use the notion "comparison level" (CL) as "the standard against which the member [of a dyad] evaluates the 'attractiveness' of the relationship or how satisfactory it is." They use CL within the context of exchange theory, the same context, of course, that is used in this volume. "CL is a standard by which the person evaluates the rewards and costs of a given relationship in terms of what he feels he 'deserves.' Relationships the outcomes of which fall above CL would be relatively 'satisfying' and attractive to the member; those . . . that fall below CL would be relatively 'unsatisfying' and unattractive. The location of CL on the person's scale of outcomes will be influenced by all the outcomes known to the member, either by direct experience or symbolically. It may be taken to be some modal or average value of all known outcomes, each outcome weighted by its 'salience.' . . ." The point is that there is strong justification, based on sound social psychological theory, for ascertaining a respondent's "comparison level" or level of perceived satisfaction in terms of varied forms of primary relations. How outside observers might evaluate

As a validity check to see that this particular item was actually measuring leisure affiliations, it was correlated with two other items. One tapped how much "time the couple spend together when neither is busy working." The other got at the degree to which the friends of each spouse are mutually held. We found that the higher one evaluated companionship with his spouse, the more likely he was to respond that he spent most of his leisure time with the spouse ($r = .62$) and the more likely he was to have friends that were mutually shared by the spouse ($r = .69$)[3] In short, shared leisure time and shared friends seem to be the core substantive elements inherent in the notion of husband-wife companionship.

At a more general level, it is plain that Americans place great value per se on nonwork activities. So-called "leisure industries" gross billions each year. Concomitant with this general stress on nonwork behaviors is that for married persons, the most "significant other during leisure time" is ideally defined as being one's spouse. Sharing leisure does not necessarily imply being isolated from others. Together the couple may interact with friends or relatives, go places with their children, or simply watch TV. The point is that a strong ideology exists regarding primary relations between spouses in the area of doing, *i.e.*, of companionship behavior. Clearly in our culture, the spouse is supposed to be deeply involved or affiliated with his alter in most leisure-time activities.

This expectation stands in contrast, for example, to many forms of extended families in various cultures where any number of individuals other than one's own mate could be the focus for primary relations in general and companionship in particular. It also stands in even sharper contrast to the current urban Japanese conjugal family. Blood, in his studies, for instance, found that "husband-wife companionship is not considered important in Japan." [4]

Vogel, in his examination of middle-class families in a Tokyo suburb, found that "for informal social life, a husband does not meet with his wife's friends, the wife does not associate with her husband's friends, and they rarely go out together as a couple." [5] Surprisingly, he claims that more

a person's primary interaction is irrelevant; what matters is how the person himself sees it—*how he feels about his own CL*. The relation of CL to conjugal cohesion is through "comparison level for alternatives," (CL-alt) or the reference point to decide whether or not to remain in the interaction, or the lowest level of reward the individual will accept in order to continue in the relationship. In short, the greater the CL of primary relations, and the more they continue above the point of CL-alt, the stronger the motivation to maintain the relationship, i.e., the greater is conjugal cohesion. See John W. Thibaut and Harold H. Kelley, *The Social Psychology of Groups*, New York: John Wiley and Sons, Inc., 1959, pp. 21 ff.

3 These figures, of course, still leave a certain amount of variance unexplained.

4 Robert O. Blood, Jr., *Love Match and Arranged Marriage*, New York: The Free Press, 1967, p. 71.

5 Ezra Vogel, *Japan's New Middle Class*, Berkeley, Calif.: University of California Press, 1963, p. 102.

modern families maintain even greater separation and less companionship than do traditional families. Not only do they not share any leisure time, neither males nor females have any desire to change this pattern. The husband's companionship is centered in his friends (both male and female) at work (called "the company gang"), whereas the wife's is centered in neighborhood contacts who are almost always females.[6] By far, the husband's round of companionship is the more active. The daily ritual after work is to stop off at bars, coffee houses, or specialty restaurants for several hours. Although these behaviors are not unlike those of some American working-class or lower-class males, it must be remembered that in Japan these are white-collar professionals. Many companies sponsor outings and trips—some overnight—which female office workers sometimes attend, but which wives never do.[7]

OBJECTIVE INTEGRATION

With this cultural contrast in mind, let us move to the first major question of this chapter, which is the relationship of the three "standard measures" of articulation into the opportunity structure to marital affiliativeness. These are the basic sociological considerations of occupation, education, and income. They are phenomena that are "out there" to a greater extent than the constructs of *alienation* and *anomie*, which we shall consider later. Compared to alienation and anomie, these objective considerations are based more on tangible artifacts, the meanings of which tend to be widely shared. For example, let us refer back to Chapter One and the illustration of the well-educated executive and the janitor. The role behaviors attached to their contrasting occupations are clearly observable. Cross-national prestige ratings consistently show that virtually everyone attributes more status to executive than to janitor. Their relative years of education can be readily certified, as can their differential income in dollars.

As noted in Chapter One, we may consider the opportunity system as a reward structure in which rewards in the form of valued means and ends are distributed unevenly in our society. Occupational status, education, and income in this sense are rewards. The more of these one has, the more one may be said to be part of, *i.e.*, articulated with, the opportunity structure. But low feelings of economic alienation and anomie are also "rewards," and the less one senses feelings of alienation and anomie, the more he may be said to be articulated (in a subjective sense, in terms of feelings or attitudes) with the opportunity structure. If we think of these different types of rewards as being on a continuum, we may say that the

[6] *Ibid.*, pp. 103 ff.
[7] *Ibid.*

objective indicators of articulation have some tangible bases and we have some evidence of shared definitions as to their meanings. The subjective indicators, on the other hand, have no certain tangible base and rest almost totally on the actor's feeling state. In short, "objective" and "subjective" should not be thought of as necessarily discrete ways of describing articulation with the opportunity structure, but instead as sensitizing us to the relative difference in emphasis between the "standard" ways of viewing achievement and success vis-à-vis the feeling states of the actors toward achievement and success. Later in the chapter, under "Subjective Integration" when we consider the subjective dimensions in greater detail, the distinctions and differences in emphasis should emerge quite clearly.

OCCUPATION OF HUSBAND

The Duncan *Socioeconomic Index* (SEI) is a very sensitive measure of occupational differences. It takes into account both the type of industry in which the respondent works and his specific job. Using this procedure, it is possible to rank occupations on a scale from 00 (low) to 96 (high).[8] Throughout the study, we shall follow a common convention by dividing the SEI into quintiles (00–19, lowest status occupations; 20–39; 40–59; 60–79; 80–96, this last being the grouping with the highest status occupations).

Another procedure followed throughout the study is to divide the sample by sex, and to compare results accordingly. There are compelling theoretical reasons for doing so. Many studies of the conjugal family have used only wives as sources of information. Consequently, their conclusions are open to the serious criticism that they reflect the bias of the female role. Perhaps, some observers note, certain generalizations extant regarding the conjugal family would have to be modified if more were known in terms of the male's viewpoint—from the perspective of his roles as husband and father. We have sought to overcome bias in either direction by including both

[8] Use of quintiles is a simple convention often employed by Blood and Wolfe, *op. cit.*, and is followed here because of its face validity. That is, given a range of scores from 00 to 96, five divisions of equal distance seem to be a reasonable and valid means to ascertain any differences that might exist between levels of occupations.

For a discussion of the Duncan SEI itself, see Albert J. Reiss, Jr., *Occupations and Social Status*, New York: The Free Press, Chaps. 6 and 7. Although the index was originally developed on the basis of the 1950 census, evidence clearly shows it to possess an extraordinarily high degree of "temporal stability." That is, comparing information with the 1940 and 1960 censuses, and "despite major changes in the value of the dollar and the generally rising levels of educational attainment," the status scale appears to remain valid over time. See Peter M. Blau and Otis Dudley Duncan, *The American Occupational Structure*, New York: John Wiley and Sons, Inc., 1967, pp. 120–21.

sexes in the sample (though none from the same household) and analyzing their responses separately.

Furthermore, given basic notions underlying this study (exchange theory and reciprocity), it seems imperative to make a distinction by sex. For instance, it might be argued that under certain conditions or situations, one sex or the other might be more or less likely to insist on reciprocity of duties and/or rights. In addition, at certain points the legitimacy of the exchange principle may break down. For example, one might argue that the exchange of income for physical affect is simply too crass for women, that for them no relationship exists between the two factors, that female affect is based solely on particularistic criteria.

Consequently, in Table 2-1, (see Appendix B for tables) we have the mean scores for companionship evaluation classified in terms of the SEI of head of household but separately for husbands and wives. The technique used to test for the significance of the difference between means is a simple one-way analysis of variance. (See Appendix A for rationale behind use of significance tests in this study.) As a result, it can be seen that husbands reveal significant differences between their occupational status and their satisfaction with affiliative interaction. The same is true for wives in terms of the occupational status of their husbands.[9]

Whereas for both sexes it is clear that companionate satisfaction increases with status, in every category husbands score higher than wives, a pattern that is general throughout the chapter. It may be that husbands expect less than wives from leisure affiliativeness and are thus satisfied more easily. Wives, on the other hand, may expect more and find reality below the level of their liking. Such an explanation would fit with the generally held notion that wives focus more of their attention and interest on conjugal interaction than do husbands. Whereas the husband's chief concern is presumably his occupational roles, "the woman must remain

[9] When examining the tables, the reader should keep in mind Lenski's argument that it is "patterns in findings" that lead us to valid generalizations. (See our Appendix A.) Whereas the actual differences in means between particular cells may not always be great, it is basically the *overall* pattern in that general relationship, plus similar patterns in relationships that are theoretically linked to it, that constitute the main foci of interest. Specifically here, we have a theoretical framework linking the opportunity system and the family through a series of pertinent variables. Our interest is in the *basic pattern* of an X-Y relationship, plus the comparison of that pattern with other theoretically analogous X-Y linkages, and finally in the overall pattern of these several relationships taken as a whole. It is when we have reached this point that generalizations regarding the opportunity system and the family attain a reasonable level of validity. But this obviously requires that we first build up to that point through close examination of specific data and meaningful interpretations thereof. (In those instances where N's vary between certain tables the variation is caused by either nonresponse or noncodeable responses to a particular item. For example, an *a–b* relationship may show 200 cases, but an *a–c* relationship may reveal 198 or 201 cases, and so on.) A copy of the interview schedule used for this report will be provided on request to the Institute of Social Research, Indiana University.

both for husband and for children the emotional hub of the family." [10] Her greater conjugal involvement leads to greater affiliative expectations—but her expectations are not satisfied as fully as she might wish, because the one who is supposed to fulfill them is relatively more concerned with other things.

Yet, the evidence does not permit us to carry such an argument to its ultimate conclusion, viz., the busier the husband is with his occupation, the less affiliative involvement he maintains. Though we found that husbands in higher-status occupations work more hours per week than those with less status, the data in Table 2-1 show that status enhances companionate evaluation. It is at this point that the exchange model discussed in Chapter One comes into use. The more status and prestige the husband's job provides, the more the wife feels that her "rights" are being met. Rights here consist, for example, of the sense of personal excellence or worth that the wife feels as a result of her husband's attainments. In our society, she and her children are judged on the basis of the husband's achievement and success. As his main sphere of interest is the *market place*, hers is the *community*. It is there that the majority of her significant others—both kin and friends—accord to her status, worth, and prestige. The same is true for her children with whom she identifies intimately.

One of the expectations, therefore, inherent within the wife role is that the husband will provide as much status as possible. This is one of her basic definitions of the task-oriented dimension of the conjugal unit. And as Homans puts it, with conformity to group norms comes approval and sentiments of liking.[11] In this case, the "contribution" of the husband motivates the wife to reciprocate in terms of the prime expectations inherent in her role as "socioemotional leader," specifically here in terms of positive affiliativeness. The husband responds in kind, and since both sexes value companionship, they define their conjugal situation as rewarding, and thus worthy of maintenance.

Obviously, this process is not coldly rational, nor do the parties methodically calculate the extent of rights and duties. Particularly in our society, where romantic love and selflessness and particularism are supposed to cancel out even the mere notion of exchange, the process is subtle indeed—perhaps even suppressed for ideological reasons—especially among those with higher status. Among the less advantaged, however, it may be more self-conscious owing to inherently greater economic strains. Homans also labels this intricate process of rectitude and gratitude as one of "mutual reinforcement." [12]

[10] John R. Seeley, R. Alexander Sim, and Elizabeth W. Loosley, *Crestwood Heights*, New York: John Wiley and Sons, Inc., 1963 edition, p. 178.
[11] George C. Homans, *Social Behavior: Its Elementary Forms*, New York: Harcourt, Brace and World, Inc., 1961, pp. 112–29.
[12] *Ibid.*, pp. 30 ff.

Both husbands and wives hold certain expectations of the duties of alter to fulfill their own (actor's) rights regarding leisure togetherness with each other, children, friends, kin—at parties, amusements, recreation. But at the same time, both are aware of the duties of the husband to fulfill status obligations to his family, and of the society-wide universalism that ascribes worth and excellence on the basis of achieved status. Both kinds of goals are essential to the maintenance of the conjugal unit. And because it is the husband's occupational role that is articulated with the determinants of status, it is from there that we must begin to trace the process of mutual reinforcement that leads to more positive affiliativeness.

It is crucial to note that Buckley has criticized Homans for failing to make explicit "notions of investment of *self* in others, exchanges of *self-identities, self*-rewards (for example, self-respect, enhancement of self) based on the concepts of social approval, interpersonal attraction, social influence, and the like. . . ." [13] Buckley cites more recent statements of exchange theory that are closer to G. H. Mead's behaviorism than to Skinner's on which Homans draws.[14] The point is that here and throughout the study we do make explicit, as part of the exchange model, notions of self-respect, self-enhancement, personal excellence, and so on. In fact, a core theoretical underpinning is that wives value the symbolic meaning of the husband's rewards as much as (or perhaps even more than) the actual rewards per se. In terms of our ascetic Protestant tradition, it is not so much the material elements alone that count, but instead the sense of worth and respectability that they signify. These kinds of elements are inextricably part of the processes of husband-wife reciprocity assumed here to exist. We identify in short more closely with Mead than with Skinner.

Furthermore, although the data might be amenable to types of explanations other than a reciprocity or exchange model, this approach seems best suited, given the theoretical considerations noted in Chapter One pertaining to the overlap or articulation of the occupational system and the conjugal family. There, in an effort to relate structural and interactional factors and also to attempt to explain conjugal cohesion in the light of much past data regarding family dissolution, this kind of model seemed to be the most appropriate. For if the opportunity system can be thought of as a reward structure, *then it is through the role of male provider that these rewards are mediated into the conjugal unit.* To whatever extent they are or are not there, they must be assumed to have certain consequences for husband-wife interaction and ultimately cohesion of the unit qua unit. Inasmuch as level of rewards varies with degree of expressive satisfaction, it can be

---

[13] Walter Buckley, *Sociology and Modern Systems Theory,* Englewood Cliffs, N.J.: Prentice-Hall, Inc., 1967, p. 112.
[14] *Ibid.,* p. 113.

assumed that a process of exchange is occurring for reasons discussed both here and in Chapter One.

"Exchange theory" as such is still primitive in its development, but the notions of interlocking role reciprocity and resultant mutual rewards seem to provide, as Gouldner suggests, an excellent means of explaining social order. The effort to apply exchange theory to the family should be considered merely initial.[15] Further work might be able to modify the theory and incorporate it with other approaches to come up eventually with a more precise explanation of the complexities of intraconjugal interaction *in conjunction with the larger social structure*. But a start has to be made somewhere, and in view of the several theoretical issues involved, the application of exchange and reciprocity theory seems the most appropriate way in which to begin to attain these objectives.

INCOME

It is significant to compare the different results, in Table 2-1, of occupational status over against income. (The distribution of incomes in the sample was divided into roughly equal quartiles: poor [\$6,500–below]=219 cases; fair [\$6,600–\$9,500] = 235; good [\$9,600–\$12,500] = 208; high [\$12,600–up] = 221. The category labels appear appropriate given the actual span of dollars encompassed in each one.) Income, it seems, is an extremely unreliable predictor of husband-wife affiliativeness. For example, husbands making \$6,500 or less per year evaluate companionship as highly as husbands making \$12,500 or more, and husbands in between vary hardly at all in their evaluations from the mean of these extreme groups. And while wives show more of a spread in mean scores, the overall differences are not great. What is more, wives in the "good" income category report slightly more satisfactory companionship than wives in the "high" grouping.

Less than 40 percent of households in the sample contain working wives. And even among those households where wives do work, because of the lower salaries that women usually obtain, the proportion of total family income contributed by wives is considerably less than that supplied by husbands. Moreover, when we removed wife income from total income and

15 The reader is reminded of the closing caveat in Chapter One, *i.e.*, our chief interest in this book is to gain "theoretical leverage" on the conjugal family, not simply to report empirical findings. Hence, the data per se, apart from any theoretical framework, may not compel one to accept exchange theory as the most adequate way to explain certain conjugal processes. Theoretically, however, it seems to be the most reasonable way to begin to analyze what are obviously complex processes. If we do no more than to stimulate dialogue and thus force others to come up with a more meaningful theoretical schema, then we shall have accomplished our chief purpose. See also John N. Edwards, "Famalial Behavior as Social Exchange," *Journal of Marriage and the Family,* 31 (August 1969).

examined companionate rankings in terms of differences in husband's income alone, the same unreliable pattern appeared as in Table 2-1.

In either case, it is clear that dollars per se are not a meaningful "medium of exchange" in so far as husband-wife companionship is concerned. Yet occupational status, particularly if it is to be transformed into social status, requires visible consumption symbols, which of course require dollars. Why then does status relate significantly to companionship, whereas income does not?

There is perhaps one major factor operating here, though it has an important corollary. Compared to occupational status, the husband may be considered less "duty bound" to provide dollars. The wife sees her rights to dollars as less significant than her rights to status and prestige. In the larger context of romantic love and particularism, sheer dollars may simply be viewed as too crass, crude, and vulgar a criterion on which to base mutual affiliative reinforcement within the conjugal unit. Yet we must remember that our sample excludes the very lowest income segments of the population. Had we included them, the resultant picture might have been somewhat different. But among those families whose income is above the subsistence level, there is a tendency for differences in income not to differentiate families in terms of companionship.

Obviously, to define status as part of the task-oriented dimension of the conjugal unit requires a minimum floor of income in order to symbolize that status to the community. But once that level is attained (perhaps defined as "respectability" in the eyes of peers), husbands and wives may be hesitant to use income as part of the exchange process between them. Instead, the focus shifts to the more subtle—though nonetheless real—consequences of status and prestige. Hence, in so far as the primary relation in view is affiliativeness, the tendency toward particularism outweighs the universalistic criteria of achievement and success inherent in income. This type of primary relation appears to be "shielded" from the "crudest" of economic criteria of personal worth. The consequences of dollars seem to be "suppressed" in favor of romantic love—but only among those who have escaped the definition of dollars as a means to survival.

EDUCATION

Education, like occupational status, is a more subtle indicant than dollars of achievement and success. It is both an end in itself and a means to valued goals. In the first instance, it is a source of self-worth, personal excellence, and prestige. It reflects such prized characteristics as intelligence, ability, and determination. As the same time, it is a potent means to jobs that provide greater income, prestige, and influence.

We see from Table 2-1 that both sexes reveal that greater education results in a more positive evaluation of affiliative-type interaction. The only exception to the pattern is found among husbands with some high school (9–11 years of schooling). They rank below husbands with only a grade school education. As before, wives at every education level rank companionship lower than do husbands. The F ratios are considerably stronger here than for occupational status, suggesting that education is more strongly linked to affiliativeness than is job status.

The reason for this stronger link probably lies in the fact that education is a resource that wives as well as husbands can contribute to the task-oriented sphere of the conjugal unit. In Table 2-1, for instance, we are reporting wives' own education in the same way that we are reporting husbands' own education. Education is something that wives have attained on their own—it represents a tangible symbol of universalistic achievement in a society that places great value on such behavior. More-over, viewed as the major resource brought by the wife to the marriage, it lends itself to being described as the functional equivalent of the dowry in certain traditional societies.

For instance, her education may have helped her to work and to support the family during the early stages of marriage, particularly while higher status husbands were going to school. Likewise, it is a kind of reserve or "emergency store" that could aid the family in the event the husband became incapacitated or deceased. Whether she is "forced" to use it, or else chooses to use it voluntarily in aiding her to find employment, it is perhaps her basic (though often latent) contribution to the task-oriented dimension of the conjugal unit.

In addition to her education's being a resource for the family, it is also an important resource for her in the community. As Parsons points out, community activities are often the setting in which the woman uses her education to fulfill the cultural demands for achievement.[16] Just as she is chief "consumption agent," she is also chief "community agent" of the conjugal family in the sense that she is often more heavily involved in the community than is her mate. Consequently, education is an important resource that enables her to gain positions of prestige and influence in the community. Inasmuch as this is still most often the chief sphere in which universalistic criteria of achievement apply to her as an individual, attainments here very likely contribute greatly to her self-definition of personal excellence. And very often her attainments in the community reflect positively back on to her family, enhancing its prestige in the eyes of significant others as well.

So from three standpoints—the inherent prestige of education, its

16 Cited in Seely, *et. al., op. cit.,* p. 278.

functions (operative and latent) for family consumption, and its functions for community prestige, women find education an invaluable resource to bring to the conjugal unit. What is more, both sexes in our sample report a high degree of educational homogeneity with their own spouses ($r = .63$). The consequences of the husband's education are very similar to those of his job status. His education is an important resource that enables him to fulfill his instrumental duties to the conjugal unit. The greater his education, therefore, the more the wife perceives her status rights as being met, and thus the more positive the ongoing reciprocal companionship between them.

From the standpoint of the wife role, her education is her one independent link to the economic-opportunity structure. Judging from the data in Table 2-1, however, it is not used as a means of rivalry vis-à-vis the husband role. If this were so, the most educated women would probably experience the least satisfactory affiliativeness. Instead, it appears to exist in latent fashion and/or as supportive to the husband role. As a result, we may assume the husband does not view educational attainment as a duty incumbent on his wife's role in the same way that it is encumbent on his role.

Role prescriptions vary in the degree of their permissiveness. "All prescriptions define given behavior as forbidden, obligatory, or indifferent, and basic to each of these is the idea of permission. If behavior is permitted, it is 'allowed'; it 'may' or 'may not' be performed, it is 'optional.' " [17] In our society at the present time, extensive education for occupants of the wife role remains more of an option than an obligation. Yet, to the degree that the wife possesses this important resource, it functions as a "medium" of exchange. The likelihood is that in our society males are increasingly coming to evaluate education for their wives as a positive value because of its symbolic or latent consequences for the conjugal unit. Because it is an actual or potential resource in terms of conjugal unit goals, and as long as it does not lead to rivalry, it evokes positive affiliative responses from the husband.

So in contrast to job status in which only the husband's attainments were theoretically meaningful, in educational efforts the wife's are too. Consequently, we have two concurrent reciprocal processes being carried out: mutual reinforcement as a result of husband's education, and mutual reinforcement as a result of wife's education. Probably, therefore, one reason that education seems so strongly linked to affiliative interaction in this study, as well as in many others, is that it is a resource that both partners may legitimately bring to the marriage. Increasing the total resources available for mutual exchange increases the likelihood of mutually

[17] Bruce J. Biddle and Edwin J. Thomas, *Role Theory: Concepts and Research,* New York: John Wiley and Sons, Inc., 1966, p. 52.

valued expressive rewards—in this case, positive affiliativeness. But this raises an important issue in view of the fact that income as resource was *not* significantly related to affiliativeness, and that is the whole question of wife employment.

WIFE EMPLOYMENT

If we accept the notion that it is the husband's occupation that is the major determinant of family prestige and position, the remaining major consequence of wife employment for the family is therefore simply sheer dollars, *i.e.*, increased family income. Whereas the resources resulting from education may be symbolic, latent, potential, or community-oriented, the resources from her actual employment are clearly tangible and immediate. What therefore are the consequences on primary interaction of the introduction of these kinds of material resources on the conjugal family system?

Whereas the total labor force increased by 14.4 million between 1940 and 1960, "married women, husband present" accounted for 8.1 million (or 56 percent) of this increase. In the decade prior to 1960, married women accounted for 60 percent of the growth rate of the labor force.[18] Approximately 38 percent of the households represented in our sample contained a working wife at the time of the interview. This compares with a national figure of 34 percent in 1964; and given the growth rate of this phenomenon, the national figure in 1967 was probably very close to our 38 percent figure.[19]

Of those wives in the sample reported to be working, 65 percent indicated the primary motivation was monetary. This was the same basic motivation reported by Hoffman in her well-known study of wife employment.[20] The remaining 35 percent reported they worked for self-fulfillment. Typical reasons included, "it gives me a sense of meaning," "fulfillment," "enjoyment," "satisfaction," "contribution," and so on. Among those wives in the sample who were not currently working, 71 percent have children at home under six years of age. Furthermore, when asked their opinion as to a married woman working with no children at home, 80 percent of the total sample were in favor of her doing so, whereas when asked about her working when small children were present, 50 percent were flatly not in favor of it. Another 20 percent were willing to allow it only under conditions of unusual economic need.

Our findings about the effects of small children on wife employment

18 Glen G. Cain, *Married Women in the Labor Force,* Chicago: University of Chicago Press, 1966, p. 1.

19 *Ibid.,* p. 2.

20 Lois Wladis Hoffman, "The Decision To Work," in F. Ivan Nye and Lois W. Hoffman, eds., *The Employed Mother in America,* Chicago: Rand McNally and Co., 1963, p. 23.

are corroborated by national census data. In 1960, of all married women, husbands present, who have children under six, only 19 percent work; and when no children under eighteen are present, 59 percent work.[21] It seems clear that at present children play a major role in the decision of the wife to work. Nevertheless, Cain shows that the rate of women working with children both in the ages 6–17 and under-age-six categories has increased substantially since 1951. He predicts that in the future this factor will become even less important in retarding wife employment, that women will work in even greater proportions, children notwithstanding.[22]

In other words, more and more women appear to be opting for the kind of behavior that the dominant society deems obligatory for males, its dominant members. For though our folk ideology praises the woman who stays by *Kinder* and *Küche,* the phrase "just a housewife" more accurately suggests the image with which many women actually view their traditional chores. For many reasons, the trend is clearly in the direction of ever-increasing female involvement with the occupational system.

The literature on the consequences of wife employment for expressive interaction contains varied conclusions. Nye, for example, concludes that any "net *adverse* effect of employment on marital adjustment is less in the higher socioeconomic families than in the lower." [23] But Blood contends there are "positive evaluations associated with [her] work in low-income households and negative evaluations when the husband's income is high." [24] From a sample of divorced women, Goode suggests that among lower status households, there is a tendency for husbands to define the wife's employment as usurping his role of "breadwinner." He states that this kind of threat to the traditional male role could negatively affect marital expressiveness.[25]

Perhaps one of the difficulties connected with research into this area has been the failure to distinguish between expressive components within the marital dyad. That is, could wife employment influence the affiliative dimension in one direction, the cathectic in the other, and the cognitive in still another, perhaps neutral, fashion? To begin to explore this possibility, we have in Table 2-2 a comparison of the companionship evaluation scores, by sex, of those households where the wife is employed, and those where she is not. The results are not significant for either sex, but the mean scores are in the direction of greater satisfaction with companionship where the wife does not work. It would appear, therefore, that the mere fact of her employment does show slight tendencies toward a negative impact on companionship.

[21] Cain, *op. cit.,* p. 3.
[22] *Ibid.,* pp. 116 ff.
[23] F. Ivan Nye, "Marital Interaction," in Nye and Hoffman, *op. cit.,* p. 280.
[24] Robert O. Blood, Jr., "The Husband-Wife Relationship," in *ibid.,* p. 304.
[25] William J. Goode, *After Divorce,* New York: The Free Press, 1956, pp. 62 ff.

A variation on the question of the impact of work vs. nonwork is the impact of occupational status only among households where wives actually do work. To get at this question, the distribution of households with employed women was divided roughly in half and measured in terms of the wife's job having high status (top three deciles on the Duncan SEI) or low status (bottom two deciles). More than 80 percent of women with higher status occupations are married to men within the same three status levels; slightly less than 70 percent of women with lower status jobs are married to men within the two similar status groupings. The results in Table 2-3 tend to confirm Nye's conclusion (and Goode's, too), at least in so far as affiliativeness is concerned. In households where the wife holds a higher status job, companionship evaluation is significantly greater in view of both sexes, than among households where the wife holds a lower-status job.

To begin to understand the phenomenon of wife employment, we must try to see where it fits in terms of the duties-rights-options syndrome discussed above. As noted there, from the standpoint of the husband, the modern wife may opt to have education. In fact, males may increasingly prefer their wives to have approximately the same amount of education as they do. Nonetheless, wife education per se is still more of an option than a duty. The same is true for wife employment, *i.e.*, the occupant of the wife role in our society is surely not obligated to work if a healthy male is present. But it seems that an increasing minority of women would prefer to move their employment to the status of a right.[26] And probably even more who are not yet to that point would still prefer to have greater independent control of their options to work.

It is logical to assume that women in these two categories (those most desiring changes in norms pertaining to wife employment) would tend to have at least a "good" education, and be married to relatively higher-status men. These kinds of men are less likely to feel their provider role is being undermined by wife employment. They are thus less apt to offer resistance to their wives' definition of their own employment as a "right" or as a very live, independently exercised option. Lower-status men, on the other hand, are less willing to concede that wife employment is a right or an extremely viable option. They are more likely to see it on the other side as a disrupting influence on the family, because it undermines their role as provider, and also because it often requires readjustment in the definition of household duty obligations.

These differences, then, help to account for the pattern of Table 2-3.

[26] The viewpoint of this minority is elaborated in Jacquelyn A. Mattfeld and Carol G. Van Aken, *Women and the Scientific Professions,* Cambridge, Mass.: The MIT. Press, 1965. See especially Alice S. Rossi, "Barriers to the Career Choice of Engineering, Medicine, or Science among American Women," pp. 51–127.

Higher-status husbands define wife employment not so much in terms of the material resources it provides, but as an exercise of her own volition, her independent choice, or perhaps even right. But they can do this primarily because they are already relatively secure in their own status. Conversely, less secure husbands see the tangible factors looming largest in import. Their occupational situation makes them unable to define her employment in other than threatening terms. The result in their case is significantly lowered levels of meaningful companionship. Among higher-status couples, in short, the wife's employment does not threaten affiliativeness, but among lower-status couples it does.

SUBJECTIVE INTEGRATION

We shall have more to say about the consequences of wife employment under "Mediating Factors, Structural Characteristics," in this same chapter, but now we must turn to what was called in Chapter One, subjective definitions of achievement and success. And so the second major question of this chapter—moving beyond objective integration—is the impact of "subjective economic articulation" on husband-wife affiliativeness. It will be recalled that the notion of subjective integration into the opportunity structure is subsumed under two widely used sociological constructs—*alienation* and *anomie*. Mizruchi points out that these are twin concepts, and are often used interchangeably by sociologists.[27] Yet they are distinguishable if one is careful to specify particular points of reference and establish clear definitions. *Alienation*, for example, inevitably requires the additional reference point—alienation from what?

ALIENATION

Mizruchi has also summarized the historical usages of alienation beginning with Marx and continuing into this century with the writings of several analysts—particularly Fromm.[28] Some definitional essence in the notion of alienation may be caught in terms used by these writers—terms such as *separation, divorcement, estrangement, opposition,* and so on. Among the several attempts to utilize this slippery construct in empirical fashion is the work of Seeman. Seeman has adopted Merton's idea of a "single term, diverse concepts," to get at alienation.[29] In other words, he sees alienation

27 Ephraim H. Mizruchi, *Success and Opportunity,* New York: The Free Press, 1964, p. 26.

28 *Ibid.,* pp. 27 ff.

29 Melvin Seeman, "On the Meaning of Alienation," *American Sociological Review* 24 (December 1959). Merton is cited in Mizruchi, *op. cit.,* p. 38. For a

as a sort of generalized construct, a step more abstract than a concept, and not directly measurable. At the same time, however, the construct alienation contains several dimensions or concepts that are amenable to operational techniques. Seeman, for instance, has suggested five such dimensions, while others such as Neal and Rettig have underlined the utility of the multidimensional approach in general toward the understanding of alienation.[30]

In recent years, other studies have sought to specify particular subsystems of the society as reference points for alienation, rather than thinking in global societal terms. These have included the political and economic systems, particular kinds of work organizations, and so on.[31] We find therefore three threads pertaining to alienation: the fundamental ideas of separation, and so on, inherent in its formal usages; the multidimensional notion; and a particular reference point. To try to tie them together, we must first specify the reference point of alienation, which in this study is, of course, the economic opportunity structure—the syndrome of occupational achievement and observable success.

So far in the chapter we have talked about objective articulation or integration with the opportunity structure. *A sense of alienation reflects subjective feelings of separation from this same structure and is the obverse of a sense of integration or articulation with it.* Given this particular reference point, it appeared that earlier measures of the several dimensions of alienation were not as appropriate as might be desired for our purposes here. Specifically, it would seem that one can feel alienated from the opportunity system in two basic senses: one, from the means to achievement and success; two, from the ends or goals themselves. This last aspect can be further subdivided into two parts: one, alienation from immediate occupational rewards—the immediate benefits of production; two, alienation from the status or class hierarchy of the society—the less tangible, more subtle factors associated with consumption patterns. It will be noted that the basic dichotomy of alienation from means and from goals follows

thorough listing of Seeman's many publications in this area, see Melvin Seeman, "On the Personal Consequences of Alienation in Work," *American Sociological Review*, 32 (April 1967), pp. 273–85.

[30] Arthur G. Neal and Salomon Rettig, "On the Multidimensionality of Alienation," *American Sociological Review*, 32 (February 1967), pp. 54–64. Neal has also recently collaborated on another report showing the utility of certain alienation variables with respect to an important dimension of the modern urban conjugal family, *i.e., fertility*. H. Theodore Groat and Arthur G. Neal, "Social Psychological Correlates of Urban Fertility," *American Sociological Review*, 32 (December 1967), pp. 945–59.

[31] This point is made in Mizruchi, *op. cit.,* p. 36. Two such examples are John P. Clark, "Measuring Alienation Within a Social System," *American Sociological Review*, 24 (December 1959); also Leonard Pearlin, "Alienation from Work: A Study of Nursing Personnel," *American Sociological Review*, 27 (June 1962).

Robin Williams' distinction between achievement and success.[32] Alienation from one and/or both is possible.

As a result of these kinds of theoretical demands, it became necessary to modify some of the earlier concepts and measurements of alienation. We suggest, therefore, three basic dimensions of alienation from the opportunity system: (1) *powerlessness* (alienation from the means to succeed), (2) *discontent* (alienation from the immediate rewards of the occupational system), (3) *status-estrangement* (alienation from the status order of our society).

POWERLESSNESS

Seeman defines *powerlessness* as "the expectancy or probability held by the individual that his own behavior cannot determine the occurrence of the outcomes, or reinforcements he seeks." [33] Mizruchi points up the similarity between this definition and Max Weber's notion of power: "the chance of a man or a number of men to realize their own will in a communal action." [34]

In terms of powerlessness vis-à-vis the opportunity structure, it is important to determine the extent to which the individual feels he possesses those means to "determine outcomes," "realize his will," *i.e.*, the means necessary for achievement and ultimately success.

To do this, we have made use of an item that has been in the literature for some years. Each respondent was presented with a list of six items and asked which one is "most important in contributing to a man's success in America today."

1. Opportunities and advantages his family gave him.
2. Hard work.
3. Knowing the right people and having pull.
4. Ability.
5. Good luck or breaks.
6. Drive and initiative.

Upon responding, he was immediately asked to compare himself with "most people" and state whether he thinks he has had "more than most people," "not as much as most," "about the same as most," in terms *only* of the one item he selected. For instance, if he replies, "good luck," he is then asked if he has had "more good luck" than most people, "not as much good luck," and so on. Hence, what we obtain first is an indicant of what the respondent himself thinks is most crucial in order to

---

[32] Robin M. Williams, Jr., *American Society*, New York: Alfred A. Knopf, Inc., 1960 edition, pp. 417 ff.

[33] *Op. cit.*, p. 784.

[34] *Op. cit.*, p. 32.

succeed. We have not imposed this definition on him except in so far as to specify six alternatives that pretty well exhaust the potential universe.

Second and even more important, we have the respondent's perception of "how much" of this "most crucial" element he possesses. If he thinks he has a sufficient amount of "means" to succeed (no matter what he perceives the particular means to be), then he believes he is "powerful" in relation to the opportunity structure. A general sociological definition of power usually includes the notion of resources sufficient to manipulate, or to use, or to influence persons or situations. If one has a "sense of power" with regard to the opportunity structure, in effect he feels capable of "using" it to his own advantage. If he does not sense this power or capability, presumably he feels unable to "use" it; he feels relatively unable to "determine outcomes" or "obtain desired reinforcements."

In terms of the response categories supplied, someone who replied that he had the same amount (of whichever of the six it happened to be) as most people could be said to have an "average" sense of power toward the opportunity structure. Someone who replied that he had more than most people would presumably have a greater than average sense of power; someone who replied that he had less would presumably have a lower than average sense of power (or the greatest sense of powerlessness).

It should be underscored again that it matters little (in terms of the issues being considered here) either theoretically or empirically which of the six attributes per se the respondent selected as being most important. This is so, theoretically, because what we are interested in is the sense of power or powerlessness per se, and not a mere ranking of the means of power. It is so, empirically, because we found no relationship whatsoever between the rankings per se and companionship evaluation. Both factors force us, therefore, to focus on the relative degree of perceived possession of means necessary to succeed. The more one feels he possesses these means, the less alienated he may be said to be; the less he feels he possesses them, the more he may be said to be alienated. Nonetheless, it is useful to note the distribution of responses to these six choices. Better than 81 percent of the sample chose numbers 2, 4, and 6. These orientations represent the traditional ascetic Protestant beliefs regarding achievement and success. In short, the Protestant ethic remains viable within our sample, and presumably within the urban universe from which it was drawn. Therefore, to the degree that a respondent actually feels powerless, he does so in terms of elements that have a long tradition in our society, plus the fact that the vast majority of "others" around him probably share these very same beliefs.

For example, in Table 2-4, we have placed those who replied they possess "more than others" in the "low powerlessness" row. Those who replied "same," are in the "average" or middle row; and those who responded "less" are in the bottom or "high powerlessness" row. Although for both sexes the relationships fall in the expected directions (the lower the sense of powerlessness, the more satisfactory is the companionship), the different levels of evaluation are not significantly different from one another.

Consequently, the generalization that powerlessness and companionship are inversely related must be viewed as only tentative. But the pattern in Table 2-4 seems pronounced enough to deserve at least some initial speculative consideration. The key question of course is, how does the exchange and reciprocity model, which seemed to apply to two objective indicators, apply here to this particular subjective criterion of economic opportunity integration?

First, we must assume that wives identify their own degree of powerlessness to be the same as their husbands'. It makes sense to think of all these subjective dimensions as complements of the objective criteria discussed earlier in this chapter. And just as the family has a social and economic position in an objective sense, so do family members have subjective feelings about this position. We saw that it is the husband's "duty" to have the level of occupation and education that will provide as much status as possible with respect to the "rights" of wife and children. The same reasoning applies to alienation, anomie, and their particular subdimensions. It is the husband's duty to reduce or allay feelings of alienation and anomie, in conjunction with the wife's right to expect this.

Now in addition to the foregoing item, we asked each husband and wife to tell us which of the six items his spouse thought was most important for success. The resulting correlation was .85, indicating very great consensus between spouses over vital means to success. It also demonstrates that almost all 916 couples represented in the sample possess traditional orientations regarding means thought necessary for success. Now while we did not ask wives how "powerful" they felt their husbands to be, given the occupational structure of our society and given evident consensus over means thought necessary for success, we can assume that even had we done so, their responses would probably not have been significantly different from what they replied in terms of themselves personally. For when we ask a wife in our society about the possession of means necessary for success, we can be almost certain that she does not visualize these means nor the ends (success) apart from identification with her husband. His success is hers—however slight or great that might be, whereas potential attainments on her job (if indeed she works) do not reflect back on his success at all.

Likewise, whatever "means" to success he possesses, these are hers also. For the means elements themselves—hard work, ability, drive—all apply chiefly to her present situation, a situation of attachment to and identification with the social status of her husband. They are not likely, for example, to have applied to her in terms of success when she was single. That is, a single girl might say "family advantages" or "good luck" are helping her to "land" a "good provider" and thus enable her to get into a situation where she can enjoy "success" in life. But given the romantic love complex, it is hardly likely that elements 2, 4, 6 would ever "land a girl a good catch." Once she is married, however, these same three factors emerge as vital if she is to "enjoy success."

And, once wed, from whence come these means factors? Presumably, just as she is constrained to make her success the same as her husband's, just so she is constrained to make her capability (*i.e.*, the means) of attaining that success the same as her husband's. To the extent he is at a certain point on the means-end syndrome, she is there too—and probably very much aware of this. Given the attachment of the wife's status to the husband's, it makes little sense, therefore, to think of her as having independent means to success. As long as she remains married, and as long as this "attachment" principle remains in our society, it seems reasonable to assume that the wife will identify her degree of powerlessness with that of her husband. That "degree of power" is a reward provided by the husband to the wife to increase the probabilities of her actually attaining and "enjoying" success. Thus, to ascertain the wife's sense of powerlessness is to ascertain something that she feels intimately in conjunction with her husband. It is something that she shares with him, because he has measured it out to her in fulfillment of his conjugal obligations.

Specifically, as powerlessness is reduced, the wife perceives that her rights in terms of success and status—the task-oriented dimension of the conjugal unit—are being met. This evokes positive sentiments—reciprocal rewards in the form of desire for and motivation to engage in meaningful companionship with the one who supplies these feelings of economic opportunity integration. Aware of these positive affiliative overtures, and aware that the wife thus defines him positively in terms of universalistic criteria, he responds with positive affiliativeness, and the reciprocal exchange process continues.

Moreover, given our finding that belief in particular elements necessary for success is held so uniformly and strongly (82 percent consensus over numbers 2, 4, 6), then it must be particularly devastating in a success-oriented society to define oneself or one's husband as having less of these attributes than most others. By the same token, it must reinforce the sense of personal excellence of those husbands and wives who define themselves as having more than most others. In short, a sense of powerlessness is crucial because there is such strong and long-standing societal consensus over the centrality of these means to success. Awareness of this should enhance our understanding of why a sense of "power" functions as a medium of exchange within the conjugal unit. Both historically and currently, it is an extremely meaningful factor.

Yet its actual potency in terms of reciprocity with affiliativeness is only tentative because of the low F ratios in Table 2-4. In the next chapter, we shall find that the relationship between powerlessness and cathectic-type primary relations is much stronger. This fact suggests, of course, that "leisure togetherness" is less influenced by this form of alienation than are other primary dimensions. Chapters Three and Four reveal several other analogous instances, but we shall put off a more detailed discussion of these differences until they appear. Suffice it here to make the point that such contrasts exist, indicating the distinctiveness of these primary dimensions, and thus the importance of treating them separately.

DISCONTENT

Just as there may be alienation from the means to success, there may also be a sense of alienation from the ends—from the goal of success itself. In this case, the ends are the immediate rewards provided by the husband's full-time job. This dimension of alienation is labeled discontent. Though the term itself has appeared in the literature on alienation, it is used here to refer specifically to the level of evaluation of job rewards. Hence, our concern here is with alienation from the occupational system in terms of the rewards it provides.

Discontent was measured by means of the following five-item scale.[35]

1. "My job ["My husband's job," in the case of wives] really doesn't provide enough money for the things we need."
2. "My job really doesn't provide enough prestige."
3. "I wish my job would give me more freedom to do the things I really want to do."
4. "I wish my job would provide more and better chances to get ahead."
5. "I wish my job had greater security."

These five items cover what is perhaps the total potential range of both tangible and intangible job rewards: money, prestige, self-fulfillment, advancement, security. The degree to which husbands feel that their full-

[35] The respondent was asked to "strongly agree, agree, disagree, strongly disagree" with each statement. Assigned weights were 0, 1, 3, 5 respectively. On another item, the respondent was asked which of these five items is the most important part of an occupation? Which is second . . ., third . . . fourth . . . fifth . . .? Based on this rank order, the most important element was weighted 5, the next 4, and so on to 1. These weights were then multiplied by the weights for the battery items described in the text. The maximum score for any respondent was 75. The distribution of total scores was then divided into quartiles on the following basis: 0–15 (very discontent); 16–30 (discontent); 31–45 (content); 46–75 (very content). The last quartile covers a larger range than the others simply owing to fewer cases in the upper levels of the distribution

time job does or does not provide these kinds of rewards is the degree to which they may be said to be alienated or separated from this particular success goal. The same is true for wives in terms of their husbands' full-time job. Viewed more broadly, job discontent is another way of viewing the level of perceived integration into the economic opportunity structure, as was the case with powerlessness. These subjective dimensions complement the objective dimensions cited earlier. The correlation of occupational status with discontent is .47, and with education it is .43 (the greater the status and education, the greater the level of content). With income, however, the correlation is only .10, suggesting that money per se does not provide the major source of job content or satisfaction.

Table 2-4 shows the relationship between levels of discontent and companionship evaluation. Both sexes reveal a strongly significant relationship between discontent and affiliativeness: the lower the discontent, the greater the affiliativeness, and the higher the discontent, the lower the affiliativeness. We continue to find that wives in every category rank this kind of primary interaction as less satisfactory than do husbands. One difference here as compared to earlier tables is the larger spread between the very highest and very lowest mean scores. Furthermore, there is less clustering among categories—each level of discontent seems substantially distinct from the ones immediately above and below it. Finally, the *F* ratios here are much stronger than any considered thus far.

Therefore, while it was not so clear in the case of powerlessness, it seems evident that this particular subjective attitude toward success is strongly associated with this kind of primary interaction. Although alienation from the means to success may not overlap too markedly on to affiliativeness, alienation from the immediate fruits of success does. It may be that individuals—especially wives, since they are presumably more consumption and community oriented—are more aware of these ends themselves than of the means to attain them. Williams, for example, has noted the overall trend in our society to use ends rather than means as a more easily recognizable (to self and others) indicant of "personal worth." [36]

As it is the husband's *duty* to reduce a sense of powerlessness, so it is his duty to reduce feelings of discontent with his job rewards. The wife defines as one of the rights or expectations of her role that she will be able to be relatively content with job rewards, *i.e.*, able to translate them into desired family consumption. Goode remarks that "the responsibility for satisfying these (family consumption) desires rests primarily with the husband, and any failure is his failure." [37] Cartoonists enjoy lampooning

[36] *Op. cit.*, pp. 417–21.

[37] William J. Goode, "Family Disorganization," in Robert K. Merton and Robert A. Nisbet, eds., *Contemporary Social Problems*, New York: Harcourt, Brace and World, Inc., 1966 (rev.), p. 510.

the wife who is *never* content with husband job rewards, the wife who continually nags her husband to bring home a fatter pay check even though they may currently experience substantial affluence. In spite of these extreme characterizations, Table 2-4 shows that discontent is not rampantly unchecked—some individuals are less discontent than others. And to the extent that wives perceive their "right to content" being met, to that degree is a reciprocal reaction set off of positive responses, to the end that both sexes tend to evaluate companionship more positively.

There are some sociologists who contend that lack of satisfaction in work can somehow be compensated for through nonwork activities. A recent government document, in a review of the literature on "Job Satisfaction and Overall Well-Being," seriously challenges this hypothesis. The overwhelming weight of evidence shows that job satisfaction is positively related to such things as mental health, *satisfactions with family and home, leisure time and community.*[38]

In our society, the centrality of the job and its meaning for identity and self-worth pervade every aspect of the total context of life outside the work scene *per se*. The allegation that husbands and wives can compensate for limited job rewards through nonwork pursuits may be more ideal or myth than reality. This is true for a host of complex reasons, but a very simple and obvious one is that, contrary to the now dated popular song, "the best things in life are *not* free." Nonwork activities cost money; positions of leadership and responsibility in the community usually go to the well off, and so on. Rather than nonwork activities compensating for unsatisfactory work situations, it would appear instead that dissatisfaction with the latter tends to undermine the former.

Nevertheless, it is significant to note that evaluation of job rewards considered in their entirety is such an important medium of conjugal exchange, whereas income alone was not. This fact tends to validate the suggestion made earlier in the Chapter, under "Objective Integration," that whereas money per se seems too crass an element to exchange for affiliative solidarity, the inclusion of more subtle achievement and success factors in the syndrome seems legitimate for this purpose. For in addition to money,

[38] *Manpower Report of the President,* U.S. Department of Labor (Washington, D.C.: U.S. Government Printing Office, April, 1968), pp. 53–55. Some of the literature cited includes Arthur Kornhauser, *Mental Health of the Industrial Worker,* New York: John Wiley and Sons, Inc., 1965; Frank Friedlander, "Importance of Work versus Nonwork among Socially Stratified and Occupationally Stratified Groups," *Journal of Applied Psychology,* December, 1966, pp. 437–441; Thomas S. Langner and Stanley T. Michael, *Life Stress and Mental Health,* New York: The Free Press, 1963; Norman M. Bradburn and David Caplovitz, *Reports on Happiness,* Chicago: Aldine Publishing Co., 1965. In addition, see Michael Aiken and Jerald Hage, "Organizational Alienation," *American Sociological Review,* 31 (August, 1966), pp. 497–507, for another attempt to link the notion of alienation to expressive elements of human interaction.

the job satisfaction scale includes prestige, status, and security factors. And while wives might feel hesitant or even guilty about discontent with money alone, they feel it is legitimate to be discontent with the other elements. The cynic may declare that they focus on these intangibles as a "cover-up" for their concern with the material. Or it may simply be that once the wives have got past the stage of defining money as necessary for survival, the intangibles actually take on added significance. In any event, it seems apparent that we cannot overestimate the centrality of this particular alienation dimension for processes of husband-wife affiliativeness.

STATUS ESTRANGEMENT

Where just now we focused on alienation from the occupational realm, we turn next to alienation from the status system. In both instances the focus is on degree of perceived success, or articulation with the economic opportunity system. Seeman has used the term self-estrangement to describe the situation in which the individual works, not for any intrinsic worth in working in and of itself, but rather for ends that are divorced from and totally outside work behavior.[39] Our usage of *status estrangement* has different connotations. We are interested in the relative position in which the respondent *sees himself* with regard to the social status hierarchy of American society. To measure this, an item was used which in one form or another has been utilized by sociologists since the late 1940's:

There has been a lot of talk recently about social classes in the United States. I wonder what you think about this. If you were asked to use one of *these* names for your social class, which would you say you belong in: lower class, working class, upper class, middle class (upper-middle or lower-middle)?

With this type of item, the respondent is free, if he so chooses, to refuse to answer and to reject the notion that there is any such thing in America as "social class." The fact, however, that only 5 responses out of 916 could not be coded in one of the categories corroborates the conclusion of many earlier studies that most Americans do have at least *some* perception of a fairly well-defined status hierarchy.[40] Presumably they define this hierarchy in terms of certain widely held and generally acknowledged visible criteria, *i.e.*, symbols of success.

It is obviously beyond the province of this volume to consider in detail

---

[39] *Op. cit.*, pp. 790 ff.

[40] See Milton M. Gordon, *Social Class in American Sociology*, Durham, N.C.: Duke University Press, pp. 193 ff., for a critique of this kind of item. However, the correlations in our sample between status estrangement and SEI ($r=.49$), and education ($r=.57$) indicate it contains a certain amount of empirical validity as far as being a "subjective" complement to "objective" status is concerned.

any of the complex issues surrounding the class and stratification structure of American society. There is, however, general agreement with Gordon's suggestion that a "status order" exists, and that this order is distinguished by different levels of consumption and correspondingly different "ways of life." [41] Furthermore, given the existence of a status order based on observable criteria, there is the related factor of the "American Dream." Most Americans desire to "move up" within the status order. If they themselves cannot do so, they at least desire it for their children. And as Robin Williams points out, the higher one is in the status order, the more one is defined as possessing worth or personal excellence.

It therefore follows that respondents in the sample who place themselves within a certain social class category perceive themselves (rightly or wrongly) as meeting the visible status criteria for that particular class. In other words, they feel they possess enough of the right kinds of visible symbols of success (car, house, furnishings, leisure accruements, addditional material objects, friendships, ad inf.) to be credibly placed in that particular category. For example, those who place themselves in the upper class probably perceive that they possess at least the minimum amounts of those symbols generally deemed by our society to accord or to indicate or to be consistent with high status and great success. Those in the upper-middle class perceive that they have a large amount of these symbols, but not quite so much as some; those in the lower-middle class probably see themselves possessing an average amount of these symbols. Finally, those in the working class perceive somewhat less than average possession, and those who placed themselves in the lower class perceive possession of only a minimum amount of these kinds of valued symbols.

Therefore, those in the upper class may be said to possess a minimum sense of estrangement from the valued symbols of status and of status placement in our society. With each succeeding drop in class placement, we may assume an increase in the sense of status estrangement—with those in the lower class sensing maximum status estrangement. The sense of estrangement is not based solely on the sense of possession or lack of certain symbols, but also on the cultural value of what Mizruchi (building on Durkheim) has called "boundlessness"—the desire for ever more symbols of success, both for their own sake and also for the sense of personal excellence they tend to nurture.

Now it is obviously the case that certain individuals located anywhere in the class structure might not be "afflicted" with "boundlessness." Particular persons, either for strong religious reasons or else because of a Humanist-intellectual orientation, might not feel estranged at all and thus not alienated from the opportunity structure though they possess only a few or else moderate symbols of success. But for the majority of Americans

---

[41] *Ibid.,* pp. 173 ff., especially p. 177, also pp. 248 ff.

at all status levels, Durkheim's words probably describe their condition quite adequately:

No matter how one acts, desires have to depend upon resources to some extent; actual possessions are partly the criterion of those aspired to. So the less one has the less he is tempted to extend the range of his needs indefinitely. Lack of power, compelling moderation, accustoms men to it, while nothing excites envy if no one has superfluity. Wealth, on the other hand, by the power it bestows, deceives us into believing that we depend on ourselves only. Reducing the resistance we encounter from objects, it suggests the possibility of unlimited success against them. The less limited one feels, the more intolerable all limitation appears. . . . The limits are unknown between the possible and the impossible, . . . legitimate claims and hopes and those which are immoderate. Consequently there is no restraint upon aspirations. . . . With increased prosperity desires increase.[42]

Observations such as these are as old as antiquity itself. That most wealthy of ancient kings, Solomon, said essentially the same thing. But what differentiates current America from Europe seven decades past, or from most previous societies, is the absence of clear delineation between affluence and nonaffluence. Durkheim's perspective was one in which certain strata were generally constrained to "limit the range of . . . needs." On the contrary, in our society, especially since 1945, "the possibility of unlimited success," the removal of all "restraint upon aspirations"—these "American Dream" notions have become almost universally diffused throughout our society.[43] One need only look at the black community to substantiate this. If ever there were a particular stratum that was "supposed" to limit its aspirations, it was this one. But in recent years a "revolution" in aspirations has occurred throughout all levels of Negro society. Furthermore, recent census data show that some blacks have joined many whites in unprecedented prosperity.[44]

In short, the desire for affluence and resulting boundlessness have become society-wide. The more one has, the more one wants—and the more he feels he deserves and indeed ought to have. At present in American society, there are few if any ceilings or restraints on consumption aspirations. And that is precisely the point when we talk about status estrange-

[42] Emile Durkheim, *Suicide,* translated by J. A. Spaulding and George Simpson, New York: The Free Press, 1951, pp. 254, 252–53, as quoted in Mizruchi, *op. cit.,* pp. 129 and 105.

[43] Blau and Duncan, *op. cit.,* pp. 437–38.

[44] Bureau of Labor Statistics, United States Department of Labor, and Bureau of the Census, United States Department of Commerce, *Recent Trends in Social and Economic Conditions of Negroes in the United States,* Current Population Reports, Series P-23, No. 26, BLS Report No. 347 (Washington, D.C., U.S. Government Printing Office, July 1968), p. 16.

ment, *i.e.*, these aspirations themselves do not supersede the reality of actual possession. Certain persons perceive that they have in fact more or fewer symbols of material success than others—they are either more estranged or less estranged than others from the status system of our society.

In summary, therefore, we may say (1) that boundlessness is a universal affliction in our society—it is not an "ill" restricted merely to the more advantaged. But (2) the more "objectively advantaged" actually have more symbols of affluence, and it is this element that enables them to place themselves in a higher class position. In other words, regardless of the universality of consumption desires, in a society that applauds the actual possession and display of those consumption symbols, the more advantaged feel less estranged, and the less advantaged feel more estranged. (This distinction between aspiration and reality is akin to Merton's well-known contrast between aspirations and expectations.) Whereas the aspiration to unfettered material display may be boundless, the reality is that possession varies systematically. And it is primarily this variation and the feelings of deprivation associated with it that are in view when we talk about status estrangement.

The "typical" middle-class individual, for example, may feel he possesses more evidence of success than those in the working class, but less than those in the upper-middle or upper class. In the majority of cases, he thus feels less estranged from the opportunity structure than those "below" him, but more so than those "above" him. Therefore, on the basis of these kinds of assumptions, it may be said that, generally, those in the upper class presumably feel least alienated from the success system and highly integrated in it. Those in the lower class feel most alienated from the success system and least integrated with it. With each rise in class placement, we may likewise assume a decrease in alienation.

Only 21 respondents placed themselves in the lower class and so they were combined with those in the working class. And since only 28 respondents put themselves in the upper class, they were combined with those in the upper-middle class. Table 2-4 therefore simply presents three categories of status estrangement—low: upper and upper-middle class; medium: lower-middle class; high: working and lower class. We find that the data verify the pattern found under discontent with respect to success and affiliativeness. An inverse relationship emerges between status estrangement and level of affiliative satisfaction. The F ratios, though significant, are not quite so strong as they were for discontent. Women continue to rank companionship as less satisfactory in general than do men. Overall, we may conclude that alienation from the status order of our society has much the same consequences for affiliativeness as alienation from the occupational reward system. And this is to be expected since job rewards (monetary, in particular) are a necessary element in obtaining visible symbols of status.

When we talk about class position in terms of visible status symbols, we are coming perilously close to the "economic crassness" that our sample seemingly rejected when the indicant in view was sheer income. But we must remember that these status symbols are just what their name implies, *i.e.,* symbolic of something more profound than the possession of mere dollars. They are likewise indicative of "virtue, worthiness, excellence." From the wife's standpoint, therefore, it is the husband's *duty* to provide as many of these symbols as possible. It is her *right* to expect him to be the major source of these symbols and of the sense of excellence they provide. She expects him to reduce feelings of status estrangement in as large a measure as possible. The more she finds this expectation fulfilled, the more she is motivated to engage in meaningful companionship, and as the reciprocal process of debt and repayment goes on, the more both partners define affiliativeness in positive terms. In this connection it cannot be stressed enough that the conjugal family is structurally inextricable from the status order of our society, because it is the hub for displays of status symbols. Moreover, to the extent that there actually are, in our society, status groups based on friendship relations, these too tend to involve the total family unit. Therefore, both in terms of objects and friendships, relative status position is linked to the conjugal family. And the more this dimension of alienation is reduced, the more solidary does this level of primary interaction become.

So far in the chapter, we have examined the consequences of "objective" articulation with the economic opportunity system, plus the consequences of feeling alienation from it. We move next to consideration of the consequences of feeling anomic toward this same structure.

ANOMIE

The history of *anomie,* this twin notion to alienation, is hoary indeed, dating back to 1897 and Durkheim's famous study of suicide. Since that time, according to Cole and Zuckerman, there have been approximately 100 "empirical studies" and the same number of additional "theoretical studies" utilizing the idea of anomie in one fashion or another.[45] Its most widespread substantive application has been of course in the field of deviant behavior. In a recent volume exploring its utility there, many of the writers expressed serious misgivings regarding its past or potential fruitfulness. Both theoretically in terms of Merton's formulations and reformulations of anomie, and methodologically in terms of techniques such as the Srole

[45] Marshall B. Clinard, ed., *Anomie and Deviant Behavior,* New York: The Free Press, 1964, pp. 243–311. This report, though somewhat dated, remains nonetheless useful.

scale, it appears that research centered on the notion of anomie seems to be at somewhat of an impasse.[46]

Merton, however, still argues that addditional research on anomie is needed and could indeed be fruitful.[47] And Mizruchi, for instance, has recently contributed certain theoretical and empirical refinements to the notion of anomie.[48] Therefore, instead of shying away from it because of its admittedly enormous difficulties, an effort will be made in this study to make use of it. As in the case of alienation, however, we shall attempt to be quite specific in definition and rigorous in measurement in order to avoid many of these past difficulties, as well as to permit the maximum adaptation possible to the purposes of our inquiry.

For example, we shall treat anomie as we did alienation—as an abstract construct with more than one dimension. At the most general level, Merton states that anomie represents "an acute disjunction between the cultural norms and goals and the socially structured capacities of members of the group to act in accord with them." [49] To test this large-scale notion, he suggests that data need to be gathered in terms of several more specific subquestions. One of these is "socially patterned differentials in the extent of discrepancy between the accepted goal and its accessibility." [50] In short, as we shift from formal theorizing to the level of propositional testing (or systematic theory), we are forced to become very specific and rigorous in our handling of constructs and concepts. Failure to do this in the past has often been responsible for at least some of the difficulties with "anomie theory." Therefore, in this study, instead of focusing on extremely global notions such as "cultural norms and goals," or "socially structured capacities" of group members, we shall define the construct anomie in more manageable fashion, yet (in order to preserve theoretical continuity) in a fashion recognized by Merton as having particular significance. Hence, *anomie* here represents *the sense of disjuncture between aspirations* (with respect to the economic opportunity structure) *and actual expectations from this structure.*[51]

The value of anomie treated in this way is that, like alienation, it is

[46] Marshall B. Clinard, "The Theoretical Implications of Anomie and Deviant Behavior," in *ibid.*, pp. 1–56.

[47] Robert K. Merton, "Anomie, Anomia and Social Interaction" in *ibid.*, pp. 213–42.

[48] *Op. cit.*

[49] Robert K. Merton, *Social Theory and Social Structure*, New York: The Free Press, 1957 (rev.), p. 162.

[50] *Ibid.*, p. 175.

[51] This particular question has also been pursued by Mizruchi, and by some others cited in Cole and Zuckerman, in Clinard, ed., *op. cit.* A very recent study, using a similar framework of means-ends discrepancy, found this kind of "gap" conducive to mental illness. See Seymour Parker and Robert J. Kleiner, *Mental Illness in the Urban Negro Community*, New York: The Free Press, 1966.

defined at the level of abstract construct rather than a macrodescription measured by the kind of tool (*e.g.,* Scrole scale) which, strictly speaking, should be an index of the order of a concept. Treating anomie in this fashion as midway between macrodescription and concept—as a type of construct—the criticism is avoided on the one hand that its generality and ambiguity make it theoretically sterile, and on the other hand, that its usage is merely empirical "fact-grubbing," with no theoretical roots in important traditions in sociology.

At the level of construct, it immediately sensitizes us to a particular process—a subjective feeling process taking place within the actor. Alienation sensitizes us to the idea of current feelings of separation-integration vis-à-vis the economic system, to the idea of being to a greater or lesser extent "cut off" from the economic opportunity structure. But to feel cut off or presently nonintegrated with a particular structure is different from feeling forever "blocked" from it. What anomie does (as used here) is to focus our attention on feelings of being blocked relatively permanently from the opportunity structure. For the idea of expectation is inherently a future-oriented notion. In both types of aspiration-expectation measures to be used, we shall concentrate on the degree of expectation that at some unspecified future date, the respondent's achievement and success goals will actually be realized.

Logically, it may be argued that one could feel "cut off" or alienated *now* from the opportunity structure, but at the same time feel that the future will be "better," that his ends will eventually be attained—that he has hope. In fact, however, there is very likely a close connection between present economic integration and future hopes of same. For in most cases failure to effectively manipulate one's current life chances does not bode well for significant future alterations. The point is that anomie so defined is a notion quite distinct from alienation. By utilizing it in the sense of perceived future blockage as over against perceived current separation, we gain additional insight into the exceedingly pervasive influence of the opportunity structure on the conjugal family. As before, we posit that the less the anomie the greater the sense of articulation with the opportunity structure. With respect to the conjugal family, we hypothesize that the less the anomie, the more positive the evaluation of primary interaction—in this chapter, *affiliativeness.*

As was the case with alienation, we will not measure anomie directly (with say, the Srole scale), but instead infer it on the basis of feelings of blocked aspirations. In other words, we describe the gap between aspirations and future expectations as *anomie.* As we did with alienation, we conceive of anomie in two senses: first, with respect to the means of success, viz., expectations regarding occupational achievement; second, in terms of expectations regarding success goals per se. And as in our treatment of alienation, where it was assumed that in our acquisitive society a sense of current malintegration with the opportunity structure is a relatively painful and threatening (and in some cases, devastating) experience, here it is assumed that a sense of future blockage—of relative future hopelessness— is equally painful and threatening. In fact, an hypothesis for later research might be that in a society such as ours which is so future-oriented in terms of progress and optimism ("The future *has* to be better"), anomie might have more significant consequences for marital interaction than does alienation.

OCCUPATIONAL ACHIEVEMENT

In this particular instance, we examine the degree of disjuncture between occupational achievement aspirations and expectations that they will actually be attained. Historically, attainment in one's occupation was a basic value in and of itself. To strive diligently was to demonstrate to one's self and to others that one possesses this particular desire to please God, a desire that was virtuous per se. Moreover, even in current American society in the secular context in which most people operate, the belief remains that occupational attainment is a *summum bonum*. It remains a legitimate arena in which every individual may "show his stuff"—may demonstrate to others and to himself his virtue or worthiness. Furthermore, as Williams notes, the belief is still part of our culture that hard work and diligent effort will bring promotion, advancement, and more responsibility as further indicants that one is a "good man." Empirical verification for this appeared earlier in the chapter when we saw that over 80 percent of the sample hold traditional beliefs that work and effort will ultimately bring success. (Note discussion under "Powerlessness.")

The following lines, though quaint, probably capture as well as anything the current secularized approach to the "virtue" of achievement held by many.

> There is no chance, no destiny,
>   no fate
> Can circumvent, or hinder or control
> The firm resolve of a determined soul.
> Gifts count for little; will alone
>   is great.
> No man can place a limit on
>   thy strength;
> All heights are thine; if thou will but believe
> In thy Creator and thyself.
> At length some feet must tread

57

> some heights now unattained.
> Why not thine own? PRESS ON! ACHIEVE!
> —Source unknown

We found, moreover, (as did Mizruchi and also Turner) that Merton is correct in the idea that high aspirations are uniformly distributed throughout the class structure.[52] Using the Duncan SEI we found no significant differences between status categories in terms of occupational achievement aspirations (the measure for this is described below). Yet, as did both investigators just cited, we found that the lower the SEI category, the lower the level of realistic expectations that aspirations will actually be attained.

Consequently, for almost all American workers there is, on the one hand, the pervasiveness of the occupational achievement theme. On the other, not all workers perceive equal chance or opportunity to fulfill this theme. Some perceive that, in spite of high aspirations, the gap between aspirations and what they can realistically expect is too great to close. What consequences, therefore, does this particular dimension of *anomie* have for conjugal affiliativeness?

To try to get some notion of this complex interrelationship, we first of all borrowed and modified a measure that proved useful in Turner's earlier study of adolescent ambition.[53] The respondent is presented with a list of "six different ways a man can look at how he stands in his job or occupation":

1. Not doing quite as well as most people in my occupation.
2. Doing as well as most people in my occupation.
3. Doing a little better than most people in my occupation.
4. Doing much better than most people in my occupation.
5. One of the top persons in my occupation.
6. Doing better than everyone else in my occupation.

The respondent was then asked which of the six ways best describes where he thinks he (she thinks her husband) "stands right now?" (present attainment). The respondent was also asked, "Which of the six best describes where you hope (you–he) will be someday?" This latter question captures their future occupational achievement aspirations. To get at expectations, a final question was put to everyone who indicated an aspiration higher than their current level of attainment: "Realistically, what do you think the chances are that you (your husband) will reach that (future) point? Are they poor, fair, or good?" When responses to aspirations alone were examined for consequences for affiliativeness, no significant or

---

[52] Mizruchi, *op. cit.*, p. 70; Ralph Turner, *The Social Context of Ambition*, San Francisco: Chandler Publishing Co., 1964, pp. 80–85.

[53] Turner, *ibid.*, p. 240.

meaningful differences emerged. Companionship evaluation did not vary systematically irrespective of aspiration level. This appeared to be the result of an attenuation of the distribution of responses around choices 3, 4, and 5. This finding, coupled with the already stated lack of aspiration difference by SEI, suggests that most respondents tend to fit the Durkheim-Merton theme of uniformly high aspirations. On the other hand, Table 2-5 shows that achievement expectations are significantly and directly linked to companionship evaluation for both sexes.

Husbands are of particular interest here for several reasons. First, the spread in mean scores between the three expectation levels is greater for them than it is for wives. And second, the F ratio for husbands is appreciably stronger than is so for wives. Hence, a case can be made that this dimension of anomie—a sense of being relatively blocked from occupational achievement—is more salient or pertinent to husbands than it is to wives. To be sure, the wife considers it the husband's duty, and her right, for him to achieve in his occupation. But the meaning of this kind of achievement is different to occupants of the two roles.

For example, husbands are obviously more involved than wives in the actual behaviors necessary to and inherent in occupational achievement. It is they after all who also play the role of "chief production agent." It is they who feel most keenly the difficulties in the world of competition and work. Therefore, it is they who are more likely than wives to sense an intimate connection between achievement and a sense of personal excellence. Because of their more extensive personal involvement they are likely to feel even more strongly than wives this sense of duty, compulsion, and obligation. What is more, they may perceive (though perhaps dimly) that the more they are able to achieve the more positively their wives reward them with respect and affiliativeness.

Because of their strong ego-involvement with occupational achievement, husbands may define their wives as sharing their same feelings about these means to success. However, the other segment of Table 2-5 suggests that the major involvement and interests of wives is in the *ends* of achievement, viz., success goals. To be sure, wives do identify with their husbands in regard to the degree of achievement they expect them to have; but in terms of a sense of excellence, or in terms of the strength of this expectation, occupational achievement per se has evidently less salience or pertinence to wives than to husbands.

The question of pertinence can perhaps be illustrated in the kinds of meanings attached to a promotion or other type of similar occupational advancement for the husband. In all likelihood, while the wife may be appreciative of the intrinsic significance of the attainment in and of itself, her chief focus is nonetheless on its outcome, viz., greater prestige and economic well-being. Whereas the latter elements are by no means lost on the husband, he is more vitally concerned than she over its "intrinsic signifi-cance," viz., the worth that accrues to him on the basis of his attainments.

Somewhat like powerlessness, achievement is a means-type dimension, and wives are primarily interested in the means only in so far as they contribute effectively to goals. The point is that though the achievement-affiliativeness relationship holds for both sexes, this particular process of reciprocal exchange, owing to the medium involved (his own achievement), is more meaningful to husbands than to wives. In short, feelings of anomie, of being permanently blocked from occupational achievement, are a more reliable prediction of male affiliative evaluation than of female. As noted under "Objective Integration," in the "real world" means and ends are highly interwoven. In the minds of most people "achievement" and "success" are difficult to separate. Both husbands and wives are greatly concerned with each aspect of the whole. But in terms of relative emphasis, husbands may be more concerned with the former, feeling that the latter will then result as a matter of course. By the same token, wives tend per-haps to be more concerned with the latter, thinking of the former only in so far as it contributes to the valued ends.

SUCCESS GOALS

On the other hand, Table 2-5 shows that when the sense of anomie or disjuncture focuses on the consumption rather than the production sector, quite a different story emerges. The item used to measure success *aspira-tions* has previously been used by Rosenberg and also Mizruchi.[54] The respondent is asked, "How important is it to you personally to get ahead in life? Is it very important, fairly important, not very important, definitely not important?" To the extent that "getting ahead in life" and "success" are interchangeable terms, this item measures aspirations for visible status in the community or in the larger society. Although occupational achieve-ment per se cannot be displayed as evidence of success, certain types of life-styles can be and are so displayed.

Mizruchi argues that lower-status groups tend to think of success more in material terms, while higher status groups think of it more in non-material terms—for example, education as an end in itself.[55] Undoubtedly with regard to relative emphasis, this distinction is valid. But as Kahl remarks, middle-class groups emphasize the nonmaterial only after the material is somewhat assuaged.[56] Moreover, it would be naïve to assume

[54] Morris Rosenberg, *Occupations and Values,* New York: The Free Press, 1957; Mizruchi, *op. cit.*

[55] *Op. cit.,* pp. 72–74.

[56] Joseph A. Kahl, "Some Measurements of Achievement Orientation," *American Journal of Sociology,* 70 (May 1965), p. 678. See also Blau and Duncan, *op. cit.,* p. 438.

that for most of the middle classes (certain intellectuals and those with particular religious orientations exempted) ever more prestigious, conspicuous, and imposing symbols of success are not continually sought after.

This "secular" orientation toward success carries with it a certain built-in status anxiety. It can be argued that the pursuit of success is even more elusive than occupational achievement. Some men past the early stages of their career or job begin to perceive certain limits on how far they can actually go, given their own propensities and the structural situation of their employment. But in a rapidly expanding economy that is continually turning out "new and better" goods and services, plus providing easy credit to obtain them, what ceiling can ever be placed on consumption desires? Add to this that personal worth is attached to visible success symbols, and there is strong "moral" reason to display them because of what they signify. Yet there is always someone else who appears to be more worthy, more successful, further ahead, and with more status than oneself. This ever-present realization would seem to engender an ever-present sense of anxiety, and thus stimulate efforts to relieve anxiety by increasing one's own status.

In the pristine Calvinist work ethic, status anxiety is absent because one is simply not competing with others for success or status. In fact, to do so would be considered sinful pride. One labors chiefly for God and for one's family, with nary a covetous glance at others' efforts. Thus, one's sense of excellence is between himself and God alone, in contrast to the current dominant secular notion of worthiness in which significant others play the "functional equivalent" of God.

As was true for achievement aspirations, success *aspirations* revealed no meaningful linkages with affiliativeness. Moreover, using the Duncan SEI, we found no significant differences in levels of aspirations. Immediately on responding to the aspiration item, the respondent was then asked, "Realistically speaking, how good do you think your chances are for getting ahead in life? Are they excellent, fair, somewhat limited, very poor?" Regardless of what the respondent wants from life in terms of the status and prestige accorded to visibly successful individuals, what does he really expect he will get?

Wives were queried as to their success expectations on the basis of the same assumptions set forth earlier in the chapter, viz., that wives do not experience success (or the means to it) apart from their husbands. There is no "independent wife success" that is distinct from the level of success got for her by her husband. Therefore, whatever the level of success expected by the wife in terms of this particular item, it is at a level accorded to her by her husband. It is a reward, a right of hers corresponding to a segment of his duties. So whatever level of success she perceives she will one day attain, she perceives this in interdependence with her husband.

Nevertheless, in contrast to the chief production agent (the husband) who senses most keenly the link of achievement to affiliativeness, Table 2-5 shows that it is the chief "consumption agent" (wife) who senses a very strong linkage of her affiliativeness with level of success expectation. Scores for the male "production agent," although in the expected pattern, are not significantly different with respect to expectation levels. This kind of anomie—of blockage—in other words, appears to be more salient in its consequences for wives than it is for husbands. For when husbands ponder status and success based on visible consumption symbols, these things are less tangible to them than their behavioral efforts to attain them.

With respect to a sense of "personal excellence," consumption and success may be for males more of an inevitable (though vital) by-product of their production efforts. They may be likely to feel that if they "make it" in the production sphere, the consumption or status sphere will *ipso facto* be cared for. The result therefore is that for husbands the by-product becomes less of a medium of exchange for affiliative solidarity than the effort itself. Wives, conversely, although necessarily concerned with the effort, are relatively more engaged with the by-product. And for them, realization of success goals is a more basic duty for the husband to fulfill, a more legitimate and pertinent means to attain affiliative solidarity.

Whereas males play out most of their major life role behaviors in the production sector, most women evidently still feel that they play out their major life roles in the community-consumption sector. If males perceive that they are continuously evaluated by work peers in the production sector, females perceive that they are continuously evaluated by peers in the community or consumption sector. It is not that males do not "consume," or that females never "produce," but the issue is rather who is most ego-involved with which set of behaviors. And just as males feel the scrutiny of other males within the production sphere, females sense the scrutiny of other females in the community, or in the perhaps larger circle of one's friends and kin.

If women are in fact judged more on their husbands' attainments instead of their own, then showing the community that the family is getting ahead or obtaining status must be the prime means to contribute to the female's sense of worthiness. The community generally has little opportunity of knowing the actual extent of her husband's attainments unless these can be translated into some kinds of visible symbols. Consequently, apart from such symbols, the female's status is generally unknown to "others" as far as she is concerned. Display of appropriate symbols signifies to the community that this particular female and her family are indeed "getting ahead in life." There seems to be no surer way for the female to be certain that she is conveying these kinds of notions.

Yet her chances for getting ahead (and thus her sense of worthiness) are inextricably bound to her husband. Consequently, she feels it is her right to expect that the husband will enable her to realize her success goals as fully as possible. To the extent he does, and feelings of anomie (of blockage) are thus relieved, she reciprocates with more positive affiliativeness. Because this is a positive situation to her, she is motivated to do all she can to maintain it. The husband in turn reciprocates in kind, and this particular exchange process continues.

MEDIATING FACTORS

Thus far in the chapter we have examined two basic questions: (1) the effect of objective and (2) the effect of subjective articulation with the economic opportunity structure. In both senses, and both in terms of achievement and success, the general conclusion seems to be that with increased articulation comes heightened evaluation of affiliativeness. Income was an exception to this generalization, powerlessness was only tentatively linked to companionship, and there were sex differences, especially in terms of the production and consumption dimensions of anomie.

These exceptions underline the utility of the multidemensional approach toward economic articulation. This procedure enables us to examine almost every possible kind of linkage of the conjugal family to the opportunity structure, and thus to consider a wide range of pertinent theoretical issues. The same rationale applies to the tridimensional aspect of primary relations. Yet, up to this point, one generic type of issue has not been raised at all, and that is the consequences of certain mediating or intervening factors. These are variables that, theoretically at least, could be expected either to reduce or increase the evaluation of primary relations within the larger context of the opportunity structure.[57] Some of them have been used in past research in conjunction with occupational status or else education. Therefore, the third and final question has to do with the consequences of these kinds of variables. Four sets of these factors have been selected for examination, and each will be described in turn.

PERSONALITY VARIABLES

Self-Esteem. The two personality variables to be considered here are

[57] The question of when certain variables are "intervening" or "dependent" rests, of course, on one's overall conceptual framework and the theoretical justification that this supplies for particular decisions. As Winch notes, certain variables may sometimes switch roles depending on one's basic research design. The variables chosen here for inclusion as intervening factors appear in the text to have both theoretical and empirical justification for being so labeled. See Robert F. Winch *Identification and Its Familial Determinants,* Indianapolis: The Bobbs-Merrill Co. Inc., 1962, p. 57.

self-esteem and anomy. As we cannot go into an exhaustive summation of the current literature on self-esteem, the reader is referred to two recent studies to which this report is indebted. Both Rosenberg and Coopersmith investigated the relationship between social class and self-esteem. They were interested in whether or not the higher prestige accorded to higher occupational, educational, and income groups actually leads to a more positive global or overall definition of oneself. Rosenberg found only a weak relationship between social class and adolescent self-esteem. The main factors he found to influence self-esteem were paternal attention and concern, which are the result of factors other than social class *alone*.[58]

Coopersmith's findings corroborate Rosenberg's and permit him to generalize still more. "Widely accepted notions of the potency of status, or physical appearance as influences in personal judgments of worthiness appear to be wide of the mark . . . self-esteem is . . . only weakly related to social status and academic performance." [59] He remarks that the "limited" relationships between self-esteem and money, education, and achievement are "surprising" because of the "great weight" placed on these objective indices of success in American life. His major point is that these "success" elements per se are not reliable predictors of self-esteem. Instead, self-esteem hinges on the *personal context* from which the individual views the impact of the objective world into his life.[60]

The conclusion we draw from both investigators is that at the personality level self-evaluation does not depend solely on one's objective position in society, but is the result of a host of complex background factors (especially parent-child relations), native biological and psychological propensities, and numerous self-other relationships existing at a current point in time. We were able to test this conclusion because the ten-item Rosenberg self-esteem scale had also been given to our respondents.[61] The distribution of total

[58] Morris Rosenberg, *Society and the Adolescent Self Image,* Princeton, N.J.: Princeton University Press, 1965, p. 60.

[59] Stanley Coopersmith, *The Antecedents of Self Esteem,* San Francisco: W. H. Freeman and Co., 1967, p. 242.

[60] *Ibid.,* p. 243.

[61] *Op. cit.* The items were
1. On the whole, I am satisfied with myself.
2. At times I think I am no good at all.
3. I feel that I have a number of good qualities.
4. I am able to do things as well as most other people.
5. I feel I do not have much to be proud of.
6. I certainly feel useless at times.
7. I feel that I am a person of worth, at least on an equal plane with others.
8. I wish I could have more respect for myself.
9. All in all I am inclined to feel that I am a failure.
10. I take a positive attitude toward myself.

Respondents were asked to "strongly agree, agree, disagree, strongly disagree," with each item. Weights were assigned to the positively worded items in 5-3-1-0 fashion

scores was divided roughly in half into "low" and "high" self-esteem and Table 2-6 presents the relationship of self-esteem by sex to SEI. Our results for adults are remarkably like those of Rosenberg for adolescents. He writes, "class differences in self-esteem are considerably greater among boys than among girls." [62] Table 2-6 shows that proportions of both low and high self-esteem are distributed almost equally among wives throughout the class structure. There are only slight nonsignificant differences between females.

Husbands, on the other hand, do show significant differences by class in the proportions of low and high self-esteem; and the question is, are these due to occupational status or to childhood socialization? Rosenberg argues that for his data "social prestige is not sufficient to explain the relationship of social class to self-esteem, since such an interpretation would apply equally to boys and girls." [63] The same applies here to husbands and wives, for if class were sufficient to explain self-esteem, then wives would report significant differences, too.

Instead, his data show that lower-status fathers are considerably less supportive psychologically of their sons than are higher-status fathers, and that there are only slight differences in paternal support for girls. (Social class is thus a necessary but not sufficient explanatory variable.) Consequently, this greater paternal supportiveness accounts for higher self-esteem among higher-status boys. Inasmuch as present occupational position is largely a function of class background, it may be that the same type of argument is pertinent here. Women do not vary much in self-esteem because of closer similarities at varied class levels in earlier socialization experiences. Men, on the other hand, do vary because of earlier differences in supportive-type socialization (related to class, among other factors) and not primarily because of present prestige differences.

One could hypothesize, however, that prestige differences among adult males at least support or reinforce levels of self-esteem developed in childhood. For example, numerous studies report that the majority of sons tend to remain approximately at the same (or perhaps slightly above) occupational level as their fathers.[64] The socialization of sons in lower or higher status homes accounts for a certain level of self-esteem, and then when

respectively, and to the negative items as 0-1-3-5 respectively. The ten scores were added for each respondent to obtain his total score. Rosenberg claimed undimensionality for his scale through use of the Guttman technique. A factor analysis of our data showed all ten items loading together strongly on one dimension.

[62] *Ibid.*, p. 41.

[63] *Ibid.*

[64] Blau and Duncan, *op. cit.*, pp. 432 ff. "The combined rate of mobility in either direction between the manual and nonmanual class is 34 percent . . . with respect to upward mobility of working-class sons into white-collar occupations, the rate in the United States [is] 37 percent. . . ."

these sons become adult workers they carry this intrinsic personality characteristic into an occupation in which there is a kind of "fit" between learned self-esteem and self-esteem engendered by the prestige of that occupation. The lower-status son often develops a low self-esteem and tends to enter an occupation where prestige is low, thereby reinforcing his previously low self-esteem. But the higher-status son often develops a more positive self-esteem and enters a more prestigeful occupation that tends to bolster his already positive self-image.

It appears, in other words, that achievement and success within the opportunity structure do not exercise a major influence on adult self-esteem—at least in so far as being able to alter it considerably. Instead, given general mobility patterns in our society, attainments merely tend to reinforce previously learned levels of male self-esteem. Self-esteem would seem to be a basic personality characteristic shaped in childhood and which more or less endures regardless of prestige and status in the case of women, and endures in conjunction with prestige in the case of males.

Moreover, this enduring global personality orientation is evidently analytically distinct from specific areas where worth might accrue to the person. For instance, the man might be a good fisherman, hunter, churchman, or drinking partner, or provider. The woman might be a good bowler, seamstress, or club-worker. These factors might bring situation-specific feelings of worth (such as Robin Williams' notion regarding the "sense of excellence" due to success), but they are not evidently the same as one's global self-esteem, which is much more basic and is tied to native propensities and early formative experiences. They might reinforce one's self-esteem (such as does male occupational success), but they are theoretically distinct phenomena. In short, a person may be objectively "successful" and/or feel that he is, and still have a low sense of global self-esteem. The opposite is also true: limited achievement and success do not preclude having a generally positive image of oneself at the psychological level. The data in Table 2-6 support both generalizations.

The significance of global self-esteem for conjugal cohesion lies in its impact on processes of reciprocity and exchange. We would expect that high self-esteem would increase the evaluations of husband-wife primary interaction, and that low self-esteem would decrease it. This expectation is based on Rosenberg's conclusions that one with low self-esteem is "more vulnerable in interpersonal relations (deeply hurt by criticism, blame, or scolding); he is relatively awkward with others (finds it hard to make talk, does not initiate contacts, etc.); he assumes others think poorly of him or do not particularly like him; he has low faith in human nature. . . . Whether [he] is right or wrong about these things—whether he is accurately reading or is misreading the effect he has on others—these are the assumptions upon which he operates; these are the thoughts and feelings that guide his actions. Similarly, [his] participation in social life will be influenced by others' reactions toward him." [65]

In short, the lower the self-esteem, the more one feels threatened and insecure in interpersonal situations, the more likly he is to "distort" the "messages" he receives and gives. In the situation of conjugal exchange, the person with low self-esteem may come to feel (consciously or unconsciously) that he is not being rewarded fully enough for his contribution to alter ("He–she doesn't appreciate me."). This may be true both in terms of instrumental and expressive contributions, and for either sex. The person may or may not feel he deserves to be limited in the rewards he gets; nonetheless, he feels he ought to have more. His definition of being under-rewarded may simply be his perception, or it may actually be the case. Or it may be a self-fulfilling prophecy, *i.e.*, he thinks he is being "short-changed," so he responds "as if" he were, and the reciprocal response to him becomes thereby limited. Conversely, just the opposite effects should occur where self-esteem is high. Lessened feelings of threat should result in a more realistic and probably more positive evaluation of conjugal rewards.

To test this notion, we have selected one objective and one subjective indicant of economic articulation (deemed to be representative of their related dimensions),[66] and in each case have controlled for the effects of low and high self-esteem on affiliative interaction. Table 2-7 shows that our expectations tend to be verified. First, we note that controlling for self-esteem does not destroy the systematic linkage between economic integration and affiliativeness. Increased articulation still results in a generally more positive evaluation of companionship whether self-esteem is negative or positive.

Second, however, low self-esteem does reduce companionship evaluation (cf. Table 2-1) at all levels of educational attainment for both sexes except among wives with 13–15 years of schooling (some college). Satisfaction with affiliativeness is likewise reduced among those with low self-esteem regardless of level of job discontent, save among husbands with least discontent (cf. Table 2-4). On the other hand, high self-esteem has precisely the opposite consequences, *i.e.*, it tends to enhance positive affiliative evaluations at all levels of education and job content. The exceptions to this continue to be women with "some college" and men with least discontent.

In short, low global self-esteem in so far as it is a basic personality characteristic does tend to influence the perceptions that both husbands and

---

[65] *Ibid.*, p. 187.

[66] The remaining independent variables yield the same overall patterns hence we follow this convention to avoid needless repetition. In remaining chapters, *different* independent variables are used to show *similarity* in the overall pattern of relationships.

wives hold of this kind of primary interaction. We must therefore elaborate the earlier generalization that the greater the integration into the opportunity structure, the greater the evaluation of affiliativeness. We must add that in adddition high self-esteem increases this evaluation, whereas low self-esteem decreases it at each level of economic integration.

The two specific exceptions to the modification may be due to various factors, not all of which are clear. Perhaps even more important than the relatively small changes among women with "some college" is the great drop in companionship evaluation among women with most education and low self-esteem ($\bar{x} = 2.42$). Wives with this personality characteristic rank considerably below wives with only "some college." In the case of "very content" husbands who rank affiliativeness so high in spite of low self-esteem, it is apparently the case that negative self-image has little effect on the companionate perceptions of men who feel so strongly articulated with the economic system. These and other "deviant situations" to follow deserve additional research that is beyond the scope of the present study. They underscore the point made in Chapter One that full-orbed understanding of the conjugal family requires both psychological and sociological type factors.

Anomy. A few pages back the construct anomie was used in the sociocultural sense, *i.e.*, the sense in which it is predominantly employed by sociologists. Although it was redefined and made more specific, our usage remains a variation of the basic theme of sociocultural disjuncture. In this case it is disjuncture between valued ends and expectations as to their future realization. The conclusion was that a sense of disjuncture, of future blockage from the opportunity structure, influences affiliativeness negatively.

McClosky and Schaar, in a critique of the traditional sociocultural approach to anomie, suggest that certain psychological notions should also be considered. They propose a generalized personality orientation to the effect that "within the same society some people are highly resistant to anomy while others are highly vulnerable, and that one's susceptibility may be determined by personality factors *quite apart from the state of society or one's position in it.* [italics supplied]." [67]

They define *anomy* as a

state of mind, a cluster of attitudes, beliefs, and feelings in the minds of individuals. Specifically, it is the feeling that the world and oneself are adrift, wandering, lacking in clear rules and stable moorings. The anomic feels literally *de*-moralized; for him, the norms governing behavior are weak. ambiguous and remote. He lives in a normative "low pressure" area, a turbu-

[67] Herbert McClosky and John H. Schaar, "Psychological Dimensions of Anomy," *American Sociological Review*, 30 (February 1965), p. 39.

lent region of weak and fitful currents of moral meaning. The core of the concept is the feeling of moral emptiness.[68]

As was the case with the Rosenberg measure of self-esteem, the authors claim anomy is the result of exposure to ineffectual socialization; and like low self-esteem, it tends to be associated with ineffective interaction and communication, and with distortions in perceptions of social reality.[69] The correlation with self-esteem, incidentally, among respondents in our sample is −.46, showing that those high on one dimension tend to be low on the other. Therefore, in addition to a global perception of self-esteem, anomy provides us with an additional personality characteristic, a global perception of one's milieu that is not necessarily class-linked.[70] The respondent perceives the milieu as more or less orderly (positive) or more or less disorderly (negative). His total social milieu presumably includes the pervasive economic opportunity structure, so that if things "out there" are perceived as disorderly, this means that conditions affecting achievement and success are disorderly too.

For this reason, therefore, and also because anomy is associated with hampered interpersonal relations, we would expect anomy to have much the same consequences for husband-wife primary relations as self-perception. Specifically here, a negative perception of the milieu should reduce affiliative evaluation, whereas a positive view should enhance it. Hence, this usage of anomy, as an intervening personality dimension similar in nature

---

[68] *Ibid.*, p. 19.
[69] *Ibid.*, pp. 38–40.
[70] The items were
1. With everything so uncertain these days, it almost seems as though anything could happen.
2. What is lacking in the world today is the old kind of friendship that lasted for a lifetime.
3. With everything in such a state of disorder, it's hard for a person to know where he stands from one day to the next.
4. Everything changes so quickly these days that I often have trouble deciding which are the right rules to follow.
5. I often feel that many things our parents stood for are just going to ruin before our very eyes.
6. The trouble with the world today is that most people don't believe in anything.
7. I often feel awkward and out of place.
8. People were better off in the old days when everyone knew just how he was expected to act.
9. It seems to me that other people find it easier to decide what is right than I do.

The authors claim undimensionality of their scale through use of the Guttman technique. A factor analysis led to the same conclusion for our data—all nine items loaded together on one dimension. Responses were "strongly agree, agree, disagree, strongly disagree." Assigned weights were 5-3-1-0 respectively. The distribution of total scores for all respondents was divided as nearly as possible in half, to get a high-low dichotomy.

to self-esteem, is to be kept distinct from the sociocultural usage of disjuncture between aspirations-expectations (anomie).

In Table 2-8 we see that this personality orientation toward one's milieu reveals patterns generally similar to self-perceptions. One's definition of the "state of the world" does not generally destroy the direct relationship between economic integration and affiliativeness. Moreover, in most instances at each integration level, those with low anomy report greater affiliativeness than those with high anomy. The fact, however, that none of the F ratios under low anomy is significant does suggest that a positive view toward one's milieu weakens differences between status levels in the degree to which companionship is judged as satisfactory. Seeing one's milieu as relatively sublime and orderly helps to overcome some of the negative consequences of differential opportunity on companionship. To the extent this is true, it may be traced to at least two factors. First, as a basic personality characteristic, low anomy may reduce distortion, misreading, and miscalculations regarding affiliative interaction. Second, seeing the milieu as sublime may reinforce one's feelings about the increased probabilities of thus manipulating it for one's own advantage. If it is orderly, it is more capable of control and thus of achievement-success.

On the other hand, a negative view of the milieu seriously threatens affiliativeness at most levels of opportunity integration. High anomy probably operates on companionate interaction in a manner directly opposite to that just described for low anomy. First, like low self-esteem, and as a personality characteristic, it may account for increased distortion of this level of primary interaction. Second, viewing the milieu as chaotic may distort one's feelings about the possibilities of increased achievement and/ or success. In this type of setting there is a perceived severe limitation placed on the possibility of available rewards. When husbands and wives define the milieu in this fashion, the result is a clearly negative influence on the level of companionate interaction experienced with their spouses.

These generalizations, however, do not fit husbands with "some college" nor both sexes who are "very content." For some reason or variety of reasons, those with low anomy show a drop in companionship satisfaction, those with high anomy, an increase. What the explanation is for these deviant cases is not clear. As was noted under "Self-esteem," additional work is required to isolate the reasons for these departures from the general pattern. All we may do here is call attention to the need for such efforts.

PERCEPTION OF SPOUSE AFFILIATIVENESS

In addition to perceptions of self and of one's milieu, we consider next perceptions of one's spouse. Whereas measures of the two former elements tapped personality orientations, the measure here is based simply on asking the respondent, how he (she) thinks his (her) wife (husband) feels about their "companionship in doing things together." [71] In Table 2-9, we see that the respondent's *own* evaluation of affiliativeness is related to whether he thinks his spouse evaluates their companionship as either "low" or "high." Once again, therefore, we must elaborate the proposition that economic integration is related to affiliative interaction. At all levels of integration, affiliativeness is reduced if one thinks that his spouse evaluates it as low (cf. Tables 2-1 and 2-4). And at all levels it is increased if one believes that his spouse evaluates it in positive fashion.

There is considerable theoretical importance of this kind of variable to husband-wife exchange. If we refer again to Figure 1 (Chapter One), the wife is reporting in Table 2-9 how she thinks her husband evaluates a segment of Y_r, and the husband is reporting the same for Z_r. The sequence behind why the perception of alter's evaluation of affiliativeness influences one's own evaluation may go something like this: If ego perceives that alter defines his (alter's) affiliative rights as not being met fully, ego may then believe (rightly or wrongly) that alter is thus less motivated to fulfill his (alter's) affiliative duties. Hence, ego may define the affiliativeness he receives "as if" it is less satisfactory.

Conversely, if ego thinks that alter believes his affiliative rights are being met and is thus relatively satisfied, ego is more likely to believe that as a result alter is more motivated to fulfill his (alter's) affiliative obligations. Ego is then more likely to define his own affiliativeness "as if" it is more satisfactory.

What would lead ego to define alter as being dissatisfied or satisfied *within the same level of economic integration* is not entirely clear. Very likely there are subtle personality characteristics that are operative. But once this cycle is in motion, it is self-perpetuating. For the more ego defines his own affiliativeness as less satisfactory (based on status rewards), the less motivated he is to fulfill his own affiliative duties, and the more this contributes to a less satisfactory evaluation by alter. It is then at this point, *i.e.*, definition of alter's evaluation, that the cycle begins that is described above. Similarly, the more ego defines his affiliativeness as more satisfactory, the more motivated he is to fulfill his own affiliative obligations, the more alter is satisfied, and so on as above.

It is particularly pertinent here to recall that whether or to what degree ego is consciously aware of these processes is not at issue here; the outcome

[71] See footnote 2, this chapter, for a complete description of the item used. Pronouns were modified to capture actor's perception of alter's feelings. The first three categories are grouped into the "low" columns in Table 2-9; the last two into the "high" columns.

is the same in any event. As Homans puts it, in amplifying a point that Merton and others have made,

> Some readers may feel that in making men profit seekers we have made them more or less "rational" than they really are. If "rational" behavior means conscious rather than unconscious behavior, the question of rationality is irrelevant . . . conscious and unconscious behavior come out at the same place.[72]

In sum, consideration of this kind of variable sheds addditional light on the complex reciprocities occurring between the Z and Y poles of Figure 1. Nevertheless, these reciprocities are not independent of the W and X poles. Table 2-9 shows clearly that these expressive reciprocities are hinged to instrumental reciprocities as well.

PERCEPTION OF FAMILY LIFE STYLE

Turning now from the consequences of perception of spouse orientations to assessment of actual family life style, Table 2-10 reveals predictable results. Respondents were asked to evaluate the kind of living standard their family currently experiences, and answers were grouped into "low" and "high." [73] We find that those who assess their family life style as *low* report lower levels of affiliativeness when compared to Tables 2-1 and 2-4. Those who see it as high consistently report increased levels of affiliativeness.

These kinds of results are to be expected because we are tapping feelings about economic rewards in so far as they are translated into family consumption symbols. Wives who view these symbols as highly satisfactory are likely, as a result, to reward their husbands more positively on the affiliative level, and reciprocally, in turn, to be rewarded at this level, and hence to evaluate affiliativeness rather positively. Likewise, husbands who view their life style in positive terms probably perceive their wives to do the same (rightly or wrongly), and thus perceive their wives to reward them positively in terms of affiliativeness. Husbands thus feel highly satisfied with this reward and respond in kind, and the process of mutual reinforcement goes on. Conversely, when family life style is seen in negative terms,

---

[72] Homans, *op. cit.*, p. 80.

[73] The question read, "How do you feel about your family's standard of living— the kind of house, clothes, car, opportunities for the children, and so forth?" The possible responses were identical to those reported in footnote 2. The first three categories are grouped into the "low" columns in Table 2-10; the last two into the "high" columns.

then these processes are reversed for both sexes in the direction of less positive affiliative evaluation at all levels of conomic articulation.

It is significant to note that even some of those with low education and relative discontent with husband's job can in fact evaluate their life style as "high."And this does serve to boost their feelings of affiliativeness compared with others at the same level of economic integration. It is equally vital to note that high education and low job discontent do not guarantee high satisfaction with family life style. These realities underscore several notions. First, in some families, no matter how great the status or how high the income, the rewards are "never enough." The cultural stress on boundlessness, *i.e.*, endless varieties of ways in which to display status and to use income, makes relative satisfaction with any level of current life style difficult for many. At the same time, some families with limited resources of status and income "make do." They are somehow able to resist cultural pressures toward built-in dissatisfaction with current life style.

Second, and related to this, is the question of husband-wife consensus over income uses. Part of the explanation for low satisfaction over life style among some higher-status families may be the feeling that available income is not being used in "appropriate" fashion. In short, there is disagreement with the spouse over how income should be spent. In these situations it is not so much that income is defined as limited, instead it is defined as "poorly" allocated. Conversely, among certain lower-status families, although both spouses may be aware that income is objectively limited, they concur strongly over the ends to which it should be allocated. This consensus therefore contributes to satisfaction with whatever life style they experience, and consequently enhances affiliative interaction.

Degree of boundlessness and disagreement over allocation provides considerable leverage in explaining differences in companionship satisfaction *within the same level* of opportunity integration. Basically, the original articulation-affiliativeness relationship is maintained in Table 2-10. The two elements just described cut across status lines and tend to appear randomly in any sample of conjugal units. Their effects are predictable, but they do not mute the more central question of economic articulation per se—they either mitigate it or else exacerbate its consequences.

In terms of explaining the complexities of family cohesion, this variable, along with self-esteem, anomy, and perception of alter, plays an important role. For it is not simply the degree of articulation with the economic system that must be taken into account in explaining cohesion; we must consider perceptions of relevant phenomena and definitions of pertinent situations as well. And what could be more pertinent than the definition of the family's "life style situation"? This, along with perceptions of self, milieu, and other, figures significantly in the maintenance of the conjugal unit as an ongoing social system.

STRUCTURAL CHARACTERISTICS

Wife Employment. Earlier in the chapter we looked at wife employment as an independent variable. It may, however, also be viewed as a factor that mediates the impact of economic articulation on husband-wife companionship. It is one of two structural factors we shall consider as over against the four perceptual elements just examined. We have seen that households with working wives report lower levels of affiliativeness, although the differences were not significant. We also saw that the status of her job, among those households where she works, is directly related to positive affiliativeness.

In Table 2-11, the sample has been divided in terms of employment-nonemployment of wife. If we examine the first column, with regard to both education and discontent, we find that at every level of economic integration, save those with least education, husbands of working wives experience a drop in companionship evaluation. Similarly, these husbands rank below husbands at the same economic level who do not have working wives. The one exception is husbands with least education, and those in the "discontent" row. Therefore, from the husband's standpoint, wife employment generally appears to threaten affiliativeness, except among husbands with a grade school education.

At the same time in column 2, with respect to husbands whose wives are not employed, the trend is in the opposite direction, viz., toward increased companionship satisfaction. There are some exceptions, notably husbands with least education. It was suggested earlier in the chapter that among households where the wife works, those husbands with higher status may be more willing than lower-status husbands to concede to their wives more "independent rights" in terms of the work role. Yet the overall comparison between all husbands, at the same status levels, with and without working wives, suggests nonetheless that employment does introduce some strain into affiliative relations. The reasons may differ with regard to status. Higher-status husbands may regard her employment as an "unnecessary" incursion into their leisure togetherness, while husbands with less status may be more apt to define her working as a threat to their provider role. The significant exception—husbands with grade school education and thus probably the lowest-status jobs—may be due to the sheer dollars that the employed wife adds to the "family till." That is, some husbands at the bottom of the opportunity structure may be so glad for the economic benefits of a working wife that threats to male ego are overridden and mutual affiliativeness is enhanced. Similarly placed husbands without this "advantage" may lack "added motivation" toward more positive affiliative interaction.[74]

[74] This was the interpretation that Blood and Wolfe, *op. cit.,* put on their findings

But the complexity grows apace when we examine wife responses. In Column 4 among wives who do not work, affiliative evaluation is down from what it was in Tables 2-1 and 2-4, and generally lower than among wives who do work. Of wives who do work those with high school education and less report a decrease in affiliativeness, those with more education show an increase. As noted earlier, less educated (lower status) wives may perceive their employment as a threat to their husbands' provider role. This includes the least educated (0–8 years) wives in spite of contrary perceptions by husbands at this same level.

Likewise, wives with high education (13 and more years) define their employment as enhancing companionship in spite of contrary perceptions by husbands at this level with employed wives. Finally, employed wives show increased affiliativeness at all discontent levels contrary to husbands with employed wives. The glaring exception to the consistency of decrease in the fourth column fits this general pattern of contrast in spouse perception. Least educated wives do not show a decrease but instead an increase in affiliativeness, suggesting that for them not working removes a potential threat to their husbands' provider role.

In summary, it is evident that the relationships between the husband's articulation with the opportunity structure, wife employment, and companionship are extremely complex. Certain generalizations, however, do emerge. Most basic of all, *husbands and wives tend to perceive the consequences of wife employment in different terms.* Husbands with non-employed wives generally see this factor reinforcing companionship, whereas nonemployed wives generally report lower affiliativeness. Husbands with employed wives tend to reveal less satisfaction with companionship, whereas working wives generally report more—except for those with lower levels of education. At the same time that the foregoing applies to the overall picture, when under "Wife Employment," we looked solely and specifically at those households where the wife works, we found that for both sexes affiliativeness tends to vary directly with social status.

Much more research is needed into this question, and one way to explore it might be through an approach raised earlier, viz., the differing definitions of norms pertaining to wife employment. Husbands may be likely to define these norms as being more toward the "options" end of a continuum, whereas wives may see them more toward the "rights" end.

that "marital satisfaction" is greater among lower income families when the wife works. For a fuller discussion of Blood and Wolfe's findings, see David A. Gover, "Socio-Economic Differential in the Relationship between Marital Adjustment and Wife's Employment Status," *Marriage and Family Living,* 25 (November 1963), pp. 452–53. See also Susan R. Orden and Norman N. Bradburn, "Working Wives and Marriage Happiness," *American Journal of Sociology,* 74 (January, 1969), pp. 392–407. They argue that whether or not the wife *chooses* to work is a vital factor in husband-wife expressiveness.

Consequently, it may be that the more the husbands perceive their wives to concur with them in defining these norms as options (and thus in practical behavioral outcome, not working), the more positively the husbands tend to evaluate affiliativeness. Simultaneously, the more wives perceive husbands to concur with their definition of employment as a right (and thus in behavior allowing them to work), the more positively they evaluate this kind of primary interaction. In any event, we shall leave discussion of wife employment until the next two chapters where the potential usefulness of this "rights-options" continuum becomes even clearer.

Length of Marriage. A frequent generalization in the literature is that time erodes expressive conjugal satisfactions. Several factors are said to account for this. Perhaps a major one can be traced to the "romantic love complex" and the enormous expectations for marriage that couples hold at the outset of their life together. Although these expectations can perhaps be met at the beginning of marriage, it becomes increasingly difficult to maintain these high ideals as time wears on. The result is what Pineo calls "disenchantment" in the later years of marriage.[75]

In Table 2-12, the sample has been divided roughly in half in terms of years married (young = 16 or less; mature = 17+).[76] Surprisingly, we do not find what we had expected, *i.e.*, a consistent decrease in affiliativeness over time. A particular pattern, however, does show itself among wives. Young wives with 12 years of school or less, and young wives in the three greatest discontent categories reveal a decrease in companionship satisfaction as compared with Tables 2-1 and 2-4. Among mature wives, the consequences of economic integration are reversed. There it is less educated wives (11 years education or less, plus two greatest discontent categories) that report increased affiliativeness. And mature wives with a higher degree of economic integration (more education, less discontent) show decreased companionate satisfaction, at the same time that young highly integrated wives report greater affiliativeness. In other words, the higher the status of the wife, the more the tendency for her to experience decreased affiliativeness over time; the lower her status, the greater is the likelihood she will experience increased affiliativeness over time.

There are undoubtedly many factors that account for these trends, but one may be especially important. It may be that higher-status young women expect more from marriage at its outset than do young women from lower status backgrounds. Higher status women may be more convinced that

---

[75] Peter Pineo, "Disenchantment in the Later Years of Marriage," *Marriage and Family Living*, 23 (February 1961), p. 6.

[76] While a dichotomy is perhaps a cruder break than the ideal, the rapid loss of cases in the cells when we attempted finer breaks moved us in this direction. Given the necessary break by sex, as well as the four or five breaks by economic integration, it appeared we had little choice.

the ideals regarding companionship inherent within the romantic love notion can and should be attained. Perhaps a "functional family course" in college has helped to reinforce these aspirations. At first, therefore, they may be highly motivated to infuse considerable energy and effort toward the goal of more positive affiliativeness. They appear to attain their lofty goals during the early years of marriage, but apparently find this ethereal plane increasingly difficult to maintain as time goes on. Inevitably, the result is decreased affiliative evaluation in later years.

On the other side, young, lower-status girls may expect far less affiliativeness at the outset of their marriages. Particularly with regard to "leisure-togetherness," they are very much aware of the lower-status "male-buddy" syndrome in which (younger) husbands spend considerable time together (apart from wives) fishing, hunting, repairing cars, or in the local pub.[77] These young wives therefore realistically expect little companionship from their husbands, though because of the romantic love complex, they might aspire to far more. And because they receive far less than they desire, they tend to evaluate affiliativeness quite negatively. The fact that their evaluation of affiliativeness rises over time may be due, among other things, to the lesser involvement of an "older" husband with male "buddies," and an actually greater involvement with his wife. Instead of "going out with the boys" as often as he did when he was younger, he may simply stay home more and thus be with his wife, even if they do no more than watch TV together. Sociologists may be less aware of this possibility and more aware of the pattern of decreased affiliativeness described above, simply because of their generally "middle-class" orientation. In any event, the disenchantment notion should be modified to take into account (1) the differential expectations for companionship associated with social status in the early years of marriage; (2) the association of status with particular changes in companionship evaluation over time.

It seems evident nonetheless that whether young or mature, the original articulation-affiliativeness pattern remains. In spite of a decrease over time, the more integrated wives maintain higher levels of companionate satisfaction. With respect to husbands, it is somewhat more difficult to identify consistent patterns that go beyond this last basic generalization. It is clear, however, that mature husbands do reveal a decline in companionship satisfaction except for high school graduates and those who are very content with their job rewards. Older husbands in these two categories actually show an increase in affiliativeness. Among young husbands, it is not at all clear that they consistently perceive more positive affiliativeness than do older husbands. In sum, while most older husbands reveal

[77] It must be remembered, of course, that families with *lowest* status have been excluded from the sample. How their inclusion might have affected these results is uncertain.

"disenchantment" with companionship, it is not possible to state the converse, viz., that young husbands are enormously enchanted with it. And this suggests a third modification in the disenchantment notion, viz., that account must be taken of the different perceptions of husbands and wives.

CONCLUSION

This chapter has introduced the major variables of the study. Its chief focus has been on companionship, or affiliativeness, *i.e.*, behavioral leisure togetherness. One's spouse, in our culture, is defined ideally as "someone to do things with." This is one of the three major goals of the expressive dimension of the modern conjugal family. Therefore the more this goal is attained—*i.e.*, defined as satisfactory by the principal actors—the more cohesive the unit will be. Using an exchange model, we have suggested that this goal is attained maximally through interdependence of the husband's occupational role and the wife's expressive role. Specifically, we found that the greater the level of rewards the husband provides—especially in terms of prestige and education—the more positively his wife is motivated to respond to him, and the more positively both tend to evaluate companionship. Income alone did not have these consequences.

But articulation with the economic opportunity structure is defined not only in terms of objective reward levels; it refers also to subjective feelings of identification with it—feelings, for instance, that one is not currently cut off from it, or else blocked from it in the foreseeable future. It is possible to feel alienated (cut off) or anomic (blocked) from the means to success and/or from the ends themselves. We found that the more the husband rewards his wife by allaying these kinds of feelings, the more positively both tend to evaluate companionship. Moreover, it appears that wives are more involved in—and thus more concerned with—the ends, viz., success goals, whereas husbands are more involved in and thus concerned with the means to success, *e.g.*, occupational achievement.

Certain personality, perceptual, and structural variables influence the processes of exchange and reciprocity. Generally, a positive perception of one's self, of one's immediate milieu, of how one's spouse feels about companionship, and of one's family life style, tended to generate more positive satisfaction with companionship at each level of economic integration, and a negative perception generated less positive satisfaction. The consequences on affiliativeness of the wife's working are perceived differently by husbands and wives. The former tend to see it as having a negative effect, the latter a positive effect. Consequences of time are similarly complicated because mature husbands in general show a decrease in companionate satisfaction, whereas only higher status mature wives report such a decrease.

CHAPTER

THREE

•

Love and Physical Affection

"FOR UNDERSTANDABLE REASONS, THE LITERATURE ON LOVE IS IMMENSE. Probably the largest body of literature on this subject is that of the poet, essayist, and novelist, all of whom use humanistic devices to arouse and communicate feelings."① So writes Burchinal in his review of sociological attempts to get at this extremely slippery notion. Americans talk about love, sing about it, believe it to be requisite to marriage, and yet they are hard pressed indeed when it comes to defining or describing it.

But this difficulty does not mean that the social scientist should consign examination of "love" solely to the Humanist. Indeed, sociologists have been studying this phenomenon since the 1930's. Most of the work has focused on premarital love relationships, or what has been termed as "romantic love." Sociologists concerned with *romantic love* have focused, for example, on its negative and positive consequences for mate selection and for marriage. In contrast, those investigating *conjugal love* have, among other things, taken up the question of "disillusionment" or "decrease in love" as marriage goes on. Blood and Wolfe, for instance, conclude that

---

[1] Lee G. Burchinal, "The Premarital Dyad and Love Involvement," in Harold T. Christensen, ed., *Handbook of Marriage and the Family,* Chicago: Rand McNally and Co., 1964, p. 658.

✳"love is most intense and satisfying in the earliest years of marriage," and with the passing of time, disillusionment sets in.[2]

We have chosen to conceptualize love as one important type of primary relation that exists between husbands and wives. Analytically, it is to be distinguished from companionship and also from empathy, which we take up in Chapter Four. In the "real world," of course, these dimensions are closely intertwined. Yet each one is sufficiently distinct, salient, and important in and of itself to be treated separately. Companionship has been defined as "shared leisure time and/or activities." What then is love?

Though the literature presents several definitions that could be useful, the definition chosen and the measurement item utilized here imply a particular emphasis. In addition to being brief and concise, Goode's definition was devised purposely to examine relationships between love and the larger social structure, which is our objective as well. Therefore, we follow Goode in defining love as "a strong attachment, a cathexis between adolescents or adults of opposite sexes, including at least components of sex desire and tenderness."[3]

There are three simple elements to this definition: (1) the idea of attachment or attraction between persons; (2) a basis of or reason for this attraction or relationship that is fundamentally *emotional* (cathectic) in nature; (3) a behavioral aspect of this emotionally based attraction that is physical or sexual. The item used to measure these emphases required the respondent to evaluate the "love and affection" received from his (her) spouse.[4] Hence,

[2] Robert O. Blood, Jr., and Donald M. Wolfe, *Husbands and Wives*, New York: The Free Press, 1960, p. 234. See also Burchinal, *op. cit.*

[3] William J. Goode, "The Theoretical Importance of Love," *American Sociological Review*, 24 (February 1959), pp. 38–47.

[4] The item read: "Please tell me which of these statements best describes how you feel about the love and affection you receive from your (wife–husband)." (See Chapter Two, footnote 2, for response categories and appropriate weightings.) The mean score for all husbands was 2.77, SD = .903; for wives, $\bar{x} = 2.70$, SD = .971. The use of this "indirect" item to approach physical relations is a convention commonly followed by sociologists in large-scale sample surveys. The rationale supplied by Orden and Bradburn for following this common convention in their study is useful here: "The reader has undoubtedly observed that specific items on sexual relations are conspicuous by their absence from both the inventory of tensions and the inventory of satisfactions in the marriage. However, the items "not showing love" and "being tired" in the tensions battery, and "showing affection" in the satisfactions battery, were designed to tap sexual problems and satisfactions. Our indirect approach to sex stems, not from modesty, but from the expectation that a general interview schedule covering a wide range of life experiences is not the best vehicle for intimate disclosures. . . . Certainly Kinsey and his associates have demonstrated that people are not reluctant to discuss sex, but the emphasis and design of an interview schedule on sexual activities would be quite different from ours." Orden and Bradburn also cite Blood and Wolfe, *op. cit.*, in support of their argument. Precisely the same rationale applies to the design of our interview schedule as well.

In the absence of a schedule purposely designed to probe sexual matters in

throughout the remainder of this chapter, *love* refers to emotional feelings connected with some sort of physical displays of affection. These may take the form of "mild" types of affection such as hand-holding, and range all the way from various types of embraces through sexual intercourse.

The question to be explored here is how conjugal love is affected by the opportunity structure of our society. In spite of another of Blood and Wolfe's conclusions, "low-status urbanites love least," [5] it has been difficult to understand the connection fully. There is some hint in the literature that love and sex serve as tension-reduction mechanisms for husbands hard pressed by occupational demands. Undoubtedly this argument contains some validity, but it tends to emphasize "male role rights" without due consideration of "female role rights." Traditionally, of course, what Rainwater calls the "central sexual norm: 'Sex is a man's pleasure and a woman's duty' " has been operative in diverse world cultures. Rainwater's comparison of studies in Mexico, Puerto Rico, England, and the United States bears this out.[6]

The idea, however, that physical affection serves chiefly the husband's interests is undergoing a significant process of change, at least within our own society. Bell suggests that with increased education come "increased demands" by wives for increased sexual satisfaction. Moreover, he argues that owing to the "sexual liberation of the modern woman" that has already occurred, some women currently have a "*greater* sexual interest than is the case for their husbands." [7] And, of course, this trend should snowball in the future as more and more women attain ever more years of education.

depth, the kind of item used herein has been found to be the next best valid indicator of physical satisfactions. Though there may be some differences by sex and class as to just what types of "behavioral specifics" constitute satisfactory love and affection, it would appear that most individuals above the lowest strata (excluded here) share some common core meaning as to what these elements "are" and "should be" in marriage. It is vital to keep in mind that in this chapter we do not focus on behaviors surrounding sexual intercourse per se. But instead, following Goode's definition and argument, we are concerned with the whole range of cathectic feelings and behaviors known as "love." In so doing, we deal with this dimension of marital primary relations in its broadest possible terms. Theoretically, this is much more meaningful than consideration solely of a narrower perspective within the total dimension. Obviously, much more work needs to be done to determine all of the varied aspects of conjugal "love." It is clear, however, that at the least love includes emotional feelings and all sorts of displays of physical affections. And it is precisely evaluation of these notions that we are attempting to explain in this chapter. (See discussion surrounding Table 3-1). See Susan R. Orden and Norman M. Bradburn, "Dimensions of Marriage Happiness," *American Journal of Sociology,* 73 (May 1968), pp. 719–20.

[5] *Op. cit.,* p. 234.

[6] Lee Rainwater, "Marital Sexuality in Four Cultures of Poverty," *Journal of Marriage and the Family,* 26 (November 1964), pp. 457–66.

[7] Robert R. Bell, *Premarital Sex in a Changing Society,* Englewood Cliffs, N.J.: Prentice-Hall, Inc., 1966, p. 138.

Significantly, Blood and Wolfe consider the wife's education to be the main factor that directly influences her satisfaction with love and affection.[8]

Therefore, while male tension-reduction is one way to describe relations between an achievement-oriented society and love, this by no means exhausts the issue. The overriding theoretical concern in this volume is to work toward an explanation of conjugal cohesion. In Chapter Two, it was suggested that reciprocal role relations between the husband's "duties" in the economic opportunity structure, and the wife's status and economic "rights," lead to mutually rewarding affiliative interaction. The combination of ongoing affiliative gratifications based on an intricate web of reciprocal exchanges was said to contribute to cohesion of the conjugal unit. Can the same be true for the affective dimension of husband-wife primary relations?

Much more so than with either the affiliative or cognitive dimensions, the problem of ideological bias emerges here. If anything should be based solely on particularistic, person-oriented criteria, most Americans feel it is "love." Nonetheless, it would be naïve to overlook the influence of universalistic, reward-oriented criteria to the extent that they do operate. As applied to this dimension of conjugal interaction, particularism implies that husband and wife will behave toward each other solely or chiefly on the basis of an ascribed person-to-person orientation, simply because of what alter is, namely, spouse who should be loved. Universalism, on the other hand, implies that certain criteria that exceed the bounds of their own *particular* relationship and apply with equal force to all persons, tend to "move into," or "invade," cathectic interaction and influence its outcomes and evaluations.[9] The organization, therefore, of this chapter follows that of Chapter Two. We shall consider first, objective-type linkages with the opportunity structure; second, subjective perceptions of same; and third, consequences of mediating factors.

OBJECTIVE INTEGRATION

Perhaps the most striking feature in Table 3-1 is the contrast between the sexes. Husbands show a significant association only in terms of education. Wives, however, report significant linkages over all three dimensions: the greater the opportunity integration, the more positively is affect evaluated. Within the context of the romantic love complex, it is surprising to find occupational status linked to women's affect evaluations, but not to men's. For in popular lore, women rather than men are supposed to be the

[8] *Op. cit.,* p. 229.
[9] See Chapter One, text surrounding footnote 16, for Parsons' distinction between *particularistic* and *universalistic*.

chief bearers of romanticism. Therefore, we would not expect women to exchange affective rewards for status in a more systematic fashion than men, but this is apparently occurring. Even more startling is the factor of income. If women really are more emotionally oriented than men, then the crass element of sheer dollars should not make the difference for them that it evidently does. Now one might argue that higher-status women define, as part of their role, the norm that they should be "highly romantic" and "love-oriented." Believing this norm, they may act upon it and in turn perceive their husbands to be "pleased" with this behavior, and thus define this expressive dimension as more satisfactory than do lower-status women.

To what extent this element may be operative, it cannot be considered apart from two other factors. First, since our sample excludes women from the "lower-lower" class culture, the data chiefly represent those who in all likelihood aspire to what Leslie calls the "dominant middle class ideal-type" of family form so widely popularized through the mass media.[10] Inherent in this ideal type is the increasing demand of women at all status levels for maximum physical affect as their intrinsic right as wife. Rainwater remarks, for example, that even "lower class wives seem to have strong needs for affection which their husbands do not recognize." [11] In short, it seems difficult to sustain the notion that there are in fact significant differences by status in female aspirations for the degree of "love, affect, romance" desired.

Second, and even more basic, if most women above the lower-lower class level (excluded from this sample) believe they "should" behave very positively in the affective realm, wherein lies the motivation to maintain this behavior? Can it be simply an internalized norm that they "should," in the Parsonian sense, or is it instead tied to the more theoretically defensible notion of reciprocity, in the Gouldner sense? That is, given the premise that most wives at all status levels feel they should behave positively in the affective sense, and given their increasingly uniformly high expectations, why do some evaluate the ongoing process more satisfactorily than others? The suggestion here is that feelings of gratitude and rectitude toward the husband for his economic and status benefits are "displaced" on to affect, *i.e.*, generate and motivate desires by wives to behave positively in the affective sense, and as a consequence, to reap greater affective rewards in turn from their husbands.

On examining Table 3-1 we find that education is the one dimension in which husband-wife evaluations concur. The more years of education the respondent has, the more positively he (she) generally tends to evaluate

[10] Gerald R. Leslie, *The Family in Social Context,* New York: Oxford University Press, 1967, pp. 255 ff.

[11] Lee Rainwater, *And the Poor Get Children,* Chicago: Quadrangle Books, 1960, p. 68.

physical affect. Applying the exchange model used for affiliativeness, we may say that education, for the occupant of the husband role at least, is described as duty that corresponds to the wife's rights to status and prestige. Not only in its symbolic but also in its instrumental aspects, the wife defines her husband's education as a "reward." This in turn evokes positive sentiments, and motivation to reward him positively in the affective as well as in the affiliative sphere. In reciprocal fashion he responds positively to meet her affective rights, and here too a cycle (or ongoing cycle) of mutual reinforcement is maintained. And, as was true for companionship, education brought to the conjugal unit by wives functions as an additional resource supporting the interactive and interwoven processes of mutually gratifying affective behaviors.

Moreover, as with companionship, it should not be assumed that this exchange process is necessarily based on conscious, methodical calculations. In Homans' study of human exchange, for example, he argues that "conscious and unconscious behavior come out at the same place." [12] His point is, of course, that whether or not human beings are consciously aware of engaging in exchange-type behavior, the practical outcome is not likely to be altered. In this same connection, another statement of his has special relevance for affect within the conjugal unit.

Let not a reader reject our argument out of hand because he does not care for its horrid profit seeking implications. Let him ask himself instead whether he and mankind have ever been able to advance any explanation why men change or fail to change their behavior other than that, in their circumstances, they would be better off doing something else, or that they are doing well enough already.[13]

In both popular and scientific literature about the modern family, it has long been argued that its major function is to provide expressive gratifications—particularly physical—that partners enter into marriage with the expectation that this right will be met, that where it is not satisfactorily met, dissolution becomes a legitimate, nonstigmatic option. What is this but "profit seeking" based on a strong ideology of pragmatism and individualism, *i.e.*, maximization of individual rights and interests? And where many sociologists see this and acknowledge it as an exchange between "interacting personalities" (the proverbial "give and take" of marriage), we are arguing that in addition (not to the exclusion of personality factors) it is also an exchange at the structural level in terms of particular role relations.

[12] George C. Homans, *Social Behavior: Its Elementary Forms,* New York: Harcourt, Brace and World, Inc., 1961, p. 80.
[13] *Ibid.,* p. 79.

Moreover, not all sociologists have ignored the linkage of economic and expressive rewards. In a discussion of marital dissolution, Winch comes very close to the model suggested here when he states that the evidence shows that families with greater economic "resources" are able to offer greater "rewards" to members than families with fewer resources, and thus are more "stable." "An obvious next step," he says, ". . . is that the presence of resources should make the individual happier than he would be in their absence. To the extent that this is so we should expect to find evidence of greater marital happiness in couples of greater than of less resources." To validate his argument, he cites two studies by Williamson that correlate income positively with "marital happiness."[14] In short, the relationship posited here between economic rewards and expressive solidarity is not unique to this study—other sociologists interested in the issue of conjugal cohesion have considered it as well.

This level of analysis (role relations) must be kept in mind when we examine the contrasts between the sexes with respect to occupational status and also income. Traditionally, the occupant of the female role had very few "rights" in the physical sector. She was chiefly to meet the needs (rights) of the male, and in such "magnificent selflessness" to be content. But in recent years the "revolution" occurring in women's rights has had profound impact on the expectations of the married woman regarding physical affection. Particularly with more years of education, wives are no longer content merely to function as passive outlets for "male sexual drives." Instead, they want to enjoy the physical aspects of marriage as much as their husbands. In short, they define physical gratification as much a part of their expressive rights as "leisure togetherness."

But Table 3-1 shows that optimal enjoyment of physical rights cannot be dissociated from optimal enjoyment of status and also income rights. So the pressing demand of modern women for optimal physical satisfaction is best met by husbands who also provide them with status and with the sense of personal worth and excellence derived therefrom. Although women may not be consciously or entirely aware of it, they apparently do tend to respond more positively to husbands who provide both status and income. These husbands in turn then reciprocate in kind, thus optimally meeting the physical rights of their wives. The upshot is that the growing trend toward greater pressure of women for physical rights makes the economic articulation of the male ever more crucial and significant for conjugal cohesion. For the more the pressures grow by females for optimal physical

[14] Robert F. Winch, *The Modern Family,* New York: Holt, Rinehart and Winston, 1963 (rev.), p. 713. Robert C. Williamson, "Economic Factors in Marital Adjustment," *Marriage and Family Living,* 14 (1952), pp. 298–301; and "Socio-Economic Factors and Marital Adjustment in an Urban Setting," *American Sociological Review,* 19 (1954), pp. 213–16.

affect, the more vital it will become for husbands to play their economic, as well as their expressive roles, as "successfully" as possible.

At this juncture, it should be noted that women in the highest SEI category, and those in the highest income bracket, actually evaluate physical affect at a lower level than those immediately below them. At least three explanations are plausible, none of which unfortunately can be verified within the scope of this study. One is that these women are married to husbands with extremely responsible positions, or with long hours, or with both, and consequently time and energy for physical affect are somewhat diminished compared to couples immediately below them in status and income. In short, there may be such a thing as "over-achievement" or "over-success" in which the husband fulfills his occupational roles with such diligence that he fails to fulfill conjugal expectations held for him by his wife.

This last qualification is the crucial element in determining the existence of "over-achievement." There is no fixed point beyond which a husband may be said to be working "too much" to fulfill his conjugal roles. Such a point is defined subjectively by the wife in her particular situation. The wife of the traveling executive who sees her husband only on weekends may not define this as "too much" attention to work roles. In contrast, the wife of the 9-to-5 accountant may be very put out on those few occasions when her husband must work late to meet a tax deadline. However, in terms of sheer probability, we would expect definitions of over-achievement to occur most frequently in the highest SEI or income categories. This might account for a slight decrease in female affect at those levels. Nonetheless, the basic reward pattern enables these wives to rank affect higher than do many other wives.

A second explanation—equally plausible—is that women in these top categories may be afflicted by a variation on the theme of "boundlessness." Having so much affluence and status may lead them to desire and to expect even much more of these same rewards from their husbands. To the extent that their already "successful" husbands are unwilling or simply unable to provide the "much more," positive feelings regarding affect may be slightly eroded. Regardless of which of these interpretations is more valid, the fact remains that there is an overall patterned increase in female affect with increased status and income.

Finally, of course, inasmuch as the mean scores of the two SEI categories in question are relatively close and there is not great dissimilarity in the range of the occupation levels involved, it may be that the reported differences are perhaps owing more to random error of various sorts rather than to any substantive or theoretical distinction. This is a third possibility and cannot be ruled out, given the empirical similarities of the two groupings.

Now let us turn back to the revolution in women's rights, and look at it from the male perspective. In a discussion of increased women's rights in Western society, Goode remarks that "men have not, however, yielded their ancient prerogatives willingly." [15] Physical enjoyment, irrespective of wives' pleasure or else hardships caused by numerous pregnancies, has been traditionally a male prerogative. Irrelevant to the husband has been his objective success—his due as a male is maximum physical enjoyment regardless of universalistic achievements. Consequently, for husbands, status or income are not legitimate media to exchange for their affective rights. Affect is regarded (albeit nonconsciously) as an ascribed right, inherently theirs, not amenable to bargaining or exchange.

This is particularly evident when income is the criterion of success. There is almost no observable difference at all in male affect between the four income categories, and those with poor incomes actually rank highest in affect. And while there is the predicted pattern in terms of SEI, aside from the top category of husbands, there is a substantial clustering of all other husbands in the sample. Interestingly, those husbands with highest SEI also possess the highest levels of education. And as we have seen, education per se apparently becomes a legitimate exchange medium even for males. This certainly suggests that difference in education is the best single predictor of the extent to which husbands recognize and acknowledge the growing demands by wives for more meaningful physical interaction. This also fits with the widely noted pattern that greater female physical satisfaction is usually associated with greater education of the wife, who is in turn generally married to a male with comparable or better education. The more exposure to the "liberalizing influences" of education, the more husbands are willing to "yield their ancient prerogatives," and to grant that it is normative for wives to expect as much physical gratification as husbands.

And yet, because the correlations between education and SEI (male = .63; female = .46) and between education and income (male = .42; female = .42) are far from unity, SEI and income fail to distinguish significant differences in male recognition of female role rights in the way that education does. SEI and income fail to be meaningful predictors because it is possible for men to attain both kinds of economic rewards in high degree (especially income) without necessarily having a "high" education. Thus, it is possible to be "high" on these two indicators of economic articulation without at the same time having necessarily been "exposed to liberalizing educational influences" in terms of female role rights. But such lack of exposure is much less likely or possible as one ascends the educational

[15] William J. Goode, *World Revolution and Family Patterns,* New York: The Free Press, 1963, p. 57.

ladder, and evidently it is education per se that contains the greatest potential for motivating males to "yield ancient prerogatives."

As soon as the husband grants physical enjoyment to be a female "right," and not solely a male right, he must *ipso facto* take into account the wife's physical satisfaction in assessing his own. So long as it is a one-way street based on ascribed sex roles, the husband can "forget" (relatively speaking) about the wife's assessments. They do not matter because she supposedly has no individual rights or interests here that she is concerned with. She has only duties to "satisfy him," and if she does this, "she should be content"—she has been a "good wife." But what education does is to predispose the husband to define affect as a "two-way street." He now has affective duties to try and fulfill her affective rights, as well as vice-versa.

Education helps to define affect as being amenable to processes of bargaining and exchange, whereas SEI and income do not. Through varied subtle influences, education tends to "undercut" traditional male role expectations and in their place substitute more modern orientations. Specifically, this means that the female has certain affective rights. Whenever the occupant of a role has rights, it is often necessary to bargain with him in order for him to feel that his rights are being met. Education therefore places males in a "bargaining situation" with females (instead of a "master-servant" situation) in so far as affect is concerned. Once they define themselves in this situation, the consequences of the "bargaining media"—economic and status rewards—become operative, whether males might wish them to or not. Because in conjunction with the male predisposition to bargain is the tendency of the wife to respond positively to the husband on the basis of the greater status rewards that his increased education brings to the family. So what emerges is a situation in which the wife is responding positively to someone who is rewarding her on the status level, and who is also seeking to meet her rights on the affective level. For both reasons, therefore, the resultant process of reciprocal affect is very likely to be highly gratifying to both parties.

But occupational status and especially income fail to discriminate between husbands with regard to these complex processes. Using these criteria, men seem more disposed to emphasize their affective rights instead of their duties, less willing to bargain with wives, less likely to exchange achievement and success for affective satisfactions. For if there actually were an exchange process occurring in terms of differential amounts of status and income, then there would be corresponding differences in affect evaluation. Instead, using these criteria, males seem more prone to demand these satisfactions as "inalienable male rights," and to evaluate them only residually in terms of female rights and satisfactions, or relative to their own objective social standing.

Wife Employment. In addition to shifts in expectations pertaining to physical affect, another great change is taking place with regard to wife employment outside the home. We saw in the last chapter some of the consequences of this for companionship. Here in Table 3-2 we find that comparing households where the wife does work against those where she does not, produces no significant differences in physical affect evaluation. This was also true for affiliativeness. The emergent pattern here is interesting, nonetheless, because of slight differences in direction between husbands and wives.

Husbands who do not have working wives are more likely to evaluate physical affect more positively than those whose wives *do* work. But wives who do work are slightly more prone to evaluate affect more positively than wives who do not work. Husbands are thus consistent for both affiliativeness and affect. But while nonworking wives reported greater affiliativeness, the opposite is true here. Moreover, in Chapter Two, when we examined only those households where the wife is employed, we found significant differences for each sex, controlling for status of the wife's job (her SEI corresponded closely to that of her husband). Inserting the same sort of control here, we find in Table 3-3 that this time only wives report a significant difference. Higher-status wives rank affect more positively than do lower-status wives. Although husbands' responses are in the same direction, the differences are not significant.

From the female standpoint, the interpretation here is analogous to that for affiliativeness. Females are seeking to make employment either a right or at least an independently exercised option in terms of the wife role. They are also seeking to contribute concretely to the task-oriented goals of the conjugal unit. Increasingly, they seek a sense of worth that in our society comes uniquely from achievement in the occupational system. Employed wives of higher-status husbands do not perceive their husbands to believe that their own provider role duties or rights are being undermined. They believe (correctly or not) that their husbands are willing to grant them this right as part of their role as wife. Conversely, wives of lower-status husbands tend to perceive less willingness to grant this right because of the greater threat it poses to the husband's ascribed role as breadwinner. One result of this tension and strain is less satisfactory female affect when compared to higher-status couples.

But the question is raised as to why there should be greater similarities in male affect evaluation, when for affiliativeness there were more distinct differences. At least two reasons may help account for these similarities. First, husbands in general—and especially lower-status husbands—may be continuing the pattern we saw under income and their own SEI. And that is simply to treat physical affect as an inherent male right regardless of "complicating factors" introduced by wife behavior, evaluations, or rights.

On this basis, wife's occupational status is to them simply another irrelevent means by which to discriminate male affect evaluation. In the face of the overriding definition of traditional male rights, it just does not enter into the process of affect evaluation.

Second, higher-status husbands married to wives with higher-status jobs may feel that the time and energy their wives devote to their jobs detracts from time and energy for love and physical affection. Because these husbands are so heavily involved with their own careers, a wife also involved in a career may be defined as intrusion into this dimension of primary interaction. This may be so in spite of the perhaps verbal willingness of these husbands to grant optimal autonomy to wives regarding their own employment. If so, this suggests that the demands of women for greater individual rights both in the affective and also in the occupational spheres may not always mesh. There may be instances in which demands in the latter sector may, in fact, undermine objectives in the former. Thus, both reasons—the traditional male definition of physical affect and also of the provider role at lower-status levels, plus the demands on time and energies where both spouses hold high-status jobs—may help account for a convergence in male affect evaluation among all those households where the wife works.

In review of the chapter to this point, we have found important differences between objective economic opportunity integration and physical affect when compared to companionship. The core of these differences seems to center in the clash of definitions of male role rights *vs.* female role rights. The tendency of women seems to be to define affect as a right to which males must reciprocate in terms of duty. They tend to make it part of the exchange process within the conjugal unit, to evaluate it in terms of the rewards (status, sense of excellence) provided by the husband. Husbands, on the other hand, do not make it part of the exchange process, at least in so far as occupational position and income are concerned. Physical affect is so much a part of ascribed male role rights that, for them, it is outs'de the realm of status exchange. Only education is a reliable predictor that a long-term change of male definitions and expectations may be in the wind.

Yet concurrent with tension at that level is tension at the level of wife employment. And as we saw in Chapter Two and now see here, the probability that males are less willing than females to define wife employment as a right tends to threaten male expressive interaction. We must visualize, in effect, two distinct dimensions of strain or tension between male-female role definitions: one having to do with physical affect, the other with female employment. But the outcomes of these kinds of strain are intermingled. The former strain alone might be resolved in the direction of female expectations given the projected increases in proportions of both sexes with more years of education. But the outcome of the second is more complex and not at all certain. To the extent it remains in its present state, it tends to have negative consequences for male affect. To the degree males may, in the future, be willing to grant greater individualism to women in this regard, it could perhaps tend to have less negative consequences. Much more research is needed focusing on both types of strain, and on their long-term intermingled consequences for each other and for other aspects of the conjugal unit.

SUBJECTIVE INTEGRATION

ALIENATION

The question then naturally arises as to the consequences of subjective feelings of articulation with the opportunity structure. (See Chapter Two for detailed discussions of definitions and measurements of the constructs and concepts involved.) It was argued in Chapter Two that the wife defines as part of the husband's economic role obligations the duty to minimize feelings of alienation as greatly as possible for the family. To the extent that the wife perceives lowered feelings of powerlessness, discontent, and status estrangement, she feels less cut off from the opportunity structure, thus less alienated from it. And to the degree that these kinds of rewards are increased, companionship evaluation is enhanced accordingly for both sexes.

Looking at Table 3-4, we find the same overall pattern with respect to physical affect. Furthermore, this time powerlessness shows strong significant differences, whereas in Chapter Two, that was not the case. In short, while two major objective criteria (Table 3-1) do not have a meaningful linkage with male affect evaluation, feelings of alienation do. Over all three dimensions in this table, the less the perceived male alienation, the greater the husband's evaluation of affect. The same is true for wives. Conversely, the greater the alienation, the less positive is the affect.

Considering wives first, it is obvious that subjective feelings regarding economic opportunity integration have much the same consequences for affect as does their objective position. If, through identification with their husbands, they feel powerless to succeed, *i.e.*, cut off from the means to get ahead, then this reduces their affect evaluation significantly. The same is true when we examine success goals. The more the wife feels discontent with immediate job rewards provided by her husband, the less likely she is to evaluate affect positively. Likewise, the more she defines herself estranged from the status system of our society—a system based on display of visible symbols and appropriate behaviors—the more likely she is to evaluate physical affect negatively.

It may be said that we find here (to use Ruth Coser's descriptive term) a certain "emotional economy of marital relations,"[16] in which the husband's duty to relieve status anxieties generated by alienation corresponds to the wife's right to this relief. To the extent this right is met, the wife "gladly" fulfills her affective obligations, leading the husband to feel his affective rights are being met, motivating him in turn to exercise his affective obligations to meet his wife's affective rights, and so on. Coser, however, warns against interpreting any exchange-type description of human kinship behavior as merely being "mechanistic."[17] In the situation just described, the partners choose "freely" to respond affectively to each other as they will, yet at the same time there are certain social constraints operating to influence the qualitative evaluation of these interactions.

Admittedly, particularistic, personality type factors play a significant role in physical love and affection. The desire for conjugal love is a pervasive feature of individuals in our society. But alienation from the means to and ends of success is equally pervasive. In a success-oriented society such as ours, where personal excellence and self-worth are tied to economic articulation, it seems reasonable to conclude that feelings of alienation do maintain a significant place in the evaluation of affective marital interaction. It appears that wives, who remain dependent on husbands for status in the community, are interlocked with their husbands in a set of reciprocal role obligations and duties involving both status and affective solidarity.

Nelson Foote notes that sociologists and social critics refer often to the "lonely individual in mobile, urban society."[18] The idea of loneliness is of course analogous to the idea of being "cut off," separated, *i.e.*, alienated from important segments of our society, and is often used in this connection. He remarks that "sex stands for many people as the symbol of the intimacy they crave, but when they reach for the symbol, the substance may yet elude them."[19] The implication drawn here is that it seems narrow to reason that physical affect can be viewed solely or even chiefly as a relief from economic alienation—as a "built in" tension-reduction or anxiety-soothing mechanism. Foote argues that love, including all of its physical and sexual components, is realized optimally under "conditions of trust, relaxation, and confidence. . . . [This is the] area of life where self is most at stake."[20] Much research is needed, he notes, to identify some of these conditions.

[16] Ruth Laub Coser, ed., *The Family: Its Structure and Functions*, New York: St. Martin's Press, 1964, p. 184.

[17] *Ibid.*, p. 91.

[18] Nelson N. Foote, "Sex as Play," in *ibid.*, p. 189. Published originally in *Sociaι Problems*, 1 (April 1954).

[19] *Op. cit.*, p. 189.

[20] *Ibid.*, p. 190.

The suggestion here is that alongside the tension-reduction idea, the trust, relaxation, and confidence deemed prerequisite to optimal physical affect are at least partly enhanced through reduced feelings of economic alienation, and conversely, eroded by the increase of such feelings. Affect, in other words, is no certain relief from alienation. Instead, it may be that the former is partially dependent on the latter, at least in so far as the latter influences certain conditions requisite for its fulfillment. For as Foote notes, "self is at stake" when physical affect is in view. But self is also strongly at stake when achievement, success, prestige, and status are in view. It is quite likely therefore that these two kinds of behavior which so strongly "influence self" are also intimately related to each other. While the totality of their relationship is complex and multifaceted, at least one thread of it is being indicated here.

In her insightful case study approach to blue-collar marriages, Komarovsky writes that "disappointment in her husband as a provider" affects the sexual response of certain wives.

Some wives are quite explicit in making this connection. A 29-year-old mother of five children, married ten years, expressed disappointment that "sex is wearing off." She is dissatisfied with her economic situation and feels that her husband is not trying hard enough to better himself. She remarked that she might have been more interested in sexual relations if he were "getting along better." [21]

In these vivid terms we get some concrete notion of how feelings of alienation undermine "conditions of trust, relaxation, and confidence." To the extent the wife feels powerless, discontent, or status estranged, to that extent she feels "unrewarded"—missing the "due" that is rightfully hers. And it is evidently this feeling of being unrequited that may help spawn mistrust, lack of confidence, and feeling ill-at-ease. And feeling this way, she is less motivated to respond positively on the affective level, and thus her husband responds in kind, which helps account for her negative views toward physical affect. But by the same token, when the wife does perceive economic and status rewards and feels requited, then trust, and so on, are generated, along with gratitude, and the motivation to reciprocate with positive affect, which, in turn, result in positive responses from the husband.

Related to this consideration is the question of why certain objective factors did not discriminate levels of male affect, whereas alienation (in terms of the three dimensions in Table 3-4) does. In a long chapter devoted to job influences on marriage, Komarovsky presents rich detail that des-

[21] Mirra Komarovsky, *Blue-Collar Marriage,* New York: Random House, Inc., 1962, p. 93.

cribes quite vividly how "trust, relaxation, and confidence" (Foote's alleged conditions for affect) may be undermined by elements that could be apprehended under the concepts of powerlessness, discontent, and status estrangement. For example, take powerlessness. Komarovsky talks about those husbands who feel "trapped in their present jobs," and uses a comment by one of them as representative: "That's as good as I could get." [22]

Furthermore, there is the case of the husband who expresses job discontent: "low pay, unpleasant working conditions, night or shift work, or low status of the job." [23] Or there is status estrangement: "economic deprivations, anxiety about the future, the sense of defeat, concern about the failure to give one's children a good start in life, the bleak existence . . . ." [24] It is not just that the husband's evaluation of affect is contingent on how fully the wife fulfills her affect obligations, there is also the very real sense in which his affect evaluation is linked directly to the *initial* step in the whole process, *i.e.*, how well he "provides" lowered feelings of alienation. To the extent he himself feels alienated, he very likely senses his wife to feel similarly.

As Komarovsky puts it, he senses his wife to be "witness" to his "economic defeat." "Men and women in general share similar aspirations. . . . One-fourth of the young husbands have to contend with an unfavorable evaluation of their performance on the part of their wives." [25] This most relevant and salient significant other within the conjugal unit (the wife) is perceived to evaluate his personal excellence and worth in terms of the same universalistic criteria applied to him throughout the society. The result is, to use a long-standing sociological axiom, that the definition of his "objective" economic situation has greater consequences for his affect evaluation than the objective situation per se. His ability to feel "trust, relaxation, and confidence" toward his wife is limited by his own sense of alienation, by his feelings that he is not adequately fulfilling his role of provider. He is, in other words, not carrying out his part of the conjugal bargain, his end of the conjugal reciprocal exchange process.

The fact that he feels this way (*i.e.*, alienated), plus the perception that his wife shares this definition, helps to undercut the conditions optimal to affect. The following quote is obviously an extreme instance of deprivation, but deprivation or alienation is after all "relative." Each succeeding level of articulation would probably feel less deprived or alienated, and thus the consequences would be less severe for affect, but relatively operative nonetheless.

[22] *Ibid.*, p. 281.
[23] *Ibid.*
[24] *Ibid.*, p. 290.
[25] *Ibid.*, p. 288.

We ain't fixed so good. . . . He got no education and he has trouble with his eyes. When we got married it looked like things were going to be good, but things ain't so good now . . . gee, I'd like to have a different house, this place is a pig-pen.[26]

It was suggested earlier that two major indicants of objective economic integration fail to discriminate between levels of male affect because males are unwilling to define (consciously or unconsciously) this kind of criterion as a legitimate exchange medium. Yet when it comes to *feelings* of alienation, we do witness what appears to be an exchange process. It seems, in other words, that traditional, ascribed male role rights to physical affect lose their "force" in the face of pervasive and powerful feelings of alienation. Whereas income and occupational status may be irrelevant to the obtaining of his affective male rights, dimensions of alienation (also anomie, see Table 3–5) are not. They become defined (consciously or unconsciously) as legitimate exchange media, and thus generate processes of reciprocity vis-à-vis physical affect.

Those writers and social critics that have addressed themselves to the theme of alienation in modern society have often referred to its depth and potency. It would appear that these data tend to substantiate this point. For male role prerogatives in the realm of physical affect have a long and strong tradition behind them. Yet in spite of this tradition, differential feelings of alienation from the opportunity structure do distinguish between degrees of satisfaction with physical affect. In our achievement- and success-oriented society at least, the particularism of male rights tend to be overshadowed—even for males—by the universalism associated with feelings of articulation into the opportunity structure.

At the same time, it must be remembered, his wife's own actual affect evaluations are entering in alongside her behavioral responses toward him, with the result that there emerges an exceedingly complex web of interdependent definitions of rights and obligations. Much additional research is obviously needed to thresh out the numerous twists and turns of these processes. The point here is that these processes are inextricably linked to how "cut off" *each* sex feels from the opportunity structure. Although particularistic criteria cannot be discounted in trying to understand physical affect, those external forces that bind the conjugal family to the larger society are equally vital in shaping this kind of primary interaction.

ANOMIE

If feeling "cut off" from the economic-opportunity system is inversely related to physical affect, what about perceptions that one's future

[26] *Ibid.*, p. 302.

aspirations are blocked? *Anomie,* for purposes of this study, is defined as the degree to which one perceives a disjuncture between achievement-success aspirations, and realistic expectations that they will actually be realized. It therefore becomes a future-oriented construct, in contrast to alienation, which taps current opportunity articulation.[27] Like alienation, anomie is thought of in two senses: first in terms of means, *i.e.,* husband's occupational achievement; and second in terms of ends, *i.e.,* success or getting ahead in life.

In Chapter Two it was suggested that the relative saliency or pertinence of these dimensions differs by sex. Occupational achievement, it was argued, was more pertinent to husbands, and therefore exercised greater influence on their affiliativeness than did success goals. Wives, on the other hand, less behaviorally involved with their husbands' job, seemed to reveal a greater affinity between status goals and companionship. These distinctions by no means imply that husbands are not vitally interested in success goals, or that wives have no concern with husband's occupational achievement. Instead, they are more a matter of emphasis, or perhaps points on a continum of means and ends. Husbands are generally to be found more at the means sector of the continuum, feeling that this will *ipso facto* meet the demands for success goals. Wives are generally to be found more at the ends sector, concerned with means chiefly as they contribute to these valued ends. But both are on the same continuum. Here in Table 3–5, however, we find that this difference in emphasis has less meaning for love and physical affection than it did for affiliativeness.

First, in terms of occupational achievement, the F ratios for each sex are virtually equal. And because both are very high, it seems evident that for each sex it is equally true that high achievement expectations and physical affect are positively related. In other words, the degree of reciprocity between occupational achievement expectations and affect exists just as strongly for women as it does for men.

Second, when we examine the data for success expectations, we find that women show a very strong F ratio—stronger even than that in Table 2–5. We would of course expect women to show a strong relationship here, because they are presumably more basically oriented toward the consumption and community sphere than are husbands. In addition, however, we find something here that did not appear in Table 2–5. And that is that husbands also show significant differences in the relationship between success expectations and this particular primary interaction, viz., affect. In short, we discover more tendency toward convergence rather than divergence between husbands and wives in so far as anomie-affect linkages are concerned.

[27] See Chapter Two for a fuller discussion of the rationale behind the use of *anomie* in this study.

In Homans' terminology, value is the degree of reinforcement or punishment that a person attaches to an activity that he receives from other.[28] Married persons may very well attach greater value or reinforcement to affect than they do to affiliativeness. There is general agreement, for example, that women in particular are increasingly demanding more satisfactory affect than previously from marriage. And given the great stress put on sex (both premarital and marital) by the popular press and the mass media in general, there is no reason to suspect that males are likewise experiencing anything but increased expectations regarding it. Therefore, the reason for the greater convergence here may lie in the *relative saliency* or importance of these two types of primary relations. For example, reference was made earlier to the comparative saliency of occupational-achievement *vs.* success goals. In similar hierarchical fashion, it may very well be that, by comparison, love and affection is the more vital of the two primary dimensions considered so far.

Therefore, if affect is indeed such a salient, highly valued reward, then we might expect that it would be associated more often and more reliably than affiliativeness with those exchange processes that will tend to maximize it. As noted repeatedly, it is not that this kind of association is the result of an explicit utilitarian calculus, but rather that *inherent in the social organization of the conjugal unit (and indeed in all social systems), there is a built-in tendency for relationships to emerge that maximize and maintain desired gratifications.* This would explain, for example, why husbands reveal a meaningful relationship, with respect to success goals, in Table 3–5 but not in Table 2–5; and also why wives reveal a much more meaningful relationship both in terms of affect and occupational achievement. For both sexes the desire for optimal physical affect may be stronger and command higher priority than the desire for affiliativeness. At the same time, affect as reward is maximized in association with rewards of achievement and success. Very simply, therefore, this kind of association between these factors is more likely to develop more often and with greater strength than is the case with companionship. (Apparently, however, this does not hold for males in terms of SEI and income, owing perhaps to the inability of these particular factors to overcome traditional notions regarding male role affect rights.)

The result is that in spite of the male's greater involvement in the production than in the consumption sphere, the consumption rewards he provides ("hope" for success, for getting ahead in life) do bring him, in exchange, significantly different levels of perceived affective rewards. Concomitantly, in spite of the female's greater involvement in the consumption rather than in the production sphere, the production rewards provided by

---

[28] *Op. cit.,* p. 40.

the husband do trigger a process that ultimately leads to very strong and significantly different levels of affective satisfactions for herself. In reference to success goals, however, the F ratio for husbands still remains considerably lower than that for wives, and the distribution of the range of male scores is not nearly so broad as that for wives. These findings, along with the virtually equal F ratios under occupational achievement, suggest not only the possible existence of a hierarchy of primary relations, but also that this hierarchy itself may vary by sex. That is, both sexes may value affect over affiliativeness, but for wives the difference in value may be greater than it is for husbands.

Much of this particular discussion is admittedly more suggestive of hypotheses to be tested than of firm conclusions. What we can conclude firmly is that feelings of anomie both in terms of occupational achievement and getting ahead in life are inversely related to physical affect for both sexes. Komarovsky presents a significant remark in describing what we have called anomie, *i.e.*, the perception that future rewards, future "cracking" of the opportunity structure, are blocked. "For these poor couples the future is not an enticing prospect to be relished . . . it is uncertain and threatening." [29]   And this kind of dismal perception, this absence of hope or optimism, has the consequence of eroding current husband-wife affection in the view of both sexes. What needs to be explored in the future is the assumption that there is a hierarchy of expressive role rights, that this may vary by sex, and that within the conjugal unit those rights with greater priority tend to be found more often and more strongly in the kinds of reciprocal relations that provide maximum fulfillment of those rights.

MEDIATING FACTORS

Up to this point, we have explored the dimension of physical affect within the context both of objective and subjective integration into the economic opportunity structure. For wives, the greater the level of both aspects of integration the greater the evaluation of affect. For husbands, this was more true for subjective than for objective integration. Reasons for this sex difference were discussed from the standpoint of ascribed male role rights, and also in terms of the ways in which feelings of alienation and anomie may undermine physical interaction. Finally, the question of the relative salience and priority of affect *vs.* affiliativeness was raised. As in Chapter Two, we turn next to the relevance of key mediating or interpretive variables, factors that in addition to economic integration also play an important role in the evaluation of physical affect.

[29] *Op. cit.*, p. 292.

PERSONALITY FACTORS

Self-esteem. In the last chapter, the representative objective and sub-jective dimensions selected as mediating elements were respondent's educa-tion and discontent with husband's job, respectively. This time for variety, and also to gain additional reliability, we shall use husband's SEI and degree of status estrangement perceived by the respondent.[30] From Table 3-6 we see that self-esteem has much the same consequences on affect within the contexts of SEI and status estrangement as it had for affiliative-ness in terms of education and discontent. Aside from one or two excep-tions, low self-esteem tends to reduce satisfaction with love and physical affection at all levels of objective and subjective economic articulation (cf. Tables 3-1 and 3-4). By the same token, high self-esteem tends to increase affect at all levels. In every instance in Table 3-6, those with high self-esteem evaluate affect higher than those with low self-esteem at the same economic level.

As before, the assumption is that global self-esteem as a basic per-sonality orientation influences processes of reciprocity between husbands and wives. Low self-esteem tends to impair their operation—to make them less effective and meaningful, whereas high self-esteem has just the oppo-site consequences. Specifically here, those with low self-esteem might be more likely to underevaluate the level of physical affect they experience—to feel they are not receiving as much as they "should" or perhaps "deserve." They might be likely to believe that they are contributing more rewards to alter (both instrumental and expressive) than the affective rewards alter is returning in exchange. As Rosenberg describes it, the *egophobe* (his term for those with low self-esteem) "assumes others think poorly of him or do not particularly like him; he has a low faith in human nature." [31] But whether he is right or wrong in these perceptions, he behaves "as if" he were correct.

The result, according to Rosenberg, is impaired interpersonal rela-tions. "They doubt that other people like and respect them and . . . they themselves do not have a very high opinion of other people." He found that they "were less likely to be described as well-thought of, makes good impression, often admired, respected by others." [32] In short, the egophobe *is* more likely to "twist" interpersonal relations (including physical affect) and to "read them" in a negative or gloomy light, as far as his own interests are concerned, irrespective of what the situation may "actually" be. So

[30] See Chapter Two for discussion of formal and operational rationale of these six mediating factors. Also as in Chapter Two, the remaining independent variables yield the same overall patterns; hence we follow the convention of using only two dimensions (different from those selected in Chapter Two) to avoid needless repetition.

[31] Morris Rosenberg, *Society and the Adolescent Self-image,* Princeton, N.J.: Princeton University Press, 1965, p. 187.

whatever the level of rewards he or she is receiving, if one is an egophobe it is quite probable that he will tend to underrate them and to perceive the reciprocal relationship as less satisfactory than would someone in the same type of situation who is an egophile (Rosenberg's term for a person with high self-esteem).

For any one or a combination of these and/or additional factors, a negative global perception of oneself has a negative impact on physical affect. At the same time, a positive self-image may encourage added motivation to contribute more fully to alter's affective rewards. Feeling less threatened and insecure, those with strong self-concept are likely less often to misread alter's behaviour in hostile and indifferent terms. For both kinds of reasons they are therefore more likely themselves to receive more positive affective reinforcement, and/or to define what reinforcement they do receive in more positive terms.

Anomy. As described in Chapter Two, the measure of anomy used here also reflects a personality orientation—the perception of the overall orderliness of one's milieu (including the economic opportunity structure). This orientation is likewise the product of early socialization experiences, and it too influences definitions of interpersonal situations and interactions. In most instances in Table 3-7, low anomy (milieu as relatively orderly) increases affect evaluation, while high anomy decreases it (cf. Tables 3-1 and 3-4). Similarly, those with low anomy almost always rank above those with high anomy at the same status level (actual or perceived). Yet the only two instances of significant differences in mean scores occur for both sexes under high anomy and status estrangement. This finding tends to reinforce the idea suggested in Chapter Two that a negative perception of the milieu is perhaps more salient than a positive one, and thus produces greater differences in interpersonal conjugal behavior.

Nevertheless, the other side of the coin emerges much more distinctively for affect than it did for affiliativeness. And that is that low anomy goes a long way toward making differences in affect disappear by status level. For instance, husbands with SEI scores from 20 to 39 under low anomy, are virtually equal in affect level to husbands with highest SEI scores. Husbands with the lowest SEI scores are not far behind, and neither are the remaining SEI groupings. An identical pattern appears for husbands with low anomy when we move down to status estrangement: those with most and least estrangement are virtually equal in affect satisfaction, and those with moderate estrangement rank closely behind. There are similar patterns for wives with low anomy, especially in terms of the narrow ranges of scores between those with most and least status.

A positive global view of one's milieu, in other words, has unusually

32 *Ibid.*, p. 203.

beneficial consequences for this type of primary interaction. Wives who possess this characteristic are evidently more optimistic about the possibilities of increased achievement and success on the part of their husbands, and this greatly increases their motivation to reciprocate in terms of affective rewards, which enhances their husbands' affect levels, which then contributes to wives' affect satisfaction. Husbands who feel positive toward the milieu may believe their wives to feel the same (rightly or wrongly), and to define them "as if" they are reciprocating positively on the affective level, which then leads husbands to reciprocate in kind. Moreover, entering also into these complex processes is the greater general competence and security in interpersonal relations that are presumably associated with this positive personality strength.

Beyond this, however, the explanation as to why positive affect has the affinity it does with low anomy requires additional research. At this point, we may only conclude that whereas high anomy tends to reduce affect evaluation at all levels of economic integration, low anomy moves in the direction of equalizing affect evaluation at various levels of objective and perceived status.

PERCEPTION OF SPOUSE AFFECT

Table 3-8 shows the results of asking each respondent how he (she) believes his (her) own spouse feels about the "love and physical affection" he (she) receives. [33] We find that a perception that alter evaluates physical affect negatively lowers affect evaluation at all levels of social status, both actual and self-defined (cf. Tables 3-1 and 3-4). When alter is seen as evaluating affect positively, actor's own affect evaluation rises substantially. Thus, it is clear that the definition of other's feelings regarding affect influences the exchange process pertaining to affect in much the same theoretical fashion as described in Chapter Two for affiliativeness. That is, the more actor defines alter as affectively satisfied, the more likely actor is to believe that alter will then reciprocate positive affective behavior; and similarly if actor thinks alter is dissatisfied, he will be less likely to expect alter's positive affective behavior.

In Table 3-8, among those husbands who believe their wives evaluate affect positively, the consequence is a blurring of objective and subjective status differences. This phenomenon partially repeats a pattern just observed under anomy. In the case of SEI, the difference in total range between lowest and highest scores is only .14, and between the lowest and highest SEI categories it is only .08. A similarly narrow range exists for male

[33] See footnote 4 for more exact wording and reference to response categories. Pronouns were altered as in Chapter Two. The first three categories are combined into the "low" column, the last two into the "high" column.

status-estrangement categories when spouse perception is seen as positive. Thus, husbands who perceive that their wives define their own (wives') affective rights as being met are likely to believe that their wives reciprocate in kind. In addition, this perception has the consequence of overcoming differences in male affect evaluation in terms of reward levels that they provide.

There are at least two possibilities to account for lower-status males evaluating affect in a fashion so similar to that in which husbands of higher status evaluate it. One is that some husbands in spite of lower status possess the personality characteristics that enable them to meet the affective demands of their wives to a great degree, so much so in fact that their wives, in spite of not having high-status rewards, respond to them very positively on the affective level. These wives do this (*i.e.*, reciprocate) because their husbands' unusual competence and skills in this area tend to compensate for and/or override the minimal status rewards they provide. This kind of situation probably accounts for some of the high affect evaluation by lower-status husbands.

The other explanation is an extension of the earlier interpretation of Table 3-1. Some lower-status husbands are likely to consider physical satisfaction as a "male right" regardless of rewards they bring to their wives—whether expressive or instrumental. As a result, these husbands are likely to misread their wives' actual feelings about affect (if indeed they have given them much careful thought at all). They may assume that their wives' feelings are positive for no good reason at all, or simply because "good wives" are "supposed" to be satisfied with whatever the husband considers "reasonable" physical affect. Or they may define their wives' affect as high (whether accurate or not) because to admit otherwise (to themselves or to the interviewer) would reflect on their own capabilities either instrumentally or expressively. In any case, some of the high affect evaluation by lower status husbands may be due to perceptual distortions traceable to traditional "male role" prerogatives.

Among husbands whose wives are defined as affectively dissatisfied, there are strong significant differences by status level in both the objective and subjective senses. We may therefore conclude for husbands that whereas increased status results in increased affect, still affect is reduced at all status levels if the wife is perceived to evaluate it negatively. If, however, she is perceived to evaluate it positively, differences in male affect by status tend to be reduced considerably·

From the wife's standpoint, perception that the husband evaluates affect as low tends to retain systematic differences by status in her own affect evaluations, although these differences are not significant. When wives perceive their husbands to evaluate affect as high, differences in wives' affect between SEI categories tend to become slight, much as they did for husbands. However, systematic and strongly significant differences in wives' affect evaluations remain with regard to status estrangement and high or positive perceptions of husbands' affect. So wives, unlike husbands, are not quite so prone to allow perceptions of alter's positive affect to blur the consequences of status rewards—specifically the consequences of perceived social status.

PERCEPTION OF FAMILY LIFE STYLE

We move now to the last of the perceptual type variables, viz., evaluation of current family life style. Table 3-9 shows that when life style is evaluated in high or positive terms, physical affect is likewise evaluated more positively (cf. Tables 3-1 and 3-4) at all status levels.[34] At the same time, both sexes reveal that a negative feeling toward life style results in reduced satisfaction with love and physical affection. Consequently at each status level those who rank life style positively evaluate affect higher than those who do not.

Status estrangement refers to the level of integration or articulation with the economic system, *i.e.*, the level of perceived rewards obtained from it. But distinct from the level of perceived status, or actual display of appropriate consumption symbols, and also distinct from objective status, is the degree of satisfaction with those rewards, especially in so far as they are manifested in family living standard. So that status—whether actual or perceived—may vary independently of satisfaction with that status or family life style. Irrespective of status a husband or wife may either wish for more success symbols (boundlessness) or else be relatively content with those already possessed.

So far in this chapter, we have seen several situations in which differences in affect by degree of economic articulation were blurred by certain of these elaboration-type variables. There is additional evidence for this blurring within the SEI dimension among both husbands and wives who view family life style positively. This is especially true among wives, where those in the lowest SEI actually equal those in the highest SEI. But husbands too show minimal affect differences in terms of objective status when they view their life style in this same fashion. Therefore when life-style satisfaction is great it tends to compensate for lowered objective status or actual rewards, so much so that status differences in affect are minimal. Defining one's life style in this way helps to mitigate the consequences of limited objective rewards.

Within the subjective dimension of status-estrangement, however, syste-

---

[34] See footnote 4 for reference to response categories. The first three categories are grouped into the "low" columns, the last two into the "high" columns. See Chapter Two for exact wording of question.

matic differences in affect remain much more evident—even among those who do perceive life style positively. Indeed among wives, unlike the case under objective status, the differences are not only pronounced but also significant. Hence, the consequences for affect, of feeling alienated from the status system, are not easily overcome even by a positive view of family living standard. When one feels that rewards are limited, it is much more difficult for even a satisfactory life style to compensate for or to mitigate the consequences of their absence, at least in so far as physical affect is concerned. There is probably a good deal of simple resignation in this situation. One feels alienated, but "what can be done about it?" If the response is "little or nothing," then one is often forced into being satisfied with whatever status symbols are available. In sum, we once again find indication of what is likely the greater potency of *subjective* feelings toward the opportunity system, as compared with one's *actual* position in it.

STRUCTURAL FACTORS

Wife Employment. Up to this point, we have examined the mediating effects of perceptions of self, milieu, other, and life style on physical affect. We now turn to the structural issue of wife employment. Earlier in the chapter, we saw that status of wife's job was directly related to positive female affect, but that her job status did not reveal significant differences in male affect. In Table 3-10 we find first that husbands with working wives report lowered levels of physical affect (cf. Tables 3-1 and 3-4) at every status category. They likewise rank this cathectic dimension lower than do husbands at the same status level whose wives do not work. Furthermore, in most categories, these latter husbands rank affect higher than they did in the earlier tables.

In the overall picture, therefore, wife employment influences male affect in much the same way as did affiliativeness: its presence tends to have deleterious consequences, its absence more positive results. However, the major exception to this generalization is among lower status husbands whose wives do not work. They either report no change or else a drop in physical affect. Yet, husbands in these same status categories whose wives do work fail to show an increase in affect. Although one might suspect that lower-status husbands with employed wives might "reward" their wives more positively at the affective level in exchange for the enlarged economic resources their wives pump into the unit, this is not so. Instead, they apparently feel their provider role being undermined and thus act negatively toward their wives, and perceive them to reicprocate in kind.

Nonetheless, it may be that husbands at these status levels whose wives do not work wish that they would do so in order to obtain greater family resources. These husbands might presently feel (albeit perhaps mistakenly) that if their wives would work, mutual affectiveness might be enhanced. Concomitantly, because their wives do not currently work, affect is reduced. But these husbands evidently do not perceive that even if their wives would work affect would not then be enhanced; instead, the likelihood is that it would actually be reduced. Thus, at these status levels—whether the wife works or not—male satisfaction with physical affect remains minimal.

Among higher-status husbands, the fact of the wife's employment or nonemployment does make a difference. And where her working does reduce male affect at these levels, it is probably owing to perceived incursions on time and energy, and to clashes over redefinitions of male participation in household duties.

In comparing wives at each status level, we find most often that those who *do* work report higher affect than those who do not. Likewise, most categories of employed wives report an increase in affect over the earlier figures, whereas most groups of nonemployed wives show a decrease. Those employed wives who report a decrease are found at the two lowest subjective status levels and at the highest objective status level. Apparently these women share with their husbands the perception that their employment threatens affect. Where status is high, these wives are probably aware of their husbands' views on the incursions and readjustments caused by wife employment. Where status is low, those wives are perhaps conscious of the "undermining effect" their working has on the male-provider role.

Overall, however, there is a basic divergence by sex in assessing the consequences of wife employment on physical affect, and at this general level it is similar to the pattern that emerged for affiliativeness. The data continue to suggest that wives are increasingly viewing employment as desirable behavior (a valued right), and that when their husbands "allow" them this right, wives define both types of primary relations more positively than when they do not. By way of contrast, husbands seem more likely to define wife employment as an option; and the less this option is exercised, the more positively are these primary relations evaluated.

Length of Marriage. When we looked at companionship, we found that the disenchantment hypothesis regarding the erosion of marital expressiveness—though for the most part valid—was modified in terms of sex, and also social status. Similarly from Table 3-11 we see that certain modifications apply also to love and physical affection. First, the original articulation-affect linkage holds for both sexes in both young and mature marriages. Second, except for some deviations, there is clear evidence of disenchantment within most objective and subjective status categories.

For example, young husbands at all status levels except those among the very top status group report greater affect than mature husbands. The same general pattern appears for wives. In most instances, mature wives show a decline in affect within each status level. Given the great stress in our society on physical attributes and enjoyments intrinsic to the romantic love complex, we might have predicted that affect would fit the disenchantment hyothesis more closely than did "leisure togetherness." Specifically, it is physical "thrills and satisfactions" that are most often culturally idealized and for which lofty expectations are established at the outset of marriage. Yet, given the inevitability of the aging process, of all three types of primary expressiveness, it is these physical goals that would seem to be the hardest to sustain. The predictable result therefore is this general pattern of erosion over time relative to status level.

Why husbands with greatest status (objective and subjective) and wives with moderate SEI (40–59) should show reversals to this general trend is not at all clear. It is likely that for some reason these kinds of respondents enter marriage with affect expectations that are so lofty as to be impossible of realistic attainment. The result is disappointment early in the marriage, but with time comes perhaps a scaling down of desired goals and thus an increase in physical satisfaction. The other deviant situation—wives with high status estrangement—are low in both young and mature marriages and show virtually no change over time. In their case, time is apparently a variable of only minor import. The low level of the status rewards they receive from their husbands generates only minimal positive affect whether young or old. The passion and fervor of youth cannot overcome the consequences of these limited rewards, and the passing of time merely solidifies a long-standing unpleasant situation.

CONCLUSION

In this chapter, we have examined some of the conditions optimal to the attainment of a major goal of the modern conjugal unit, viz., the cathectic, or affective, dimension. In general, the proposition holds that with greater articulation into the economic opportunity structure comes more positive evaluation of physical affect. In terms of objective criteria, however, this is much more true for women than for men, though it holds equally for both sexes when subjective criteria are being examined. Given the differences between sexes over objective criteria, it was suggested that there is a cleavage between husbands and wives over male-female role rights centering around the cathectic aspects of marriage. Education seems to be the one objective element that brings about a convergence between the sexes regarding affective rights and expectations.

At the same time, however, that the trend seems to be toward granting female rights at this level, females are moreover defining employment as a right. Husbands, on the other hand, appear to see wife employment as more of an option which, when it is exercised, tends to undermine physical affect. The outcome of this particular clash on role definitions and its long-term consequences for affect, as well as for the organization and cohesion of the conjugal unit, are difficult to foresee at present.

Though physical affect is often thought of as a means of tension-reduction, *i.e.*, as a relief from the pressures of modern society, it was suggested that the pervasive and salient character of economic alienation may have adverse consequences for both male and female affect. The same was true for anomie, *i.e.*, feelings of disjuncture between aspirations and future achievement and success expectations. The issue was also raised as to whether there may not be a priority of expressive behaviors within the conjugal unit. Moreover, to the extent the exchange model posed herein has validity, we would expect a convergence of "valued elements," *i.e.*, strong and frequent relationships between "high priority" economic and expressive factors. In this regard, it has been continually reaffirmed that exchange within the conjugal unit is not of a crass, materialistic sort. In fact, reciprocity here is basically at the level of deep feeling states derived from cultural definitions of personal excellence related to achievement and success. These deep feeling states are linked to equally deep feeling states surrounding physical affect.

Finally, we saw that the consequences of positive perceptions of self, of the milieu, of spouse feelings toward affect, and of family life style tended to enhance affect, whereas negative perceptions in terms of these four dimensions had the opposite influence. Controlling for these kinds of elements often revealed a blurring of status differences in affect, although the patterning here was not consistent over the several variables. Aside from some deviation, the "disenchantment hypothesis" was predictably validated in terms of affect, although differences by status remained.

CHAPTER

FOUR

•

Empathy

It has been suggested that primary relations between husbands and wives could be conceptualized in three ways: companionship, love and physical affection, and empathy. Put more colloquially, "someone to do things with, someone to love, someone to talk to." We have discussed the first two types of primary behaviors as they are affected by the economic opportunity structure of American society. We come now to the last basic form of primary interaction, viz., empathy.

And what is meant by empathy? The term may be defined formally as "the intellectual identification with or vicarious experiencing of the feelings, thoughts, or attitudes of another." Stryker distinguished between this notion of empathy (or of "sympathy" in the Cooley sense of "feeling with") and role-taking. Role-taking, or taking the role of the other, "refers to the anticipation of the responses of others implicated with one in some social act. There is no necessary element of 'feeling with,' that is, of sympathy in this conception of role-taking. . . ." [1] He argues that it is possible to "anticipate the behavior" of other without becoming "identified" with him.[2] His point is that it is on this basis of identification that role-taking is to be distinguished from empathy. Identification is requisite to the latter, but not to the former. For our purposes in this study the process of empathy or identification contains at least two essential components: communication and understanding.

[1] Sheldon Stryker, "The Interactional and Situational Approaches," in Harold T. Christensen, ed., *Handbook of Marriage and the Family*, Chicago: Rand McNally and Co., 1964, p. 138.
[2] *Ibid.*

Both these terms, particularly the former, have received considerable attention in the popular press, the clinical and counseling literature, and in the research literature as well. It is even fashionable in some circles to talk about the "failure of communication" as being at the root of much marital discord. Although in itself this represents an oversimplification, it is nonetheless true that, given the structural position of the nuclear family in modern society, empathy relations take on great significance.

Parsons' notion of the "isolated nuclear family" has been shown to be invalid at the level of visiting patterns and other kinds of shared behaviors with the extended kin. But there is some indication that this "isolation" from the kin exists at the level of empathy. Particularly where the nuclear unit has become upwardly socially mobile relative to other parts of the kin, we would expect communication and understanding between them to be especially impaired.[3] Furthermore, the so-called "generation gap," although perenially present, is probably intensified these days by rapid social and technological changes and by the increased levels of education attained by the young. Thus, unless the several parts of the kin unit keep pace equally with these changes, with advanced education, and with social and occupational mobility, processes of empathy—of identification—between them tend to become extremely difficult. To this may be added the effects of increasing geographical mobility, in which nuclear units move repeatedly away from peers. These peers, since they are on the same social level as a particular nuclear unit, could potentially "empathize" with its members. But the accomplishment of in-depth communication and understanding takes time, and at just about the point where certain couples may achieve this between themselves, often one or more of them moves away.

These two structural factors, *i.e.*, "social" separation from the kin and "geographical disruption" from peers, tend to develop and reinforce the widely held cultural prescription that the husband and wife should be able to "talk" to each other. Indeed, even though they may be able to maintain empathic relations with kin and/or friends, it is thought that ideally they should be able most of all to communicate with and to understand each other. This value or belief has its roots originally in the Judaeo-Christian-Humanist tradition referred to in Chapter One. Part of this tradition is the stress on the mutual optimum development of both marital partners. This development as "persons" is substantially enhanced if one's spouse is an effective and meaningful sounding board for problems and ideas.

But the current widespread acceptance, strength, and intensity of this

---

[3] Adams argues that "upwardly mobile and stable blue collar young adults" will "feel less close" to their parents than "stable white-collar and downwardly mobile young adults." This issue is very complex, and Adams' work is useful as a beginning toward an understanding of it. Bert N. Adams, *Kinship in an Urban Setting,* Chicago: Markham Publishing Co., 1968, pp. 68 ff.

value in our society are due in large part to certain structural factors. On the one hand, we have the value that marriage should provide empathy relations. On the other, we have the fact that it is often difficult to establish these in depth to any lasting extent outside of marriage. The result is that this type of behavior becomes part of the essential core of marital primary relations. Its therapeutic and richly satisfying consequences are sought for in prospective as well as in actual mates. The "need" of the "social animal" to express himself, to be aware that channels are clear to alter, that alter "gets the message," that in turn actor believes that alter feels free to express himself, that he (alter) perceives clear channels and that he feels he is "getting through," this "need" is what is involved in empathy —in communication and understanding.

But it is one thing to believe that empathy should be part of marital primary relations, and quite another to discover conditions under which it is maximized or else limited. Bernard, for example, comments that "a review of the research literature and reports on husband-wife relationships has turned up the interesting and salient fact that conversation, 'just plain talk,' between husbands and wives almost never happens. A general social apartheid between the sexes has also shown up." [4] In this chapter, we will continue to test the hypothesis that articulation with the economic opportunity structure of our society is linked systematically to primary interaction —in this case, empathy. As before, our prime concern is with the conditions of cohesion within the conjugal unit. Empathy, like affiliativeness and affect, is thought to be a major goal in modern marriage. Partners enter marriage defining this as a right. It will be suggested that this right, like its two related expressive components, is part of a larger complex process of interlacing duties and obligations, hinged closely on the opportunity system. Finally, throughout the chapter we shall treat empathy as both valued means and valued goal. This has already been implied in our discussion thus far, and we shall have occasion to elaborate and to emphasize one or the other of these intertwined aspects.

The empirical index of empathy used here is built, in turn, on measures of the twin concepts of communication and understanding. Communication is measured by an item in which the respondent was asked to evaluate how he feels about the way he and his spouse "can confide in each other and discuss anything that comes up." [5] These two capabilities, to confide and to discuss anything that comes to mind, are indicants of open lines

---

[4] Jessie Bernard, "Developmental Tasks of the NCFR—1963–1988," *Journal of Marriage and the Family,* 26 (February 1964), p. 33.

[5] The exact wording was, "Please tell which of these statements best describes how you feel about the way you and your (husband-wife) can confide in each other and discuss anything that comes up." The response categories were identical to those used for the affiliative and affect items (see Chaps. Two and Three) and were similarly weighted: 0-1-2-3-4. The mean score for this item alone was 2.60).

of communication. We are viewing communication here primarily as a process of transmission in much the same way that a radio beam is communicated from a transmitter. The one transmitting can exercise volition in the kinds of things that may or may not be transmitted, how often he may do so, and so on. In addition, transmission involves choice as to the depth of things to be communicated, as seen in the notion of confiding. When one confides, he generally emits something that is very close to the core of his being.

But this process cannot be viewed in full-orbed perspective without its projected and valued end, viz., understanding. For signals may be transmitted, but they can be blocked, garbled, misunderstood, or not understood at all. Awareness that signals are not getting through may, in turn, cause the sender to limit, alter, or even terminate his signals. Thus, both communication and understanding are reduced in significance. Therefore, the two processes—transmission and meaningful reception—are inextricably linked together.

To measure "reception" or understanding, we asked each respondent to evaluate "the understanding of your problems and feelings that you get from your (husband-wife)." We therefore assumed the prior existence of problems and feelings, the desire and/or "need" to communicate (share, transmit) them with the spouse, and a certain level of response in the form of understanding, *i.e.*, sympathy, solace, comfort, helpful comments or behaviors, and so on. This further underscores the cyclical nature of transmission and reception within the total process of empathy. Each element tends to reinforce the other; together, both make up the complex process of empathy. Finally, therefore, responses to each item were added together for each respondent to form a total empathy score.[6] On the basis of the correlation between the communication and understanding items ($r = .58$), it is clear that while these notions are empirically as well as theoretically linked, they are not totally identical. Both notions are inseparable aspects of or emphases within the same phenomenon—identification or empathy. But they seem sufficiently distinct to measure separately and then combine into a composite index. In this way, when we define empathy as both transmission and reception, we can have a more certain basis for this claim than if only one item were used as our indicant.

Communication here emphasizes the transmission aspect, *i.e.*, the feeling that one can emit certain "messages." In popular literature, communication often carries the connotation of "getting through." That is not

---

[6] "Please tell me the statement that best describes the understanding of your problems and feelings that you get from your (husband-wife)." Response categories and weightings are the same as in footnote 5. The mean score for this item alone was 2.57. After adding the two scores together for each respondent, the mean score for husbands on the *empathy* index was 5.37, for wives it was 5.00.

primarily what is meant here. The emphasis of "getting through" is reserved for the notion of understanding or "reception" in response to transmission. Now it is likely that the more one feels he does get through, the more he will be motivated to emit messages, and, contrariwise, the less perceived meaningful reception, the less the motivation to emit in the future.

Empathy or identification, then, consists of both necessarily related elements. Analytically they are distinct emphases; but substantively and empirically they are a package. This kind of husband-wife primary interaction consists of the feeling that between spouse and self there is open transmission plus open reception. The more open is the one aspect, the more open we can expect the other to be, and the more satisfied we may then expect actor to be with the total process of empathy.

OPPORTUNITY INTEGRATION AND EMPATHY

Table 4-1 *permits the generalization that objective criteria of articulation with the opportunity structure are directly linked to positive empathy.* The increase of empathy with greater articulation is evident for women with regard to occupational status, education, and income. For men, income remains a somewhat unreliable predictor for their empathy evaluations, as it was for their affiliative and affect rankings. Yet the pattern of male empathy evaluation by income, except for the reversal of the "fair" and "good" brackets, does fall into the expected pattern. Hence, while still weak, income predicts male empathy better than it does companionship or physical affect.

Furthermore, the F ratio for SEI and especially education is greater for males in Table 4-1 than it is either for affiliativeness or affect. Wives also reveal stronger F ratios in income and education for empathy than for either of the earlier primary dimensions. With regard to SEI, the F ratio for female empathy ranks below that of affect but ahead of affiliativeness. So generally speaking, of the three types of primary relations, empathy seems to be consistently the most strongly related for both sexes to objective criteria of success and achievement.

Moreover, from Table 4-2 it is apparent that alienation and empathy are inversely related for both husbands and wives. This is true whether the alienation dimension be powerlessness, discontent, or status estrangement. And furthermore, as was true for the objective indicators, the F ratios for both husbands and wives are consistently higher in Table 4-2 than they are for either affect or affiliativeness in conjunction with alienation. And this is so for each of the three alienation dimensions.

Finally, the same kinds of generalizations apply to anomie as well. First, anomie and empathy are inversely linked. Second, in terms of success expectations, the *F* ratios for both sexes are stronger in Table 4-3 than in either of the other two expressive elements in relation to anomie. The same holds for wives with regard to occupational achievement expectations. For husbands, the *F* ratio between achievement and affect is highest, followed by virtually identical *F* ratios over empathy and companionship.

In short, the linkage between husband-wife empathy and degree of articulation with the opportunity structure emerges more often and is consistently stronger than the linkage for the other two types of primary relations. First, therefore, let us examine in detail some of the processes that are probably part of this relationship. And second, on the basis of these data, we shall posit a generalization regarding the theoretical significance of empathy in terms of conjugal unit cohesion.

To attain the first objective, we must ask ourselves how the exchange model used before applies in this situation. We may begin by positing objective and subjective economic rewards as duties of the husband role corresponding to rights within the wife role. Komarovsky grasps the significance of this approach by arguing that "the relative failure of the husband as provider disturbs the reciprocities inherent in conjugal roles." [7] To the extent, for example, that the husband is able to provide just these sorts of rewards, the more he defines himself and is defined by others—especially his wife—as having a sense of excellence, of worth, of respect, and also of providing feelings of these kinds for his wife. A sense of respect and self-worth tend to lead the husband to expect greater understanding and communication. In addition, a sense of respect and confidence probably enable him to be more effective per se in communication and understanding.

It is also quite likely that satisfactory empathy itself can act back on and enhance one's sense of personal worth or excellence. That is, once these complex processes are in motion, it is never merely a one-way relationship between economic-status (instrumental) rewards and empathy (expressive rewards). At the same time that the instrumental-expressive exchange occurs, the expressive gratifications can, in turn, stimulate further "subprocesses" of exchange. For example, meaningful empathy per se can enhance person's sense of excellence, thereby resulting in still greater positive empathic responses toward other. Concomitantly, these gratifications per se can stimulate other to reciprocate even more positively in kind.

Furthermore, the greater sense of worth, respect, and excellence attributed to the husband by the wife, alongside the rewards he provides her—economic elements per se, status in the community, the feeling that others accord her worth and excellence, too—all this has implications for empathy. They tend to generate greater motivation on the part of the wife in the

---

[7] Mirra Komarovsky, *Blue-Collar Marriage,* New York: Random House, Inc., 1962, p. 290.

direction of "rectitude and gratitude." Specifically here, they lead to greater efforts on her part toward more meaningful communication-understanding. These kinds of efforts reinforce the husband's expectations that on the basis of his attainments and excellence he should receive meaningful empathy. The result is a positive response on his part toward his wife, which, in turn, contributes to a pattern of ongoing reciprocity that initially has important roots in the objective and subjective rewards provided by the husband. As these kinds of rewards are continually supplied, processes of mutually satisfactory empathy are generated that, in turn, contribute to reinforcement of additional such processes, and so on.

Komarovsky, on the basis of her case studies of blue-collar families near the bottom of the opportunity structure, presents a vivid description of how the processes of empathy break down when the husband's objective rewards are minimal and when feelings of alienation and anomie are great.

Many wives restrain their criticism [of husbands providing limited rewards] out of pity, or expediency, or because they do not hold their husbands completely responsible for the plight of the family. . . . But even the wives who do not voice any criticism could not conceal their disappointment—a worried face can be enough of a reproach. Eventually, however, all but the most compassionate and restrained wives are provoked into some criticism.

The women's deprivations and anxieties lead to a more critical scrutiny of their husbands' personalities. A barely perceptible weakness, one which might be tolerated in a good provider, tends to be seized upon as a possible cause of the husband's failure. This excessive sensitivity to the husband's faults unhappily feeds into another typical tendency: fault-finding is easy because economic failure is likely to magnify shortcomings. The poor providers are, themselves, frustrated and anxious. Not many men can handle these destructive emotions without further painful consequences, such as drinking, violence, irritability, increased sensitivity to criticism, and withdrawal. Whatever temporary relief some of these reactions may provide for the men, their long-range effects are to deepen the husband's sense of guilt and to antagonize his wife.

There is another reason why even the more considerate wives are drawn occasionally into disparagement of their husbands. The poor providers offer their wives too obvious a weapon not to be used in a fit of anger. Thus, a wife insisted that her child finish the food on her plate and her husband took the daughter's part, saying that he sympathizes with his daughter's dislike of this particular dish. The wife "hollered at me at the table and said if I'd make enough money she could get the food they liked."

The extreme shortage of money might be thought to rule out quarrels over expenditures because every dollar must be spent on necessities. But this is not the case. The couples quarrel over the order in which bills are to be paid—the milk bills first, so that the children can be fed properly—or the electric bill, so that the light is not turned off. They quarrel over the few discretionary expenditures that do remain—beer, cigarettes or clothes. Every minor difference in economic preferences may cause a conflict because the shortage of money necessitates choices.

Conflict is intensified also because lack of money deprives some husbands of the use of certain rapport devices to decrease marital tensions. When money is available, an apology often takes the form of a gift to break the ice after a quarrel, even if it is only a coffee ring and "Let's have some java to go with it." Thus husbands lack the resources to alleviate marital strain at a time when the strain is exacerbated by poverty.

Some common means of coping with the problems of poverty often provide temporary relief only at the cost of long-range losses. A certain remoteness in marriage and a loss of spontaneity are a case in point. To talk about what matters most—the bills, the fear of sickness and of the uncertain future—is only to intensify the anxiety, and by suppressing these topics one hopes to find some relief. But avoidance of one's uppermost concern blocks other sharing as well. A slightly dishonest tinge to the whole relationship is given by still other suppressions. For example, the wife curbs her irritation out of pity and, more frequently, out of fear of driving her husband to drink or intensifying some other defensive reaction. Again, among the economically more secure and aspiring couples, common aspirations for the children, the purchase of a house and other plans constitute one of the strong ties of marriage. But for these poor couples the future is not an enticing prospect to be relished in repeated discussions; it is uncertain and threatening. Asked whether she and her husband ever discussed their dreams for the children, a 29-year-old woman said: "Nah, that's too sore." The avoidance of painful subjects in turn increases the loneliness of each partner, at the time when each is most in need of emotional support.[8]

Komarovsky's discussion provides us with a detailed portrayal of the wife's negative empathic responses to limited economic rewards. She describes quite vividly how processes of communication and understanding tend to break down in this type of situation. Because the wife does not feel her economic rights are being met, she does not respond positively in terms of her empathic obligations toward her husband, which in turn leads him to define his empathic rights as being fulfilled negatively. This generates a correspondingly negative empathic response in terms of his expressive duties, and so the cycle continues. But as our data suggest, to the extent that the husband does fulfill his economic obligations and provides those kinds of rewards, the more positive and satisfactory become these sorts of interpersonal husband-wife processes.

[8] *Ibid.,* pp. 291–92.

The second objective noted above was to try to pinpoint the theoretical significance of this form of primary interaction. Let us therefore state the proposal and then discuss why it is plausible. In terms of the cohesion and solidarity of the conjugal unit in modern society, empathy is very likely the most crucial of the three forms of expressiveness considered so far. By *crucial* we mean that the more positively it is evaluated by both partners, the stronger the feelings of conjugal solidarity and cohesion, and thus the greater the probability that the unit will be maintained, whereas the less positively it is valued, the weaker the feelings of cohesion and attraction, and the less the probability that the unit will be maintained. There are at least three reasons for its unusual significance.

One is its function as a highly valued goal in and of itself. Komarovsky describes the expectations that most individuals bring to marriage regarding empathy. "We expect that a married person will be his mate's closest confidant, with whom he will share his deepest feelings and thoughts. The romantic ideal calls for completeness of communication—no secrets from the mate." [9] Moreover, the importance of empathy as compared with affiliativeness and affect takes on added significance the longer the marriage continues.

For example, it is believed by many that when "leisure togetherness" loses some of the unique thrills experienced by the couple during their dating, courtship, and early married years, and/or when physical affect becomes relatively predictable, processes of empathy may still become an ever-expanding, ever-deepening area of satisfying interpersonal exploration. Later in this chapter we shall examine data which show that empathy does in fact become more positive in the later years of marriage. Hence empathy is crucial for system maintenance, not only because it is such a highly valued goal, but also because as the luster of togetherness and physical affect wears down somewhat, the significance of empathy tends to assume even greater proportions.

But secondly, throughout the life of the marriage, empathy functions as a vital means factor. The greater the degree of empathy, the more possible it is to resolve conflicts in the remaining two forms of primary interaction, as well as in the several instrumental sectors of husband-wife interaction, including decisions about money, children, kin, friends, and so on. The importance of this function cannot be overstressed in modern society, where norms specific enough to cover all the numerous and varied situations that could potentially emerge in a marriage simply do not exist.

It may have been possible for the ideal-typical agricultural family of the last century to maintain itself with a minimum of husband-wife communication. Most situations were probably covered by long-standing and

[9] *Ibid.*, p. 112.

highly legitimate norms. Where there may have been uncertainty, kin and community provided direction for the conjugal unit. Wives "knew their place," were subservient to their husbands, and rarely challenged their wishes seriously. In modern society all this has changed, and if the conjugal unit is to have solidarity, the major figures in it must be able to "talk" to and "understand" each other. To the extent this element is missing, the unit will be unable to resolve the numerous issues that confront it qua unit continually. To the extent this is present, the likelihood that the unit will be ongoing is increased.

Third, in addition to its functions as goal and means, empathy is theoretically important because of its special significance to the wife in modern society. In Chapter Two the suggestion was made that the wife, as the "expressive hub" of the conjugal unit, probably desires a higher level of all three forms of expressive gratifications than the husband and yet receives less than she would like. This may help account for the generally lower levels of reported female expressive satisfactions in all three areas. And when it comes to empathy, wives' desires may be extraordinarily high, and yet the realities disappointingly low—especially at the more disadvantaged levels.

Komarovsky reports that "the findings on dissatisfactions with communication add up to one major result: the women are by far the more dissatisfied sex and what they want is more interaction. They certainly want their husbands to be better listeners . . . [to engage in] sharing for its own sake, or for reassurance, counsel, appreciation and encouragement."[10] In short, what Komarovsky implies on the basis of her studies and also of others, and what our data point toward as well, is that wives desire positive empathy far more than husbands do, and at the same time are far less satisfied than their mates with what they receive. And it appears that this gap between the sexes is greater for empathy than for either affect or affiliativeness.

For example, in Table 4-4, the proportions of each sex reporting a "high" level of satisfaction with each type of primary relation have been standardized and then compared.[11] Only the dimension of education is presented because it is representative of the generally consistent pattern of the remaining seven dimensions. These data clearly concur with Komarovsky's conclusions—women in general are far less satisfied with empathy

10 *Ibid.*, pp. 197–98.

11 In the case of affiliativeness and affect, "high" scores represented those in the two top response categories, those with a 3 or 4 score, or those in the upper 40 percent of the potential range of scores. The closest standardization possible for the range of empathy scores (0–8) were the scores 5–8, or those in the upper 44 percent of the potential range of scores. All those who are found in Table 4-4 are thus in the upper 40 percent of potential range of scores, with those in the empathy columns stretching slightly to 44 percent of potential range of scores.

than are husbands. In addition, Table 4-4 shows that this kind of gap is generally greater for empathy than for the other primary dimensions. The data reveal further, as we might expect, that the "empathy gap" is inversely related to status.

There are several reasons for this "empathy gap." The most obvious is in the difference in fields of significant others potentially available to each sex. Because of the structural separation of the work place from the home, the wife is relatively more isolated from others with whom she might interact intimately at this cognitive level. The popular literature is replete with cartoons and stories about the wife who interacts all day with pots, pans, and cooking utensils, dirty clothes, and the family car in which she incessantly buses screaming children to and fro over the neighborhood.

Meanwhile, throughout the day her husband participates in a meaningful and highly valued activity (work) in the company of other adults. Even at lower status jobs there is ample opportunity for talk over a whole range of topics—from sex to baseball—deemed relevant.[12] When he comes home, his "needs" for empathy have largely been fulfilled so he hides behind the newspaper or in front of TV. On the other hand, his wife tries hard to get him to talk or else at least listen to her. At the same time, she must fight the competition of interruptions and demands made by the children both on her and the husband-father. In short, this kind of interaction with her husband is deemed vitally important because her range of potential listeners is severely restricted, whereas his may extend from work mate through bartender.

Nevertheless, Komarovsky points out that many women in her blue-collar sample have outside female confidants who are the "functional equivalents" of the male work mates possessed by husbands.[13] Thus, it is not isolation alone that accounts for greater female demands for empathy. It must be noted, however, that blue-collar wives are less likely than white-collar wives to be geographically mobile, and consequently to have more extended periods of time in which to develop intimate friendships. They are also more likely to live nearer female kin and thus, in addition, to be intimate with them. Hence, we need to make an important distinction in reasons for generally greater female desires for empathy. The isolation hypothesis, in which the wife is tied to home and children and perhaps a host of superficial contacts in community activities, probably fits the white-collar wife more adequately than the blue-collar wife.

In the latter case, there are two different but perhaps even more cogent reasons for female demands for empathy. One is traceable to the different patterns of socialization experienced by blue-collar boys and girls. Much

---

[12] Robert Dubin, *The World of Work*, Englewood Cliffs, N.J.: Prentice-Hall, 1958, pp. 289–309.

[13] *Op. cit.*, p. 208.

more than in white-collar homes, there is a sharp distinction made in terms of ascribed sex roles. These distinctions carry over into the marriages of the less advantaged.

The phrase "trained incapacity to share" aims to convey a certain view about the men's inarticulateness. The ideal of masculinity into which they were socialized inhibits expressiveness both directly, with its emphasis on reserve, and indirectly, by identifying personal interchange with the feminine role. Childhood and adolescence, spent in an environment in which feelings were not named, discussed or explained, strengthened these inhibitions. In adulthood they extend beyond culturally demanded reticence—the inhibitions are now experienced not only as "I shouldn't," but as "I cannot." In explaining instances of reserve in marriage many more husbands than wives say: "It is hard to talk about such things."
"I used to try to ask him when we were first married," said a 26-year-old woman about her husband, "why he gets into those real flippy moods, but he used to say nothing was wrong, and asking seemed to make him worse. The more I tried, the worse he'd get. So I found out that if you just don't bother him, it wears off." [14]

In short, the more disadvantaged the husband is, the less likely he is to be able to engage in meaningful processes of reciprocal communication and understanding. And in large measure this inability is caused by circumstances beyond his control, stemming from earlier childhood experiences, so that even if he might wish to respond positively to his wife on the cognitive level in order to overcome some of the negative consequences of his limited job rewards, he finds it extremely difficult to do so. His difficulty, of course, then has the consequence of limiting still further the wife's evaluation of empathic processes.

The other factor accounting for greater female empathy demands, and one more directly related to the exchange model, pertains to the extent of communication over the husband's job itself. Almost every textbook on the family points out that one of the reasons for high stability rates among traditional and current farm families is the behavioral interdependence of husband and wife with regard to agricultural labors. Sharing these behaviors, they are bound together in cohesive fashion. The thesis of this volume is that in modern society economic interdependence has this same function, but that the nature of this interdependence has changed and become exceedingly more complex. Interdependence currently is based on the kinds of processes of reciprocity discussed throughout the book.

Analogous to joint participation in the husband's economic labors—

[14] *Ibid.*, p. 156.

and from the viewpoint of the wife in modern society, the next "best" thing—is communication about the husband's job. In this way, the wife participates vicariously with her husband in the major activity affecting the present and future state of the conjugal unit. But this type of participation varies by degree of economic integration.

Many studies reveal that the greater the status of the husband's job, the greater the degree of communication regarding it. That the "working man," remarks Komarovsky, engages in almost none of this type of communication is because in this way he "enjoys a greater immunity from his wife's scrutiny of his daily performance." [15] The lower his economic integration and thus the lower the level of economic rewards (objective and subjective) he provides, the less he wishes to open his efforts to close scrutiny by the significant other who evaluates him so meticulously in terms of those rewards. The less "successful" he is, the less he wishes to talk about it (Komarovsky reports that job matters "head the list of topics that the husbands admittedly disclose least to their wives"),[16] and the more success, the more willingness to discuss it.

And this kind of discussion—of "joint participation" in the husband's occupation—helps to reinforce the whole reciprocal process between status and empathy. At the very same time that the higher status husband is providing status rewards, he is also providing a highly valued form of a highly desired expressive reward, *i.e.*, communication regarding his job. As a result of rewards at both levels, the wife is thereby motivated even more strongly to reciprocate in terms of meaningful communication and understanding. Conversely, the absence of this kind of empathic reward among lower-status wives lowers still further her satisfaction with this expressive dimension.

The question can be raised as to whether "silence" on the part of lower-status males might not have certain positive consequences for conjugal cohesion.[17] That is, if there were, for instance, a fuller and more frank discussion of husband's "daily performance" or of other sensitive areas, would this not threaten the husband and serve to "upset" him, whereas "avoidance" may avert open clashes? In this way is not cohesion furthered? This possibility might hold under those conditions in which the wife did not herself desire maximum levels of empathy. If she is willing not to expect empathy from her husband, then his "silence" might not undermine cohesion. But in those cases where she desires and expects it, yet discovers a

15 *Ibid.*, p. 154.
16 *Ibid.*, p. 151.
17 See Stryker, *op. cit.*, also his "Role Taking: Accuracy and Adjustment," *Sociometry*, 20 (1957), pp. 286–96. He raises the point that accurate role-taking can lead to "maladjustment" within the family. The same might be true for extensive identification. But as discussed in the text of this chapter, this is likely to hold chiefly where the wife does not desire maximum levels of empathy.

certain element of unwillingness on the part of her husband to engage in this kind of behavior, her sense of solidarity with him is probably weakened.

In short, the answer to this question depends on the wife, and suggests once again the greater salience of this primary dimension to wives than to husbands. Indeed, in the perception of the "less successful" male, "silence is golden" and probably preserves cohesion. But from the female standpoint, "talk is desirable" and its absence is threatening to solidarity. Moreover, the question may be moot in those cases where the wife actually desires high levels of empathy. For it is not at all likely that she will be silent, and thus the potentially beneficial function of husband withdrawal falls short of attainment as a result of her consistent prodding.

By way of caution, it should not be naïvely assumed that among higher-status couples, this kind of "joint cognitive participation" is automatic, nor as extensive as wives at that level might like it to be. The differences between the sexes in Table 4-4 among even those with greatest economic integration makes this point clear. There are other kinds of factors besides fear of scrutiny that hinder communication regarding the husband's job at all status levels: beliefs that there are technical and esoteric aspects of the job beyond the wife's ken, feeling that talking about the job at home constitutes griping, which is thought to be unmanly, the idea that work and home should be kept separate, and so on.[18] Overall, however, it seems that the presence of achievement and success generate a greater willingness to discuss the world of the job, their absence a corresponding reticence.

In sum, by reason of these three factors—valued goal, significant means, special pertinence to women—empathy takes on particular theoretical significance for conjugal unit cohesion in modern society. To the extent it is attained as goal, functions as effective means, and is regarded as especially meaningful by wives—to that extent is the conjugal unit likely to be more cohesive. Therefore, if empathy is actually as crucial to system-maintenance as it appears to be, then in turn even more basic is the question of the optimum conditions for empathy. Undoubtedly, variables such as personality factors and complementary needs play an important role in this dimension, and we shall consider some of these in a few pages. But it is equally clear that certain structural factors as well can optimize conditions for positive empathy. Specifically, as economic and status rewards are increased, and feelings of alienation and anomie are allayed, these benefits generate feelings of rectitude and gratitude, and in general structure the organization of husband-wife interaction in such a way as to help account for the particular level of empathy attained.

Wife Employment. Table 4-5 continues the pattern noted under the other two primary relations, viz., employment *vs.* nonemployment seems to make no significant difference in empathy from the standpoint of either sex.

[18] Komarovsky, *op. cit.*, pp. 152 ff.

Nevertheless, the data fall in the direction of at least suggesting that among those households where the wife does *not* work, empathy is evaluated by both sexes at a higher level.

Table 4-6 repeats the divergence of Table 3-5. Among those households where the wife is employed, there is no significant difference between husbands in so far as their satisfaction with empathy is concerned. (There is only some tendency toward more favorable evaluation among husbands whose wives hold higher-status jobs.) But among wives, those with higher-status rank substantially ahead (with a very strong *F* ratio) of wives who hold lesser-status jobs.

The most plausible explanation for these differences by sex is one advanced in Chapter Three pertaining to physical affect. Higher-status husbands married to wives with higher-status jobs may find that the time and energy their wives necessarily devote to their jobs detracts from the time and energy necessary for satisfactory processes of empathy to take place. The fact that both partners are heavily involved in demanding careers may erode somewhat these kinds of primary interactions (from the male perspective) in the same way that this situation might erode affect. And the demand of wives for more satisfactory empathy, as for more satisfactory affect, at the same time that they desire greater freedom for employment, may actually place them in the ironic situation of undermining the former through the latter. These combined factors operate to minimize differences in male empathy among those with greater SEI. At the same time lower-status husbands perceive reduced empathy when their wives work because of the threat posed to their male role as provider. So for basically different reasons, the consequences of wife employment on male empathy are similar even though there is variation in female job status.

Yet higher-status wives do not evidently perceive strains of these sorts. Or even if they do, the differences between them and lower-status wives may be owing to a larger perception or awareness on the part of the latter that their employment threatens their husbands and thus reduces empathy. Very likely two elements are operative—the "threat element" among lower-status wives, and elation among higher-status wives that "employment rights" are being attained.

SPECIFYING FACTORS

PERSONALITY ORIENTATIONS

Self-esteem. If self-esteem is, as cited in Chapter Two, intrinsically related to effective interpersonal processes in general, then we might expect it to have considerable bearing on processes of husband-wife empathy.

"Someone to talk to,"—to communicate with, to understand—one's evaluation of this kind of primary interaction would seem to be especially liable to the overall view of self. Table 4-7 indicates this is so. (*Success expectation* is used in this chapter as representative of the several subjective dimensions of economic opportunity integration.[19])

Not only do we find that those with low self-esteem report lower levels of empathy, and those with high self-esteem show higher levels of empathy (cf. Tables 4-1 and 4-3), we also find that these relationships are more consistently reliable and stronger than for either affiliativeness or affect. For example, in seven out of eight instances in Table 4-7 there are significant relationships. Five of these are at the .01 level or beyond, of which wives account for four. This recurring degree of strength did not emerge when self-esteem helped to interpret the other two expressive dimensions. We do not discover here, moreover, the tendency toward blurring of empathy differences that we frequently discovered with regard to affect (Chapter Three) among those who ranked high on a particular control variable. The original direct linkages remain between education and empathy (though not always linear), and between success expectations and empathy.

Take, for instance, those with eight years or less of education—those at the bottom of the opportunity structure. As we noted earlier, there is considerable homogamy of educational level in the sample, particularly at the lower-status levels, and this reflects the general pattern of the larger society. Wives in this situation receive low levels of rewards from their husbands in the form of status, prestige, and economic benefits. As a result they are in turn motivated to reciprocate less positively in the empathic sphere, their husbands then respond to them in kind, and so on.

But both sexes at this reward level with low self-esteem may be prone to several additional factors that negate empathy still further. Such persons may be more insecure and feel more threatened and hostile in general, thus underrating and distorting the effects and competence of the other in communication and understanding. They may also tend to be more "distant" and unwilling to "bare themselves" out of fear of threat and insecurity. In addition, wives in particular are quite likely to carry to extremes the criticisms and "harping" that occur, as Komarovsky noted, where success is minimal.[20] As a consequence, channels of "interpersonal competence" (already impaired owing to limited rewards) are blocked still further—particularly from the wife's standpoint, as seen in Table 4-7. (Wives' mean empathy score in this education category is 3.88; husbands', 4.53.) And because these families start from a disadvantaged position, viz., minimal educational rewards, they immediately drop below other families

---

[19] As in Chapters Two and Three, the remaining independent variables yield similar results, but are omitted to avoid needless repetition.

[20] *Ibid.,* p. 291.

with more education, who may at the same time experience similar "block-ages" owing to poor self-esteem, but who nonetheless, because of greater status rewards, maintain more satisfactory processes of empathy.

Finally, referring back to an alternative hypothesis (discussed earlier) that there may sometimes exist certain conditions in which silence, avoidance, and withdrawal may be conducive to conjugal cohesion, we should not overlook the possibility that low self-esteem may be one of these conditions. At times, for instance, low self-esteem might inhibit the desire and/or capability for meaningful empathy; thus, discussion regarding the husband's "underachievement" is less likely to occur, with the result that a potential "sore spot" is removed from husband-wife interaction. Given the propensity of the "modern wife" toward husband-wife dialogue, however, it is not at all certain that even a negative self-conception could have this inhibiting consequence.

We should also take note of the possibility that a perception on the part of actor that he is experiencing positive empathy could react back on his sense of self-esteem. That is, it is not simply that this personality dimension influences the level of empathy experienced—that it does. But it is likewise possible that the level of empathy experienced also reinforces or else negates one's image of himself, particularly in those cases where there is a great deal of this kind of "primariness" desired but little being attained. In short, there is very likely operating here a complex network of cyclical, highly interdependent processes. Economic-status rewards and self-esteem have a certain impact on empathy, but empathy also has a certain impact on self-esteem, which in turn influences empathy, and so on. It is beyond the scope of this present study to trace with great precision the conditions that affect the varied directions in which these processes operate. All we may do here is call attention to some of the relevant variables, and some of the potential processes involved. Further investigation (perhaps by laboratory or case study techniques) is required to analyze these complex phenomena in more exact fashion.

But even where a strong and positive self-image exists and the "channels of communication" are thereby opened (and hence, insecurity, fear, misreadings, are lessened), these husbands and wives with minimal education still experience significantly less satisfactory empathy than those with more education. (Though wives with high self-esteem and minimal education in Table 4-7 score higher than wives with "some high school," they still fall below high school graduates.) Because they start with a lower level of reward (limited education), their levels of empathy are lower to begin with, and it becomes that much more difficult for them to rise beyond a certain point in meaningful empathy. Those with more education start with more positive empathy, and their positive self-esteem builds on this "higher" base of rewards.

The same general reasoning applies (in spite of minor deviations) to each ascending level of education with regard to both low and high self-esteem. It applies similarly in the case of ascending levels of success expectations. Hence, the effects of negative or positive self-esteem on empathy are tied closely to the level of empathy initially associated with a particular reward level. Empathy, compared to affect, is less susceptible to the blurring influences of self-esteem on status differences. Even in the presence of this significant type of personality variable, processes of communication-understanding still remain systematically linked to degree of articulation with the opportunity system.

In sum, there is a strong relationship for both sexes between economic integration, self-esteem, and empathy. Greater integration elicits and generates more positive empathy. The level of global self-esteem either erodes communication-understanding, or else enhances it. Therefore, the greater the integration and the stronger the self-esteem, the higher the levels of perceived empathy. Conversely, the less the integration and the weaker the self-esteem, the lower the levels of perceived empathy.

Anomy. The conclusions we may draw from Table 4-8 are in some respects similar to earlier observed consequences of anomy, but in one important element they are different. First, there is the predictable increase in empathy among those who see their milieu in a positive light, and a decrease among those who view it in negative and threatening terms (cf. Tables 4-1 and 4-3). This is true at each level of economic-opportunity integration with the result that at the same level, those with low anomy evaluate processes of communication-understanding as more satisfactory than those with high anomy.

Second, among husbands with low anomy, differences in empathy by opportunity levels (objective and subjective) tend to be extremely blurred. But the major difference here compared to affiliativeness and affect is based on sex. For the first time among the three forms of primary relations, we find significant differences by opportunity level among those with low anomy—but only among wives.

Even when the milieu is perceived in optimistic fashion by wives, this is not sufficient to overcome differences in levels of their communication-understanding generated by educational attainment and also perceived future success. Earlier arguments in the chapter that empathy is extremely important to wives probably help account for the persistence of these differences. It was noted there that as objective and subjective rewards drop, empathy becomes extensively impaired, particularly from the wife's viewpoint. And though certain wives possess a positive personality orientation regarding the world "out there," their relative satisfaction with empathy vis-à-vis wives at other opportunity levels does not change.

Further indication of the salience of empathy to wives even when controlling for additional factors is seen in the very high F ratio for wives with high anomy under success expectations. Note too the substantial differences there in empathy by level of success expectation. (It will be recalled that in Table 4-7 a similarly large F ratio plus substantial empathy differences appeared in the subjective dimension for wives holding the analogous negative view of self.) Therefore, we conclude that whether wives perceive their immediate milieu as benign or threatening, this does not alter, in so far as they are concerned, their comparative satisfaction with the processes of empathy exchange with their husbands based initially on level of opportunity integration. On the other side, for husbands who possess a personality orientation in which they see the milieu as orderly, differences in levels of empathy satisfaction with respect to status tend to be minimal. But among husbands who perceive their milieu as disorderly, the status differences in empathy evaluation remain, though empathy becomes systematically lowered at all opportunity levels.

PERCEPTION OF SPOUSE EMPATHY

Table 4-9 verifies the expectation (based on the theoretical rationale outlined in Chapter Two) that how actor defines his spouse to evaluate empathy influences how he himself will evaluate it. We find therefore that not only do increased levels of opportunity integration (both objective and subjective) generate increased empathy, but also that at each reward level empathy is enhanced where other is perceived as satisfied, and eroded where other is perceived as dissatisfied.

Further inquiry into the impact of other's evaluations on actor's would seem to be especially called for within this cognitive dimension of husband-wife interaction. Specifically, it might be hypothesized that, compared to affiliativeness or to affect, actor will have a more accurate perception of alter's empathy feelings. This is because empathy (at least as we have measured it) involves largely verbal and thus overt symbols. Perhaps such symbols make it simpler than in the case of the other two elements to interpret how alter feels about empathy. Indeed, among lower-status couples and others with whom empathy is particularly unsatisfactory, actor may often be told outright by alter that "you don't understand," or "we simply can't seem to communicate," or other words or obvious emotional behavior or outbursts to that effect. Such overtness is probably less likely less often in the case of the other two primary dimensions. And even among those couples whose empathy is generally satisfactory, any tendencies toward poor communication or understanding by one partner or the other are likely to be pointed out sooner and more unequivocally than is likely true for either affiliativeness or particularly affect, where covertness, subtlety, and coyness are more predominent.[21]

The suggestion has been made that empathy may be the most crucial and salient of the three primary dimensions; it is a *right* of actor's that alter has a strong obligation to fulfill. It was further suggested (see Chapter Two) that definition of other's perceptions (in this case, of empathy) influences actor's, because actor comes to feel that alter is motivated to respond positively to him based on the degree that he (alter) is being satisfied. Therefore, if it is in fact the case that actor's perceptions of alter's empathy evaluations tend to be rather accurate, then this provides added insight into cohesion of the conjugal unit. We would expect the probability of cohesion to be greatest among those units where empathy (highly valued reward) is actually greatest, because where it is, each partner is quite likely to have an accurate reading that alter defines it so and is thus reciprocating in kind toward actor, and so on. By the same token, where empathy is actually minimal, there is a strong likelihood that both partners will generally see it "the way it is," instead of misreading it as perhaps "better" than it actually is. In other words, added to the notion of the centrality of empathy and the import per se of alter's perceived evaluations, is the idea of the accuracy of these perceptions or definitions. To the extent that they tend to be accurate with regard to empathy, to that degree do they add to its already great theoretical significance in explaining the cohesion of the conjugal family.

In other words, what we are doing here is making use of Stryker's distinction between empathy (identification) and role-taking (anticipation of other's responses).[22] The argument is first that empathy is extremely important to the cohesion of the modern conjugal unit for its own sake as valued means and end. Next empathy, because of its very essence (tendency to overtness compared with affiliativeness and affect) stimulates accurate role-taking or anticipation, in terms of communication-understanding. The possibilities of inaccurate role-taking in terms of other's responses over this particular primary dimension are thereby reduced. Ultimately, therefore, the relationship to unit cohesion becomes more important.

What we have, in short, is a highly valued and significant process within the conjugal unit, which stands a high probability of being accurately

[21] There is always the possibility of the alternative hypothesis that there is a "halo effect" operating in both directions. Actor thinks that empathy is either "good" or "bad" as far as he is concerned, and merely *assumes* alter feels likewise, without grounds other than this mere presumption. The validity of this argument is uncertain, however, since the original relationships (cf. Tables 4-1 and 4-3) are firmly maintained. If a strong "halo effect" were actually operative, we might expect much more of a blurring between status levels than does in fact occur. There should be no reason, in other words, for the "halo" to exist more forcefully at some degrees of articulation than at others.

[22] *Op. cit.*

assessed by the actors involved. That is, they are likely to be able to anti-cipate how alter will and does respond to them over this dimension with a fair degree of accurateness. They tend to possess a more or less "reliable feeling" as to the extent to which alter fulfills what is presumably an extremely important role expectation. The result is that the theoretical meaningfulness to conjugal cohesion of empathy is broadened. Not only is its place within the structure of the unit per se important, but the likeli-hood that its processual aspects are accurately anticipated makes its function all that more crucial. Among higher-status couples, for example, we would expect that positive empathy plus keen and accurate assessment thereof would tend to reinforce cohesion more than would just the identification alone. Likewise, among lower-status couples, low identification coupled with accurate anticipation and assessment thereof would probably tend to undermine cohesion more than would the processes of impaired empathy operating alone. To "feel" something is desirable and to be keenly aware that it is either being attained or denied would seem to have larger conse-quences than the same "feeling" alongside lesser awareness of its actual outcomes.

PERCEPTION OF FAMILY LIFE STYLE

In Table 4-10, we find that perception of a low family life style reduces empathy evaluation at every level of economic opportunity integration (cf. Tables 4-1 and 4-3). This holds for both sexes, and for both education and success expectations. In all four such instances in Table 4–10, differ-ences by integration level are significant, with those in the subjective dimen-sion being especially strong. Thus, the lower the opportunity integration and the lower the perceived life style, the less satisfactory to each sex are the processes of communication-understanding.

At the same time, the opposite generalization also holds, though some-what less strongly since only one of the four instances under high life style evaluation shows significant differences. Empathy is enhanced at all oppor-tunity levels when life style is perceived positively; and by and large, the original differences by education and success expectations tend to persist—though perhaps less under education than under success expectations. Thus, perception of family life style, along with perceptions of self, other, and milieu all play a similar role in their influence on the degree of perceived empathy. Where these are positive, they tend to generate more satisfactory empathy at all levels of achievement and success. Where they are negative, they have the opposite effect.

STRUCTURAL FACTORS

Wife Employment. Repeatedly, we have been impressed with the complexities of trying to analyze consequences of wife employment on conjugal primary relations. Nonetheless, we can safely conclude that the two
major "wedges" to an understanding of the issue are sex of respondent and
degree of economic integration. For example, from Table 4–11, we may
derive the following generalizations:

1. The greater the opportunity integration, the greater the reported
empathy by both sexes regardless of whether the wife works or not.

2. Higher-status husbands (9+ years of education, "fair" or better
success expectations) report decreased empathy when their wives work
(and increased empathy if they do not work); but higher-status wives (same
kinds of success expectations, 13+ years of education) report increased
empathy when they work (and less empathy if they do not work).

3. Lower-status husbands report increased empathy evaluation when
their wives work (and less if they do not); but lower-status wives report
decreased empathy when they work (and more satisfaction if not working).

In short, the lower the status of the male, the more likely he is to
define money supplied by the wife positively, and in exchange respond
positively to her on the cognitive level, and then in turn define her responses
on this level "as if" they are positive. And if she does not work, his
feelings of empathy with her are threatened, presumably because he feels
she does not contribute concretely to the task-oriented goals of the conjugal
unit. At the same time, the lower the status of the female, the more likely
she is to perceive that money she supplies is defined as a threat by her
husband to his provider-role, and as a result, processes of communication-
understanding suffer. Yet, if she does not work, this threat is removed and
her empathy is enhanced. The possibility that husbands and wives can
"read" the identical kind of situation very differently is seen again in the
following circumstances.

The higher the status of the male, the more likely he is to define the
time and energy required by wife employment as an incursion on empathy
relations, and thus a threat to them. If she does not work, the incursion is
removed and male empathy is enhanced. At the same time, the higher the
status of the female, the more she feels certain rights are being granted
to her by her husband, and in exchange, the more positively she responds
to him on this level and then in turn defines his responses "as if" they too
are positive. If she does not work, she perhaps feels these rights are not
being exercised and female empathy suffers.

Of these eight different situations (Table 4-11) it is difficult to state
which is most conducive to conjugal cohesion, which is least so. Certainly
this is an important question for future research. One might speculate that

higher-status couples in which the wife is most satisfied with both her expressive and employment rights would be most cohesive, and that lower-status couples in which the employed wife is least satisfied with her expressive rights yet feels the husband resents her employment rights would experience least solidarity.

In the former instance, cohesion is reinforced through husband status, subsequent female satisfaction with empathy, plus female gratification over fulfillment of employment rights. Though her husband may consider her working a nuisance, given the remaining additional positive elements that are operative or "going" for the unit, her employment is not a serious threat to the unit per se from his standpoint. And from hers, employment is an additional benefit added to an already positive situation. But, in the case of lower-status couples, none of the positive elements just mentioned are operative; and to the husband, the wife's employment is probably perceived as far more serious than a mere nuisance. If these two kinds of situations do in fact represent the polar extremes, then the six remaining situations would fall somewhere in between.

In this regard, a question merely implied thus far throughout the study needs to be made explicit, viz., the significance of the wife to conjugal cohesion. In future research, one might hypothesize that she is the more significant of the two principal figures. If cohesion is conceived of as an ongoing process, rather than as a static state, then we may describe the husband as Goode does as the bearer and defender of traditional male rights, *i.e.*, a kind of *status quo*.[23]. If change in the *status quo* is to come about, it must be most often through the wife who challenges it by assertion of individual rights in one or more sectors of the conjugal unit. To the extent her husband is willing to grant her these rights and give up some of his prerogatives (*e.g.*, such would be most likely in the case of the more educated husband, or the one with higher SEI, who can be less threatened in terms of his job), the more cohesive the unit tends to be. To the extent he resists her demands, the less cohesive it might tend to be.

In this type of model, the husband is significant chiefly in reaction to his wife—most often he is probably content to "leave things as they are," not to "stir up difficulties." As long as the wife (*e.g.*, one with a traditional

[23] William J. Goode, *World Revolution and Family Patterns,* New York: The Free Press, 1963, p. 57.

In another place, Goode speculates that when it comes to the actual "strategy of divorce conflict" it is the husband "who first wishes to escape from the marriage," but who nonetheless goads the wife into taking the initial formal and legal steps toward dissolution. (William J. Goode, *After Divorce,* New York: The Free Press, 1956, p. 135.) To whatever extent this may be valid, it does not undercut the notion that it is the wife more than the husband who agitates for change within the conjugal unit. Indeed, it may be precisely because she continually presses for change that certain husbands grow weary of the situation and begin to think of dissolution. But as discussed in the text, his attitudes are in reaction to her agitation.

image of the wife role) accepts the situation, cohesion is probably enhanced, even among lower-status couples. The point is that whether she "acts by inaction" or by "agitation for her rights," she is the one who acts (in relative comparison to his reaction), who either maintains or disturbs traditional conjugal patterns. Therefore ultimately, in most cases, the cohesion of the modern conjugal family depends in large measure on how the female defines her own role rights, and to what extent she perceives these rights as being met. Without question, the husband's attitudes and behavior are vital, but in terms of ongoing process, they perhaps follow in order (and thus in significance) the wife's actions with regard to traditional orientations.

Length of Marriage. To a certain extent, affiliativeness, and to a very large degree, the data on physical affect confirmed the widely held notion that primary relations decline as marriage wears on. Table 4-12 shows, however, that this hypothesis does not apply to processes of communication-understanding. Quite the contrary—*at each level of education* (save one) *and of success expectations, the longer the marriage continues the more satisfactory is the empathy in the view of both sexes.* The sole exception occurs among husbands and wives with 16+ years of education. Moreover, throughout these eight instances, the original articulation-empathy linkage does not appear to be weakened in the least.

Actually, it is just as logical to predict that empathy would increase over the length of marriage as it is to predict that physical affect will decrease. By its very nature physical enjoyment generally tends to peak in the early years of marriage and then slowly decline. But interpersonal competence, the capacity to communicate and to understand, and so on, do not peak quite so quickly. Capabilities and skills in these areas usually take years to develop. And with each passing year, as partners get to know, understand, and "read" each other more deeply and fully, these skills are enhanced still further. Moreover, as couples grow more mature and "leisure togtherness" and physical affect lose some of the charm attributed to them in the dominant popular lore of romantic love, couples are forced to fall back onto empathy as the prime basis for mutual attraction.

Finally, the correlations between the three types of primary relations are both strong and consistent enough to minimize greatly the possibility that empathy, as we have measured it, is not of the "same order" as affiliativeness and affect. For husbands, the figures are as follows: affiliativeness and affect ($r=$ .62); affiliativeness and empathy ($r=$ .59); affect and empathy ($r=$ .65). For wives, the figures are these: affiliativeness and affect ($r=$ .64); affiliativeness and empathy ($r=$ .66); affect and empathy ($r=$ .70). In other words, there is ample reason to conclude that empathy is as much a part of the "expressive syndrome" of the conjugal unit as are the other two dimensions. There is no evidence to suggest that we are measuring "something other" than one aspect of this syndrome, and that therefore the differences due to time are the result of empathy not being of the "same order" as affect or affiliativeness. If these three expressive dimensions are thus so highly interrelated, then differences associated with time are not so much the result of empathy being outside the core expressive syndrome, but are instead probably due to the arguments presented herein.

For example, these data supply additional fuel to the argument that has been building up so far in this chapter, viz., empathy may be the most theoretically significant primary element in explaining conjugal unit cohesion. First, it has already been suggested that empathy is valued not only as an important goal per se, but also as a means factor, an element that enhances other aspects of conjugal interaction. Specifically, couples with positive empathy may be more able than those with negative empathy to resolve difficulties in the affiliative and affect realms, as well as in certain instrumental areas. Second, as the unit goes on in time, affiliativeness and affect as valued goals and rewards are in general becoming increasingly less satisfactory and meaningful to the significant partners. Yet this kind of deprivation does not necessarily threaten cohesion because concurrently empathy is assuming greater importance as both means and end and is becoming more satisfactory and meaningful. Indeed, it must take on greater significance or else the system will be threatened, because given the nature of affiliativeness and affect, they are less likely to take on greater meaningfulness over time. The longer the marriage persists, therefore, the more crucial becomes the function of empathy for system-maintenance. For if two of the three system goals are inherently more difficult to attain, but the remaining one presents no such inevitable obstacle, then it is bound to take on greater significance as both means and end.

Why extremely educated couples should not fit the general pattern of change is not totally clear any more than why the highest SEI couples did not fit the pattern in Table 3-10. It may be that these people enter marriage with highly toned interpersonal skills plus a strong ideological commitment to attain meaningful empathy. As a result, they may develop peak levels of empathy in their marriages much earlier than those with less education. But as time wears on, these great peaks may be difficult to maintain, plus the fact that both sexes who are highly educated and also "mature" may be extensively involved in occupational and/or community demands. Consequently, there may simply be "less time to talk" now than there was in earlier—perhaps less hectic—years. In any event, we must note that their empathy levels—especially wives'—remain quite high vis-à-vis those with less education.

One question that might be raised, and one that unfortunately cannot be tested within the scope of this research design, is whether mature couples show an increase in empathy partly because of a selective process that "weeds out" marriages with extremely poor empathy. That is, by the time the couple reaches the sixteenth year (or beyond) of marriage, unless a "minimum floor" of empathy interaction is attained, the marriage may not be likely to survive and thus not appear in our sample. To the extent this hypothesis has some validity, it too serves to underscore the crucial nature of empathy vis-à-vis affect and affiliativeness. For the data in Chapters Two and Three showed that mature marriages do tend to experience reductions in the latter two expressive dimensions and yet they obviously survive. This occurs at the same time that there is little evidence of ongoing mature marriages that experience reductions in empathy. Thus, even if a "selective process" is going on, it evidently tends to occur more frequently in reference to empathy than to the other two dimensions, thereby emphasizing its potentially greater significance.

Furthermore, if we accept this line of reasoning, then we may still suspect that among those mature marriages that are in the sample, empathy continues to remain a major expressive factor. For if so far these marriages have been maintained in spite of reductions in affect and affiliativeness and in conjunction with positive empathy, then if for one reason or another empathy levels drop "too far," what is to prevent these marriages from also falling into that "selective weeding" process? In short, the "selective hypothesis" is just that—a hypothesis that needs to be tested. But even if it is valid, it does not substantially weaken the generalization that time tends to enhance marital empathy. Future work may show the hypothesis to be part of the total complex process. That is, marriages begin with relatively lower levels of empathy, and these levels increase as time goes on. Among certain marriages in which the rise is minimal, the probability of dissolution is increased. In those cases in which the rise continues, the likelihood of dissolution is decreased. So that there may be both a "selective process," and yet also in those mature marriages that remain intact, increasing empathy versus decreasing satisfaction with affect and affiliativeness.

A major point emerging from this discussion is the distinctiveness of marital primary relations, as well as the variability of their impact on marital cohesion at different points in time. Affiliativeness (someone to do things with) and affect (someone to love) assume major significance early in marriage—although empathy is by no means unimportant, if for no other reason than to be able to "talk" about what goes on in the other two primary dimensions. But later in marriage, empathy assumes major significance because by default the other forms of expressiveness (though by no means unimportant) become less prominent. So it is not that one or another expressive dimension is *ipso facto* more valued or crucial at all times throughout the life of the conjugal unit. Complexity is introduced by the inherent fact that certain structural situations either impede or enhance the attainment of particular conjugal unit goals at particular times. One of these kinds of situations appears to be the length of the marriage itself. Undoubtedly, there are other such considerations, and their explication is necessary for a more complete understanding of the intricate processes of conjugal cohesion.

CONCLUSION

This chapter completes our discussion of the three major forms of conjugal primary interaction. Empathy was defined in terms of processes of husband-wife communication and understanding. We found that the frequency and strength of relationships between the economic opportunity structure and empathy generally exceeded those for affiliativeness and affect. It was suggested that communication-understanding is particularly vulnerable to "failure" of the husband to fulfill his provider role duties in terms of wife expectations. On the other hand, "adequate provision" seemed to generate in exchange considerable empathy satisfaction. The strong and direct linkage of economic articulation and empathy suggests that empathy may perhaps be theoretically the most significant of the three expressive dimensions. This is because of its definition as highly valued goal in general, its means-function with respect to other conjugal elements, and its particular meaning to the modern wife.

In general, the personality and perceptual type variables produced predictable results. Those with a positive orientation toward self, milieu, family life style, and other's evaluation of empathy tended to rank it higher themselves. Those with a negative orientation toward these four elements tended to view empathy in quite the opposite direction. Compared to the remaining primary dimensions, use of these control variables here revealed considerably fewer deviant type situations, indicating once again perhaps the strength and consistency of the original articulation-empathy associations.

Next, the impact of wife employment on empathy illustrates vividly how husbands and wives may perceive similar situations differently. At higher status levels, males define its consequences negatively, females define them positively; and just the opposite occurs at lower-status levels. Then we found reverse outcomes again where the wife is not employed. To explain these data, a model was utilized suggesting a tension over definition of female role rights. Finally, empathy reverses the disenchantment hypothesis in that it tends to increase in evaluation as the marriage continues. This finding tends to reinforce the notion of the centrality of empathy for conjugal unit cohesion.

CHAPTER

FIVE

•

Husband-Wife Hostility

CHAPTERS TWO, THREE, AND FOUR ARE BASED ON THE PREMISE THAT BEHAVIOR on the part of role-occupant A that is defined as reward by role occupant B will, in turn, elicit rewards by B toward A. More concretely, we have focused on the exchange of economic and status rewards for expressive rewards within the conjugal unit. In Homans' terminology, rewards produce "sentiments of liking." But Homans also suggests the converse of this proposition, *i.e.*, "the withdrawal of a reward stimulates the emotional reactions of hostility and aggression." [1] Persons do not need to be in competition to feel deprived and thus hostile. If A and B are interdependent, and A feels that B is "depriving" him of rewards due him, he might be likely to feel hostile to B. B might then reciprocate with hostility toward A. Moreover, A might also tend to withhold expected rewards from B and thus generate added hostility on the part of B. And so a certain amount of ongoing hostility becomes part of the processes of interaction between A and B.

This brief chapter is an attempt at further validation of the basic proposition underlying this book, viz., articulation with the economic opportunity structure promotes cohesion of the conjugal unit. So far we have looked at cohesion in terms of degrees of positive expressiveness. But if the theory has some validity, we should also be able to demonstrate the opposite side in terms similar to those suggested by Homans. *To the extent*

[1] George C. Homans, *Social Behavior: Its Elementary Forms*. New York: Harcourt, Brace and World, Inc., 1961, p. 144.

*that economic opportunity rewards are lacking within the conjugal unit,
not only should expressiveness decline, but hostility should increase.*

A formal definition of hostility might be worded in somewhat the following fashion: feelings of anger, opposition, and antagonism that may
often—though not inevitably—eventuate in behavior that could be described as offensive and/or aggressive. What is basic here is the *feeling* of
acrimony and distaste on the part of person for other. Whether or how
often these kinds of feelings may result in overt behavior that patently
reveals hositility is more problematic. The hostile behavior may take the
form of withdrawal or avoidance as in item 2 in the following list, or it
may consist of open "acts of aggression" (items 1, 3, 4 on the list).

Goode has used the term "negative affect" (or more broadly, as in this
study, "negative expressiveness") to refer to attitudes of wives toward
their ex-husbands.[2] "Negative affect" in his work covered such diverse
feelings as merely being indifferent, or else negative, and perhaps even
antagonistic. Furthermore, within existing marriages as well, it is quite
plain that a certain amount of negative feelings and behaviors toward one's
spouse are inevitable. Negative expressiveness or hostility is just as likely
as are feelings of positive expressiveness.

Shibutani remarks:

Because men generally deny hating those with whom they are in close
contact, it is frequently contended that one cannot hate someone he knows
intimately. Actually this is not the case. Relationships in which social distance
is reduced have far greater potentialities for the development of intense hatred.
Indeed, probably the most intense form of hatred is the vindictiveness that
develops when one turns against someone he had once loved and trusted.[3]

Hatred, of course, is an extreme form of hostility in which attitudes of
hostility are institutionalized or have become permanent. Although the
question of the degree of institutionalized hostility in ongoing marriage is
problematic, there is no doubt about Shibutani's main point. Intimacy
is no safeguard against hostility—indeed, it may be the breeding ground
for its most severe forms. And in marriage, where there is a high degree
of familiarity and thus cultural inhibitions regarding hostility are probably
less operative, there is every reason to suspect—the romantic love complex
notwithstanding—that hostility could be present and act as a significant
factor in the degree of conjugal cohesion, or lack of it.

As a measure of hostility, we used the following four items read
in this sequence to each respondent in the sample:[4]

[2] William J. Goode, *After Divorce*, New York: The Free Press, 1956, p. 292.
[3] Tamotsu Shibutani, *Society and Personality*, Englewood Cliffs, N.J.: Prentice-
Hall, Inc., 1961, p. 348.
[4] The basic source of these items is a series of unpublished papers by Professor
James L. Hawkins. See his "Associations between Companionship, Hostility, and

1. How often would you say you have a big "blow-up" with your husband (wife)?
2. How often do you get so angry with your husband (wife) that you refuse to talk?
3. How often do you get so angry that you swear at your husband (wife)?
4. How often do you get so angry that you tell your (husband-wife) you don't love (him–her) anymore?

Tables 5-1, 5-2, and 5-3 show the scores of the hositility index in terms of the several objective and subjective criteria of economic articulation.[5] For both sexes the evidence falls consistently in the predicted direction: *As objective integration decreases, and as alienation and anomie increase, hostility increases correspondingly; and vice-versa.* Wives show a very strong significance level in all eight instances. Moreover, at each articulation level, wives generally report a greater level of hostility than husbands at that same level, although the differences between sexes tend to be greater at lower levels of articulation.

In Table 5-2, there are two types of alienation dimensions (powerlessness, status estrangement) in which differences in hostility are not significant for husbands, and one such (success expectations) appears in Table 5-3. These several indications, along with the generally higher female hostility scores, suggest that the linkage of economic articulation and hostility is somewhat stronger and perhaps somewhat more salient to wives than to husbands. Theoretically, we might expect this to be so. For according to the model in Figure 1 (Chapter One), it is the wife who assesses the husband's status rewards and reacts accordingly. Her status is totally dependent or grounded on his achievements and successes. To the extent that rewards of this kind are minimal, and she is thus "deprived," to that extent will she react with greater hostility. And the more she does this, the more likely her husband is to respond in kind.

Because the wife is so thoroughly dependent on her husband for these rewards—especially those status and prestige rewards that she could only rarely attain through her own employment—the relationship between economic articulation and hostility is more pervasive and consistent for her than for her husband. She is the one being "deprived" of her rights and who is thus presumably resentful. Her husband is not likely to feel hostility towards his wife on the basis of his attainments per se, but instead in reaction to her hostility toward him on the basis of her assessment of

Marital Satisfaction," *Journal of Marriage and the Family*, 30 (November 1968), pp. 647–50, for a discussion of the substantive significance of hostility in husband-wife relations.

[5] The response categories were very often, often, sometimes, seldom, never. The respective weights were 7-5-3-1-0. The four scores were added for each respondent to obtain a "total perceived hostility score." Overall mean score was 3.83; S.D.=4.49.

his rewards. Since for him the relationship between articulation and hostility is thus more indirect, it is more open to influence by other kinds of variables, and thus likely to be weaker and less consistent.

It is not that status exchange is necessarily the major reason for particular hostility levels, or that husband or wife would not initiate hostility on *other* grounds. The point simply is that when one of the major "rights" of the wife role is relatively denied, this type of deprivation sets up, or becomes intrinsically part of, a resultant process that generates hostility on the part of that role occupant. Occupants of the husband role then tend to respond systematically in kind to the level of hostility emitted by their wives. Obviously, husbands may and do act in a hostile manner toward their wives for reasons other than wife hostility. This is undoubtedly an additional factor that helps account for the lesser consistency of data describing them in Tables 5-2 and 5-3. But it does seem that one element accounting for systematic differences in husband perception of hostility attitudes and behaviors is the hostile behavior of his wife toward him, based, in turn, on the sense of deprivation that she feels because of the particular level of rewards he supplies to her.

We must not, however, fail to take account of at least two other explanations for the relationships shown in these data. These explanations are in fact complementary to the reward-deprivation-hostility hypothesis, and together all three would probably account for a good deal of the total variance in husband-wife hostility. The first is built on the premise that persons from lower-status homes learn hostility and aggression as children and accept them as part of their "normal" way of life. Overt acrimony is taken for granted, in contrast to the setting in higher-status homes where attempts are made to "smooth over" hostility and aggression and to institutionalize "politeness" and "calmness." Having learned these contrasting patterns in childhood, individuals carry them over into many phases of their adult lives, and into their respective marriages as well. As a result, lower-status marriages tend to be characterized by greater hostility than are higher-status marriages.[6]

Although this line of reasoning is plausible, it leaves unanswered the question as to why, in the first place, there might be greater hostility among lower-status families. This then leads us to a second possible explanation for the reported data. McKinley has suggested that the lower the status of the husband's job, the more frustrated he feels, and the more

---

[6] One might wish to argue that *feelings* of hostility are less apt to vary by status level than are *behaviors* of an aggressive nature. The higher the status, the more the tendency to suppress aggression or overt hostility. Further research might attempt to distinguish between covert feelings of hostility and overt aggressive behavior within the husband-wife dyad. But for now, we are assuming that the two are related, and that tendencies toward increased covert and/or overt hostility are stimulated where expected rewards are not forthcoming.

aggression he thus emits toward his family members.[7] Conversely, the fewer deprivations the father feels in the occupational realm, the less frustrated he feels in terms of his own sense of "personal excellence," and the less hostile he will be in the home—especially toward his sons, according to McKinley. This hypothesis goes a long way toward explaining why lower-status children experience and learn to accept greater hostility, and also why higher-status children experience less of it. McKinley claims it is the adolescent son who feels the brunt of his lower-status father's frustration, and consequently the overt hostility and aggression. The higher-status adolescent son is said to receive greater support, warmth, and acceptance from his father.

Thus, McKinley's conclusions contribute further to the explanation of why husbands as different status levels engage in different degrees of hostility. The suggestion has been made that one factor is based on their response to their wives' differential hostility, hinged, in turn, on rewards that they themselves provide. But, in addition, it seems likely that husbands also engage in differential amounts of hostility as a reaction to differential amounts of frustration experienced in the occupational sector. This would help to explain, and to add additional force, to the systematic decrease in reported husband hostility at greater levels of economic articulation. (As noted in Chapter One, status deprivation and frustration are not necessarily directly related in every instance. Some higher-status husbands may feel very frustrated in their occupations, whereas some lower-status husbands may not feel that way at all. In general, however, it would seem that McKinley's expectations would hold true at least in the majority of cases.)

But by itself, the frustration-aggression notion would not help to explain the strong and consistent relationships reported by wives. McKinley, for example, cites the many studies that indicate that compared to lower-status boys, girls from lower-status homes receive more emotional support and less rejection and hostility—particularly from their mothers.[8] The point is that since lower-status girls experience and learn less hostility than boys, they should carry this with them into their own families of procreation.[9]

[7] Donald G. McKinley, *Social Class and Family Life,* New York: The Free Press, 1964, pp. 243 ff.

[8] *Ibid.,* pp. 200–201.

[9] One might also interject at this point the notion that girls in the lower-lower class (especially from Negro families) learn a generalized male hostility from their mothers, and that they carry this over into their later marriages. To the extent this is true, part of this hostility is due to the inability of the lower-lower class male to be even a *stable*—much less a *good*—provider. Since, however, our sample excludes most persons of these kinds, it is not likely that the data here reflect much, if any, *institutionalized* hostility or contempt on the part of females toward males. Instead, hostility here is more likely to develop chiefly in response to situations that emerge afer marriage, viz., those described in the text.

But the data suggest that these girls later as women experience very high levels of hostility. One could argue this is merely a response to their husbands' occupational frustration-hostility syndrome. Undoubtedly this is part of it, but by no means a complete picture. For if childhood socialization were the prime factor operating, then presumably lower-status girls would be better able to cope with their husbands' hostility. They would be less likely to respond in kind and would try to make every effort to "calm troubled waters" rather than to "stir them up." At the very least, the strength and consistency of the reported relationships would not fall so heavily in the direction of wives as they do. We might, for instance, expect a frequent blurring of female hostility levels over the range of various articulation levels.

In short, to explain fully the different hostility levels as reported by wives, we need to draw on Homans' notion of reward deprivation. Although the other two explanations contribute, they lack sufficient force by themselves. This is so, not only because of the relative merits per se of these several arguments in terms of the data in Tables 5-1, 5-2, and 5-3, but even more fundamentally, because of the overall theoretical linkage to our four earlier chapters. For there the exchange model was elaborated in terms of "sentiments of postitive liking." Here it is being elaborated and "filled out" in terms of a logical requisite converse, *i.e., conditions of disaffection.* The frustration-aggression model is too ambiguous by itself to account for husband-wife hostility. Even more significant, it is particularly unsuitable to explain husband-wife primary relations. Instead, it needs to be incorporated under the rubric of the more general and comprehensive social-exchange model. For example, even though McKinley drew heavily on the frustration-aggression hypothesis to explain certain patterns of child socialization, he acknowledges that at a more general level the exchange model actually subsumes the major points he has made.

What I have borrowed from economics and through Homans has been rather simple. . . . Social life is an exchange of not only goods but emotional sanctions, and a position of high status means the receipt of large positive resources. The person of high status enjoys or has accumulated emotional "profit" which can be reinvested in the child to bring about socialization . . . into the mode of life of the adult.[10]

In analogous fashion, with regard to the issue being discussed here, viz., husband-wife hostility, the point is clear that the frustration-aggression theme per se is too narrow to account satisfactorily for the kinds of relationships that emerged. To explain more fully the differences in hostility levels, and equally vital, to be able to link these data with those pertaining to

[10] *Op. cit.,* pp. 251–52.

positive expressiveness, we must make use of a more inclusive model based on human exchange. In other words, the systematic differences in levels of hostility experienced by wives in the sample cannot be totally understood apart from the varying levels of economic and status rewards received from their husbands.

Moreover, granting the validity of the exchange model as it is being applied here, hostility, particularly as we have measured it, very likely operates in conjunction with numerous personality and need-complementarity variables. Here we shall consider only one such variable, viz., the measure of global self-esteem used previously. In Table 5–4, the results seem to fall in expected directions. First, the original inverse articulation-hostility association remains, even in the presence of so crucial a personality variable as self-esteem. One might have predicted that an overall positive view of oneself would enable one to "cope" effectively with hostilities, and hence tend to blur interstatus differences in these kinds of feelings and behaviors. Instead, it appears that reward level continues to exercise considerable influence on hostility levels even when self-esteem is high. To be sure, this positive personality orientation has some effect—for example, the husband-discontent, high self-esteem table does fail to show significant differences. Yet the same is true for the low male self-esteem discontent table. So that these particular results may be owing as much to the lesser saliency in general to husbands of this kind of relationship as to the influence of this personality orientation alone.

Second, in general, within most economic-articulation levels we find that low self-esteem increases hostility scores, whereas high self-esteem decreases them. The reasons for the few exceptions are unclear but, overall, we may conclude that a negative image of oneself tends to exacerbate feelings of perceived hostility. As Rosenberg has described his measure of self-esteem, a low score would tend to suggest impaired communication with, and misreading of, alter. These factors, plus a certain amount of defensiveness associated with a negative self-image, would probably help to accentuate hostility and perhaps to make it more intense and even bitter.

Conversely, a positive self-image apparently mitigates feelings of hostility and resentment. There is undoubtedly among persons of this kind a greater capability to cope with the anger and outbursts of both oneself and one's spouse. Likewise, potential intensity and bitterness are probably softened, and "blow-ups" are more quickly and easily forgotten. In short, particularly for wives, but generally for husbands as well, whereas positive self-esteem does not eliminate the consequences of differential status rewards, it does provide at each status level a "personality resource" whereby the presumably deleterious impact of hostility on conjugal cohesion is effectively reduced.

CONCLUSION

This brief chapter is essentially an attempt to add additional validity to the notion that greater economic opportunity articulation generates greater feelings of conjugal solidarity and cohesion. In earier chapters, our concern was with the impact of the opportunity structure on expressive interaction. In these last few pages, we have turned the coin over and asked whether deprivation of status rewards would generate feelings of husband-wife hostility. We found that it does, particularly for wives. The frustration-aggression hypothesis was considered as a possible explanation for the data, but although it is an important complement, it can be subsumed under the more general model of social exchange.

Furthermore, we found that a negative self-image tended to increase feelings of hostility, a positive self-image to reduce them, although the original relationship between economic opportunity integration and hostility held in both directions, and once again especially for wives. These findings, therefore, do serve the function of providing added validity to the theory underlying this entire volume. For it appears that with greater articulation with the economic opportunity structure, come not only increased satisfaction with primary relations, but also decreased feelings of hostility toward one's spouse. And both kinds of elements, in complex interrelationship, presumably generate feelings of solidarity and thus promote conjugal cohesion. On the other side, decreased economic articulation decreases perceived expressiveness and also increases feelings of hostility. Acting together, these factors probably decrease feelings of solidarity and thus undermine cohesion of the unit qua unit.

CHAPTER

SIX

•

Authority Relations

As stated in Chapter One, the major objective of this book is to work toward a theory of conjugal cohesion. The previous chapters have spelled out in considerable detail ways in which the opportunity and success structure of our society impinges on husband-wife primary relations. A major inference so far has been that primary satisfactions are a basic indicant of conjugal cohesion. In this chapter, we wish to shift the focus from expressive-type to instrumental-type relations—and in particular, to husband-wife authority relations. The discussion will continue to focus, nonetheless, on the larger theoretical question of what sort of impact the opportunity structure has on this variety of conjugal interaction, and how it, in turn, may be ultimately linked to cohesion of the conjugal unit.

The very notion of "authority relations" sensitizes us to the premise that every social system, including the conjugal family, must solve the "functional problem" variously described as authority, power, policy and/ or decision-making and/or execution, conflict resolution, and so on. Theoretically, we should expect this question to be an intrinsic element in conjugal cohesion and thus also in the even broader issue of the order-disorder of the conjugal unit. The "problem of order" in terms of any social system would seem to necessitate "satisfactory handling" or "system management" of the issue of power.

Indeed, the earliest studies of marital adjustment and divorce were cognizant of the presence of conflicts and disagreements in marriage. They were also aware that inability to "solve" major conflicts is associated with the decision to become separated or divorced. More recent studies of the general phenomenon have been labeled as investigations of "family power," and have focused primarily on existing marriages, as does this study. A thorough critique of these latter kinds of studies was made by Heer.[1] He outlines the numerous methodological problems that attend the measurement of family power. The two major categories of efforts are said to be Strodtbeck's experimental-observational technique, and the reputational technique. The latter depends on a report by one or more family members (husband, wife, adolescent) as to the exercise of power.

Heer notes that a crucial problem common to both techniques is that "power is not unidimensional. Persons having greater power in one area of family decision-making do not necessarily have the same degree of power in other areas . . . this lack of unidimensionality presents a problem in that some way must be found to assign a proper weight to each of the various areas in which decisions are made." [2]

The work of Blood and Wolfe is then cited in which eight areas of household decisions were given equal weight in constructing a "final index of conjugal power." Heer points up a weakness in this approach in that "no research has been conducted to determine whether a method that taps only specified areas of decision-making is tapping areas of conflict for any given family. In addition, no research has been conducted to determine whether it is justified to give equal weight to each of the decision-making areas. For instance, are decisions concerning 'what type of car to purchase' of equal importance with decisions concerning 'what job or house to take' ? " [3] In short, some areas may be extremely vital in the power process, others irrelevant. Related to this is the question of saliency of these areas. Since they were imposed arbitrarily on the respondent, there is no way of knowing whether there are additional untapped areas, more crucial to the couple and over which a good deal of conflict takes place.

An alternative to assigning weights to specified areas of decision-making is known as the "generalized question" approach and has been used by Heer and others. In this procedure, the respondent is asked to report who "wins out," "gets his way," "usually decides," when an "important" or "major" or "frequent" disagreement arises. The chief strength of this approach is that it clearly pinpoints for the respondent and researcher the area(s) of most salient husband-wife conflict, and the direction of its (their) resolution. Heer acknowledges the major failing of this method to be its inability to obtain a precise measure of family power, based on

[1] David M. Heer, "The Measurement and Bases of Family Power," *Marriage and Family Living*, 25 (May 1963), pp. 133–39.

[2] *Ibid.*, p. 135.

[3] Heer, *ibid.*; Robert O. Blood, Jr., and Donald M. Wolfe, *Husbands and Wives*, New York: The Free Press, 1960.

an overall view of the processes of decision-making. "When a generalized question is used, it is difficult to be more precise than to place each family member into one of several categories." [4] In other words, both the "predesignated areas" and the "generalized" approaches have their methodological strengths and weaknesses.

Heer notes that much more research is needed to determine the relative validity of each, as well as those situations in which perhaps one or the other approach might be more appropriate. In this study, we shall make use of the "generalized question" approach, chiefly because of its presumed capability of tapping that area (out of many) of husband-wife dissensus which is most salient or pertinent to any particular conjugal unit. Detailed discussion of our procedures will be presented shortly, but first let us consider two further points made by Heer.

He points out that while Blood and Wolfe actually measured only *one* aspect of family power (household decision-making), they nonetheless imply that this is all there is to authority within the conjugal family. Specifically, they assert that the notion of formal authority, tradition, and normative ideologies is now defunct simply because they found no evidence of consistent male dominance within their eight areas of predesignated decision-making. Even though they had no actual measure of the patriarchal ideology whatsoever, they nonetheless dismissed it on the basis of their measure of a separate and distinct aspect of power.[5] Heer suggests that they may have oversimplified this highly intricate issue, and he cites other studies that make some effort to include measures of beliefs regarding family power, and that also try to relate them to the actual processes of authority.

In this study, we have made a deliberate effort to measure beliefs about family power, as well as the actual behaviors involved. It seems far too simplistic to assert that certain traditions regarding male authority and/or dominance do not still persist in our society—at least without actual empirical demonstration of same. In earlier chapters, we have drawn on the work of Goode and others describing the "struggle" between male role rights and duties versus those of the female role. Our discussion took place within the context of physical affect and employment. Here we continue to examine male-female role tension, only now we focus on the realm of authority and power.

If what Blood and Wolfe say is valid, *i.e.*, that traditional beliefs regarding male dominance are no longer operative, then a significant change has indeed occurred in definitions of certain role rights by males (and by females, too). Males, in effect, have come to define conjugal authority simply as an option (based on the Blood and Wolfe concept of "resources,"

[4] Heer, *op. cit.*, p. 136.
[5] Blood and Wolfe, *op. cit.*, pp. 11–46.

discussed below), rather than as a traditional right based on their sex role. Females, on the other hand, have been able to bring about a shift in the definition of authority inherent in the female role from the traditional one of "obligation to defer" to the option to exercise power apart from sex role. Given the generalizations drawn from our earlier discussions of physical affect and employment, a "cultural change" of this magnitude in this particular realm seems doubtful. And indeed, as our data will show, it does not appear to have taken place.

An additional point made by Heer pertains to the linkage of power to marital cohesion. It was noted in Chapter One that Heer has made an initial effort in this direction through use of exchange theory. He proposes this as a more comprehensive revision of Blood and Wolfe's "resource theory." Heer argues that his "theory explicitly states that each partner to the marriage conceives the possibility of separation, divorce, and subsequent remarriage." He states, "the greater the difference between the value to the wife of the resources contributed by her husband and the value to the wife of the resources which she might earn outside the existing marriage, the greater the power of her husband, and vice-versa." [6]

Support for his expanded theory comes from those studies that have found that husbands' power increases with social status. Women married to "successful" men, says Heer, may be less likely to contradict their husbands out of fear of losing the "good catch" they have made, or lest they endanger or jeopardize an economically "beneficial" situation. By the same token, wives of "unsuccessful" men are less afraid of endangering their situation by insisting on their own way or else contradicting their husbands, because they have less to lose if the relationship dissolves. Blood later criticized Heer on several counts to which Heer himself responded in turn. One major divergence between them is over the meaning and implications of exchange theory. Blood asserts "such an economic calculus," with reference to the contemplation of divorce, finds little support in the literature.[7]

Heer responds that the thin support may be due to a preponderance of "socially acceptable" answers when the respondent is asked if he had ever "contemplated separation and/or divorce." [8] But the crux of this matter lies in the point that Homans, Merton, and others have made and that has been reiterated often in this volume. And that is that the notion of

---

6 *Op. cit.*, p. 138. The reader will note the similarity between this formulation and the "comparison level for alternatives," or "the lowest level of outcomes a member will accept in the light of available alternative opportunities." See John W. Thibaut and Harold H. Kelley, *The Social Psychology of Groups,* New York: John Wiley and Sons, Inc., 1959, p. 21.

7 Robert O. Blood, Jr., "The Measurement and Bases of Family Power: A Rejoinder," *Marriage and Family Living,* 25 (November 1963), p. 476.

8 David Heer, "Reply," *Marriage and Family Living,* 25 (November 1963), p. 478.

human exchange and reciprocity do not require nor even imply a "rational calculus," but are instead the result of exigencies structured by the social organization of a particular situation. In short, Heer's theory may have validity apart from any of the conscious, rational thought processes that Blood believes are implied.

It does not follow, however, that we subscribe totally to Heer's initial formulations. For instance, his specific hypothesis may be a bit narrow in its potential application. That is, it may be quite relevant for couples who aspire to or who actually experience rapid upward mobility, but less pertinent for couples who are socially "stable," whether at low or high status levels. Likewise, there may be a flaw in his assertion that higher-status wives are less likely to "contradict" their husbands. There is nothing in exchange theory to suggest that disagreement per se (or conflict) should necessarily be less in higher-status situations—even disagreement over production and especially the use of money. (See Footnote 23.)

Perhaps the most serious bias of some of the older "adjustment" studies was that conflict per se is somehow inimical to functioning of the conjugal unit. This, of course, reflected a general anticonflict bias in sociology, but in recent years most sociologists have come to agree that conflict per se does not necessarily threaten a social system. The real issue is the manner of its resolution. Exchange theory, as we shall apply it in this chapter, deals precisely with this more vital matter. Higher-status couples may disagree as much as those with less status over any range of things, including finances. The basic question, therefore, in terms of unit cohesion, is the manner of conflict resolution.

Finally in the light of our earlier chapters, particularly Buckley's comments in Chapter Two modifying the crassness of Homans' purely economic notions, plus Buckley's introduction of self-worth, and so on, into the exchange process, an expansion of Heer's ideas in this direction is to be expected. Nonetheless, in spite of the fact that we wish to modify his formulations, they remain an important contribution.

Recalling Chapter One, it was noted that, in our society, great stress is put on achievement and success. An important element in the "success syndrome" is the sense of "personal excellence" that derives from it. As McClelland notes, the "achievement motive" is far more comprehensive and complex than the Marxian-type "profit motive." [9] Therefore, if we refer again to Figure 1, Chapter One, we may say that the more the husband fulfills his economic duties (Wd), and thus the more the wife defines her status rights (Xr) are being met, the more she will allow her husband to define the norms for Xd and Wr. She will accede to his expectations regarding his rights and her duties in terms of household decision-making.

[9] David C. McClelland, *The Achieving Society,* Princeton, N.J.: D. Van Nostrand Co., 1961, p. 391.

Thereby she, in essence, gives him power to shape this dimension of the conjugal unit, in exchange for the economic rewards and status benefits he provides for her vis-à-vis the larger community. She is more motivated to "go along" with him, to "give in" to him, to let him "have his way" to the extent that he provides maximum economic rewards. But to the degree that these rewards (including the respect and sense of excellence that inhere in them) decline, she is thus less motivated to accede to him.

Earlier chapters suggested that increased economic articulation of the husband sets off a chain reaction of reciprocal behaviors that result in maximized primary satisfactions and in minimized hostilities. It is then a simple step to surmise that these types of goal-attainments, in turn, contribute to enhanced marital cohesion. But how do economic-instrumental reciprocities contribute to cohesion? Heer suggests that the "less rewarded wife," by being willing to challenge her husband, is thereby indicating greater willingness to end the union. In the *extreme* case, she is willing to make the conflict intense enough actually to bring about dissolution. This explanation may be valid as far as it goes. But it leaves out at least one additional step in a complex process that we shall attempt to identify shortly.

First, let us see if our data fit the exchange model described above. Using a variation on Heer's "generalized question," the respondent was asked to name in rank order four things he and his spouse disagree about most often. After each stated disagreement the respondent was then asked, "When you disagree about [the item named] who usually gets his way, you or your (husband-wife)? Some respondents (9 percent of the sample) claimed they never disagreed about anything with their spouse, although 91 percent acknowledged at least one frequent disagreement. Seventy percent of the sample could name two areas of conflict, 52 percent could name three such areas, and only 37 percent could name four.

In Table 6-1, we have used education, and level of success expectations, as representative of the several dimensions of objective and subjective articulation with the economic opportunity system.[10] The data are based on the resolution of the first conflict named by the respondent. Presumably, to him, this is the most salient and most frequent altercation, and thus the most significant for purposes of analysis. Moreover, it encompasses better than 90 percent of the sample. The tables also take into account those who replied that neither spouse decided the contested issue alone, but who, instead, volunteered that they resolved it "jointly," or "together," or "by mutual compromise," and so on.

Contrary to what we had expected, there is not a consistent pattern of increasing male dominance corresponding to increased opportunity inte-

[10] Representative, as in earlier chapters, of similar patterns that emerge when the remaining indicators are used.

gration. Take the first educational level. The less the education, the more power husbands attribute to themselves, although the differences are not statistically significant. But theoretically significant is the concomitant decrease in joint conflict resolution that husbands also report as education level drops. So it is not simply that lower-status husbands more frequently resolve conflicts unilaterally than do higher-status husbands; in addition, they tend to be less apt to "work with" their wives in the processes of conflict resolution. Conversely, at higher status levels, it is not that wives necessarily have more power than husbands, but rather that they participate together with them in the processes of resolving contested issues. Consequently, we may say that as level of economic articulation drops, husbands tend to exercise more power, both in terms of unilateral conflict resolution and also in terms of less shared conflict resolution.

When we examine wives' perceptions in terms of their education level, it is again quite apparent that as articulation level drops, degree of shared conflict resolution systematically drops as well. Likewise, wives with most education report lowest husband dominance, and wives with least education show the greatest husband dominance. In between, however, from those with "some high school" through those with "some college," we do note a corresponding rise in male dominance. Yet the concomitant rise in shared decisions at these three levels tends to weaken the notion of absolute increases in male power within these same levels. That is, for each increase in unilateral male conflict resolution, there is also an increase in joint conflict resolution. Specifically, along with the 7 percent increase in the frequency of the exercise of male power between the three categories, there is also a 9 percent increase in the frequency of shared power.

Third, when we examine the top three categories of male success expectations, we find only minimal differences in unilateral and shared conflict resolution. But interestingly enough, when we note the thirteen cases in the "poor" category, there is overwhelming evidence of female dominance. This seems to be the one instance where our original expectation is clearly verified. That is, where husbands provide "very poor" rewards in terms of future success expectations, they do not feel they can claim much authority over conjugal conflict resolution. Lacking almost any bargaining power whatsoever, they see themselves as deferring often to wives' demands. In spite of these few cases, the occurrence of this finding among the most anomic males certainly merits further investigation, if for no other reason than to see if the pattern would continue to hold up at this articulation level with a larger *n*.

Finally, when we examine wives' success expectations, we find differences in degree of husband dominance and in joint conflict resolution that are now statistically significant. Once again we see that the lower the articulation level of the husband, the more unilateral is the frequency of his power, and the less he tends to share decisions with his wife, and conversely, the higher his articulation level, the less unilateral is his power, and the more he tends to share decisions with his wife. The fact is that this "double-faceted" generalization sums up our behavioral data regarding this dimension of conjugal power. It is noteworthy that wives with "poor" expectations do not see themselves with the same overwhelming dominance that husbands in this category ascribe to their own wives. There is almost a complete reversal in terms of the 60-odd percent of the frequency of power that each sex ascribes to the other. So even in this high-anomie category, verification of our original expectation must be tempered by the realization that perception varies by sex of respondent.

Basically, therefore, except for some isolated indications, we seem unable to validate the hypothesis that status is exchanged for power—at least in so far as this particular aspect of power is concerned. Instead, it would appear that, as Goode puts it, lower-status men "demand deference as *men*, as heads of families." [11] But unlike his prediction that they would not be able to gain this deference because of the limited inputs they bring to the family system, they seem to "take it" anyway. Now it may very well be that with regard to day-to-day decision-making, such as was measured by Blood and Wolfe, lower-status men may be willing to settle for minimal power, simply perhaps because over many household questions they "just don't care." But when they do care about a contested issue, they seem to get their own way and, moreover, to limit in general the participation of wives in the process of conflict resolution. Finally, we should note in any event that overall, at most status levels, husbands, more frequently than wives, resolve conflicts in their own favor. What tends to vary systematically by status level is the size of the differences in power between the sexes, and also the relative frequencies of shared conflict resolution.

Our study is not alone in failing to confirm clearly the status-power hypothesis. Komarovsky also found that "the expectation that the better providers and the better-educated husbands would wield superior power in marriage is belied by the fact." [12] She, too, was surprised by her results, which showed, as do ours, that upper blue-collar husbands exercise less power than lower blue-collar husbands. In an attempt to explain her "different" findings, she explored (among several possibilities, including personality characteristics) the presence of patriarchal attitudes in her sample and

[11] William J. Goode, *World Revolution and Family Patterns,* New York: The Free Press, 1963, p. 22.

[12] Mirra Komarovsky, *Blue-Collar Marriage,* New York: Random House, Inc., 1962, p. 234. She further notes that Blood and Wolfe (*op. cit.*) also found "relatively high power [among] men at the bottom of the occupational and social hierarchy," but aside from their suggestion that "these lower status men may be older," she points out that Blood and Wolfe do not elaborate further on their finding. (Komarovsky, p. 225)

found they "are more prevalent among the less-educated." [13] She suggests that this may be one factor helping to explain her results, and also indicates that the phenomenon of family power may be exceedingly more complex than some investigators had supposed. Komarovsky's conclusions add force to Heer's contention that "Blood and Wolfe's findings do not destroy the argument that tradition is an important base of family power." [14] This is so simply because they failed to measure it. Rodman also argues that Blood and Wolfe's treatment of family power is incomplete apart from consideration of the "influential role" of "cultural factors" such as the emphasis on the "equalitarian ethic." [15]

We do, however, have a measure of that particular dimension of family power described earlier as beliefs regarding traditional male authority *vs.* the equalitarian ethic. This orientation was tapped by means of a two-item index of "authority ideology."

1. "The wife should have equal authority with the husband in making decisions."

2. "The husband should be the head of the home."

The items were read separately during different stages of the interview, and the structured responses were "strongly agree, agree, disagree, strongly disagree." The items were combined, and strong agreement with item No. 1 was weighted 4, agree = 3, disagree = 2, strongly disagree = 1. Precisely the reverse weighting was followed with item No. 2: strongly agree = 1, and so on. The result is that the lower the respondent's score, the more traditional he is in terms of patriarchal authority; and the higher the score, the more equalitarian he reveals himself to be.

There is no doubt that what is in view here is a continuum of beliefs about male authority from traditional to modern. Those nearer the traditional end of the continuum tend to deemphasize the idea that the wife should share equally with the husband in decision-making; and at the same time, they tend to emphasize the belief that the husband is the head of the home, or the "court of final appeals," in terms of deference over contested issues. On the other hand, those who fall nearer to the modern end of the continuum tend to emphasize the notion of the wife sharing equally in decision-making. They also tend to deemphasize the idea that the husband—simply because of his sex role—should *ipso facto* command

---

[13] Komarovsky, *ibid.,* p. 225.

[14] Heer, *op. cit.,* May, 1963, p. 136.

[15] Hyman Rodman, "Marital Power in France, Greece, Yugoslavia, and the United States: A Cross-national Discussion," *Journal of Marriage and the Family,* 29 (May 1967), p. 322.

the traditional reverence and respect "due" the male, and thus be the ultimate arbiter of conflicts and disagreements.

Furthermore, as is generally the case with belief systems, this kind of description—in terms of relative emphases—still does not apprehend the full extent of the complexity involved. Specifically, 15 percent of the sample "strongly agreed" and 67 percent "agreed" that the wife should have equal authority in decisions. At the same time, 15 percent and 74 percent of the sample "strongly agreed" and "agreed," respectively, that the husband should be the head of the home. In other words, among our respondents, there is a basic tendency toward believing in shared authority, yet at the same time feeling that because some means of final arbitration is often needed in the family (as in any social system), it might as well—or perhaps "ought"—to be the traditional means, viz., a resort to the will of the male figure.

Thus, the idea of relative emphases on a traditional-modern (right-left) continuum must be juxtaposed with the notion that there is concurrently a basic pull to the "center." While most respondents favor the modern view of shared authority, they also favor the traditional means of resolving deadlocks by an appeal to ultimate male predominance. Whether this latter orientation will undergo substantial change during the next few decades is not clear at this point. Nonetheless, in spite of this "pull to the center," it is possible for a husband or wife to possess a combination of these two orientations that, relatively speaking, more or less tends to lean in either the traditional or modern direction.

For example, Table 6–2 shows the several relationships of male authority ideology to varied indicators of the three types of economic opportunity integration used throughout the study.[16] Over all five dimensions, wives show significant differences in their orientations. Without exception, *the greater the degree of objective and subjective economic articulation, the more traditional the wives are with respect to male authority.* Conversely, *the less the articulation, the more "modern" the wives are with respect to male authority.* That is, lower-status wives are much more equalitarian or egalitarian in their beliefs than are higher-status wives. The latter are more likely to believe their husbands should have greater power than wives; the former are more apt to believe that power should be shared.

On the other hand, no such significant differences emerge for husbands. Although there may be a slight tendency for higher-status husbands to

[16] The remaining three indicators revealed patterns similar to those seen in Table 6-2, *i.e.*, greater spread in mean scores for wives than for husbands, with lower status wives being more "modern" than higher status wives. But since the F ratios for wives fell just short of the .05 level of significance, these indicators were not shown. And, as in Table 6-2, relationships for husbands were never significantly different.

be more "modern" than lower-status husbands, the range of scores between categories is quite narrow indeed. Moreover, in actual scores, husbands only once exceed the 3.0 mark ("fair" income), whereas wives do so often. Husbands, in other words, regardless of level of economic articulation, do not differ significantly from each other in terms of traditional male authority. At all status levels they are likely to believe that the husband should be the dominant figure in the household, that power should not be shared so equally. Goode implies that upper-status men are more likely to concede more rights ideologically to their wives than are lower-status men.[17] But this argument, *i.e.*, that higher-status men are necessarily more favorable toward the equalitarian ethic, is not borne out by our data.

There is, in short, a divergence between the sexes over legitimate male authority. Moreover, this divergence is sharpest and widest at lower status levels. For although less articulated men are the most traditional of all men (even though the differences with higher-status men are minimal), wives at these same lower levels are the most modern of all wives. Hence the conflict of male versus female role rights discussed in connection with wife employment and with physical affect appears once again—this time with respect to the issue of family power in general. And it appears to be more salient the lower the economic articulation of the family. In fact, Table 6-2 shows that within higher-status homes, wives are more traditional even than husbands at their same levels.

The tension over egalitarianism takes on considerable significance when we compare the ideological aspect of family power with the data on the "conflict resolution" dimension of power (Table 6-1). For there we found that the lower the economic articulation, the greater the tendency of the husband to dominate in conflict resolution—both unilaterally and also in his unwillingness to resolve contested issues jointly. The greater the articulation, the less his exclusive dominance, and the more he tended to share power with his wife.

In other words, among "more advantaged" families we discover a combination of lesser husband dominance in actual conflict resolution, plus the belief on the part of wives that the degree of power that their husbands do actually exercise is in fact legitimate. Thus, the greater the articulation, the less the actual husband dominance; and yet, the more wives belief in husband authority. More succinctly, the greater the articulation, the more legitimate is male exercise of power. Higher-status wives believe that it is "right and proper" that their husbands should settle issues more often than they, though in fact they tend at least to share in these decisions more frequently than do lower-status wives.

Ideologically, at higher status levels, there is greater consensus over

[17] *Op. cit.*, p. 21.

beliefs about power (or more correctly, as Buckley puts it, authority, which he defines as "the direction or control of the behavior of others for the promotion of collective goals, based on some ascertainable form of their knowledgeable consent. Authority thus implies informed, voluntary compliance, which is a definite psychological state. . . ."[18]). There is, at the same time, behaviorally, greater actual sharing of authority. The fact that these higher-status wives share authority even though they possess no strong "ideological push" to do so should not be disruptive to the solidarity of the conjugal unit. On the contrary, we would expect that in any social system, to actually share more authority than one actually expects or defines as right and proper would increase feelings of solidarity and thus contribute to the cohesion of that system. Therefore, we would propose that the particular combination of beliefs and behavior in terms of legitimate authority found among higher-status families actually contributes to the likelihood of their greater cohesion.

But among the "less advantaged" families, in which husbands more frequently dominate conflict resolution, wives do not believe that this exercise of male power is legitimate. Rather, they are more likely to hold that power should be shared to a greater extent, that contested issues should be settled on a more equalitarian basis. This kind of situation, therefore, we may presume to be a source of strain within the conjugal family as it would be in any social system. Specifically, Buckley defines power as "control or influence over the actions of others to promote one's goals without their consent, against their 'will,' or without their knowledge or understanding. . . . The emphasis here is on the lack of ascertainable 'consent,' considered as something socially and psychologically deeper than mere acquiescence or overt compliance. A closely related characteristic is the emphasis on private goal-orientation rather than on collectivity goal-orientation." [19]

Hence, whenever power is exercised against those who perceive it is adversely affecting their interests (in this case, less advantaged wives who "lose" contested issues they feel they ought to "win" or at least help to resolve) at the same time that they believe this power has only slight legitimate basis, we may assume that system solidarity is potentially being threatened. In terms of the tension over female rights, the lower the articulation of the wife, the more she feels it is her right to share in conjugal authority, yet the more she is denied her self-defined right by a husband who does not share her belief. This denial of shared authority may be assumed to weaken feelings of solidarity and thus pose a threat to conjugal

18 Walter Buckley, *Sociology and Modern Systems Theory,* Englewood Cliffs, New Jersey: Prentice-Hall, Inc., 1967, p. 186.
19 *Ibid.*

cohesion. Therefore, this particular combination of beliefs and behavior undermines, rather than reinforces, the conjugal unit.

The question naturally arises as to why contrasting combinations of legitimate-nonlegitimate authority occur at different levels of economic articulation. To answer this, we may now make use of the exchange model, which did not appear to apply to the dimension of conflict resolution alone. At the most general level, we may say that the greater the level of objective and subjective rewards provided by the husband, the more the wife deems his authority legitimate. That is, in exchange for material and prestige factors, she accords him deference at the ideological level. She believes that his inputs have "earned" him the "right to govern" or to "lead" the conjugal unit. Recognition of his legitimate authority is tied to the sense of worth, respect, and personal excellence he provides for the wife through his achievements and successes.

On the other hand, the less the objective and subjective rewards provided her by the husband, the less is his authority deemed legitimate by his wife. Because he has fewer rewards that he can exchange for ideological deference, he obtains less of the latter reward. As Homans states it so very simply, "the most important single factor in making a man a leader is . . . the ability to provide rare and valued rewards for his followers." [20] In short, the less successful is the husband, the less he is able to earn or merit this legitimate authority. The less his success, the less he is able to demonstrate his worth and his "right" to respect; hence, the less his wife is willing *ipso facto* to accord him deference. Instead, she sees no reason why she ought not to share more effectively in processes of conflict resolution. Because he has not "proved himself," or is not "proving himself," adequately in the crucible of the occupational sphere, there is a tendency for the wife to believe that his power ought to be limited in the sphere of the home as well.

The exchange model, in short, is useful in explaining actual differences in legitimate authority from the standpoint of the wife. And in terms of conjugal cohesion, because she is the one who is "acted upon," *i.e.*, is the object of authority, her perspective is probably the more theoretically significant. That is, given the general traditional state of family power, few husbands are likely to complain "if things are as they always have been"—if wives remain subservient. If family power is to become an issue and thus a potential source of tension, then we would expect that the wife would generally make it so. Thus the exchange model becomes an important vehicle for isolating some of the conditions under which she would make power an issue, viz., limited economic-status rewards.

[20] George C. Homans, *Social Behavior, Its Elementary Forms*, New York: Harcourt, Brace and World, Inc., 1961, p. 287.

From the standpoint of the male, even though differences in ideology are not significant, it is probable that the exchange model also plays a significant role in explaining the views of higher-status husbands. That is, in addition to whatever traditional orientations they possess regarding male dominance, they probably also feel that their achievement and success merit them greater authority in the family. The sense of "personal excellence," worth, and respect attained in the occupational realm probably lead the husband to think that these ought to "carry over," to overlap onto conjugal conflict resolution and/or decision-making. Though perhaps unconscious, but potent nonetheless, is the notion that his successes can and should be exchanged for authority.

But the exchange model is less appropriate for explaining the views of lower-status husbands. Since the husband possesses relatively fewer attainments, there is less "medium of exchange," less bargaining power as far as he is concerned. Nevertheless, in spite of less achievement and success, he feels he ought to have greater power simply because of his sex role, *i.e.*, because of traditional orientations. The fact that he possesses fewer attainments in no way limits his thinking (or acting) regarding his "rightful place." He does not have to "earn" authority on the basis of achieved criteria; he feels he already possesses power on the basis of sex role ascription.

But if there are no significant differences between husbands over ideologies regarding traditional authority, and if higher-status husbands believe that their greater attainments merit greater authority, why then do lower-status husbands seem to exercise more power in conflict resolution, and why do higher-status husbands seem to share more authority with their wives? McKinley has explored child-rearing practices from the same theoretical perspective as this volume, viz., the impact of achievement-oriented society on the modern conjugal unit. He concludes that "the father's deprived social position in the lower levels of society also results in a greater general hostility toward and a reduced involvement in the emotional life of the adolescent son." [21] The "less integrated" male, claims McKinley, is frustrated in the occupational sphere, and so one outlet for his aggression is his adolescent son. Limited in his capabilities to assert himself in the opportunity system, he tends to "lord it over" his son.

The same kinds of arguments might also apply regarding his adherence to traditional male authority, and especially to his dominance in conflict resolution. Precisely because he feels relatively limited in the universalistic-achievement sector of the society, he is more willing to retain the particularistic-ascribed male authority status. It is, in fact, the one type of power

[21] Donald G. McKinley, *Social Class and Family Life,* New York: The Free Press, 1964, p. 243.

he has anywhere in his existence that is effectively unchallenged, as Komarovsky notes. Consequently, he is not going to part with this traditional male prerogative lightly. And what is more, since he believes that the male has the right to decide qua male, he is going to try insistently and aggressively to exercise this authority whenever a pertinent, controversial issue arises between him and his wife.

The "less successful" husband may in fact leave the major share of uncontested day-to-day decision-making to his wife by default, simply because he cares very little about the kinds of areas that the interviewer puts to him. But it is highly unlikely that he is going to give in or become docile vis-à-vis his wife with respect to something that really means something to him. In other words, it does not follow that the male who is forced to be subservient in the success system will also be subservient to his wife. On the contrary, the application of the "frustration-aggression hypothesis" to our data on conflict resolution and authority ideology suggests, in fact, that he is not.

The kinds of disagreements named by respondents in terms of the first altercation shed additional light on this question: 38 percent indicated conflict over the production and consumption of money, 19 percent responded in terms of issues connected with children, 10 percent said friends, 3 percent referred to kin, 21 percent were combined in the miscellaneous category (conflicts common to only a few families—too few numbers to warrant a special code category), and 9 percent reported nothing.[22]

Economic issues, of course, show up in almost every study as the major source of husband-wife conflict. And theoretically, we should expect this, because of the nature of our acquisitive society.[23] Combining McKinley's

[22] Interestingly, the percentage of respondents who reported sex as the first area of disagreement was only 0.7 percent. Thus, they were placed in the miscellaneous category. A similarly diminutive finding is reported by Blood and Wolfe, *op. cit.*, pp. 243–44.

[23] In our consumption-oriented society, disagreement over a plethora of matters pertaining to the production and especially the consumption of resources is to be expected at all status levels. Unfortunately, we did not measure intensity of economic conflict, and this may indeed vary systematically with level of resources. But when we talk about intensity we are moving away from the sheer fact of conflict, and into the realm of process and resolution. Surely future studies of family power and authority ought to consider carefully the issue of intensity. For example, a higher-status couple may disagree over money five times in a month, and this may be their most frequent altercation. A lower-status couple may disagree twenty times over money during that same month for their most frequent disagreement. Our measure would rank them equal as far as the thing disagreed about most often, but it leaves untouched one aspect of intensity, *i.e.*, relative degree of conflict within a certain span of time. It is this kind of issue that needs future investigation in relation to opportunity integration.

Significantly, most respondents who reported disagreements over money matters indicated that substantively they had to do with the allocation of family income. Almost all American families (no matter how large the income) face the task of allocating relatively scarce resources to almost limitless ends. And as the following

observations with the mass of literature on child-rearing, it is not unusual to find, as we did, that husbands and wives also experience considerable disagreement over the relative amounts of control and nurture they should expend on their children.

The third large category (miscellaneous) is particularly significant here. It consists of what is called in the "practical" marriage literature the *tremendous trifles*—those areas which are often particular to certain marital situations but are seldom, if ever, on a researcher's list of items to be included as part of the decision-making dimension of family power, and yet have tremendous psychological import to the actors involved. (Some of the trifles in our sample included items such as "keeping in physical trim," "what colors to decorate interior of house," "punctuality," and "what temperature to keep the house at.") We may assume that matters of these kinds take on especially great sgnificance for husbands who perhaps perceive that their sense of excellence is being called into question as a result of limited universalistic attainments. Chances are good that they will attempt to conmpensate (and perhaps overcompensate) for this lack and try to assert their excellence by demanding their own way in these areas, as well as in money matters and in issues related to child-rearing. But it is precisely because of their adamant stand and their wives' rejection of traditional male unilateral power that strain and tension are introduced, and that feelings of solidarity and conjugal cohesion are threatened in these marriages.

Conversely, it would appear that higher-status husbands feel less compulsion, actually to resolve contested issues in a unilateral fashion. Perhaps because they are less "frustrated" in the occupational realm, they tend to

---

data suggest, the proportions of respondents who report this is the thing "disagreed over most often" are relatively similar at various status levels.

For example, family income is representative of the pattern that emerges when we run the objective indicators against frequency of economic conflicts. Among husbands in the "poor" category, 41 percent report economic disagreement; in the "fair group" it is 35 percent; in the "good" category it is 49 percent; and in the "high" group it is 40 percent. Wives in these four categories report 36, 34, 38, and 39 percent, respectively. Likewise, "discontent" (under *alienation*) is representative of the same pattern when we run the subjective indicators against the very same dependent variable. For husbands who are "very discontent," the proportion is 46 percent; "discontent," 38 percent; "content," 42 percent; "very content," 41 percent. Wives in these four categories report 40, 42, 33, 34 percent, respectively.

But sheer disagreement is one thing, how it is resolved, quite another; and this distinction is taken up in the text. Intensity might enter in here in that wives at lower-status levels press a contested issue with greater intensity than higher-status wives. That is, the lower-status wife, because she feels her husband has not "earned" the right to deference, feels more strongly or intensely that she ought not to "give in" very soon or very often. The higher-status wife, on the other hand, although disagreeing most often over the same particular matter, may simply not press it with as much intensity and may just give in, owing to the deference her husband has earned.

be less "aggressive" in the realm of conjugal power. In spite of traditional ideology, and in spite of what authority they believe they have earned, they nonetheless are willing to behave in a more or less equalitarian fashion in so far as resolution of contested issues is concerned. They may also have greater authority than their wives in daily decision-making, but this is evidently less consequential to their wives. For after all, when a conflict actually arises, these wives often get to share in its resolution, and this in itself is probably ego-gratifying.

Moreover, being actually able to share in conflict resolution means that female role definitions are being reshaped—from the "duty to obey" to the right (or at least the option) to "participate" in family authority. To the extent that this shift is defined as "good" by higher-status females, its positive effect in terms of conjugal solidarity is not lost on them. Thus the fact that higher-status males less often or unduly "press their advantage" either in terms of traditional male role rights, or else in terms of rights based on success, even when they could because of their wives' beliefs, permits us to assume that feelings of solidarity and thus conjugal cohesion are thereby enhanced. There is, in short, a more harmonious "fit" of beliefs and behavior as economic articulation increases. As the latter decreases, the "fit" becomes correspondingly less harmonious.

The sum of all this, then is a refinement of the status-power hypothesis. It is not merely that with greater status comes greater male power. More correctly, greater status generates greater legitimate authority. Wives are more likely to define their husbands' leadership role as right and proper at the same time that they actually enjoy greater fulfillment of female rights, *i.e.*, greater participation in conflict resolution. This, in turn, presumably generates greater satisfaction on the part of both spouses with the authority dimension of instrumental conjugal interaction. Wives in this situation are more inclined to feel that their own rights are being met, and yet so do their husbands. Both spouses therefore are more motivated to perform their role "duties" in this sphere (she to defer, he to attempt to share authority), and thus the fulfillment of rights is enhanced. In this way, the reciprocal process continues.

But with less articulation comes authority—or rather power—that is defined by wives as less legitimate. Males are more likely to exercise their traditional rights, and females more likely to feel their rights are not being met. Wives then are even more likely to feel less motivated to perform their "duties" in this realm (to defer), and thus reciprocity in this instrumental area suffers, as does general satisfaction with it. And dissatisfaction with authority relations, as with primary relations, lessens the probability of conjugal cohesion.

The impact of wife employment on conjugal authority warrants attention. The juxtaposition of these elements is, theoretically speaking, highly significant. Both authority and employment represent part of the long-term "struggle" or "tension" in terms of role rights as defined by males vis-à-vis females. In Chapter Three, there was some indication that the realization of female employment rights might possibly undermine the attainment of desired female rights in another sector, *i.e.*, physical affect. In terms of the literature on wife employment and authority, there appears to be no substantial disagreement with Heer's finding that "both in the working class and in the middle class, the working wife exerts more influence in decision-making than the non-working wife." [24] It would thus appear that as the wife increases her "economic inputs" into the conjugal family, her participation in processes of authority increases.

In Table 6–3, seen from the perspective of the wife, Heer's conclusion appears to be validated. Using education as representative of the remaining dimensions of economic opportunity integration, we find that the wife's power in conflict resolution is increased at *all* education levels when she works (cf. Table 6–1). Correspondingly, when she does not work, her participation in conflict resolution is reduced. It is important to note, however, that in both instances it is not so much that the husband is less or more active in unilateral conflict resolution; instead a shift occurs in joint conflict resolution. Where the wife works, the frequency of shared resolution generally drops. Decisions that were once shared are now decided by the wife alone. Except for the lowest education category, husbands are perceived as having about the same level of power as before.

On the other side, where wives do not work, frequency of joint conflict resolution increases at all levels except among those with least education. And except for this latter category, there is not much perceived change in terms of husband power. Evidently at most education levels, the consequence of wife employment is to reduce joint conflict resolution; the consequence of nonemployment is to increase it. In the former instance, it is probable that the wife's economic resources give her a better bargaining position, so that when a contested issue arises there is a greater likelihood that she will be able to attain her desires. In the latter instance, lacking this kind of bargaining position, she is forced into greater compromise and joint resolution with her husband. Which alternative influences conjugal solidarity (if at all) more positively or negatively is uncertain.

The picture is less simple when seen through the eyes of husbands. Those with less than a high school diploma see their wives having more power when they work, and less power when they do not. But husbands with more education than that see wife power reduced by employment and increased by nonemployment. As before, except for least educated

---

[24] David M. Heer, "Dominance and the Working Wife," *Social Forces*, 36 (May 1958), p. 347.

husbands, most of the shift takes place between joint resolution and wife acting alone. Husbands' unilateral power changes little in terms of the actual frequencies involved. Why better-educated husbands should reverse the expected pattern is not at all clear and deserves further investigation. At the very least, it reveals once again how husbands and wives in the same social situation can "read it" in opposite fashion.

Turning to ideology and using "discontent" as representative, we find in Table 6-4 that most husbands who have an employed wife show a rise in modern orientations toward shared authority, whereas those with a nonemployed wife report more traditional orientations. Least articulated husbands show a reverse trend. Whether having a working wife makes most males more modern, or whether their orientations were modern before the wife worked cannot be ascertained from these data. Neither can we know if wife employment would change the traditional orientations of most males whose wives are currently not working. Similarly, most wives who work show an increase in modern values regarding conjugal power, whereas most of those who do not work show a trend toward traditional orientations. Once again, it is difficult to know whether egalitarian values preceded or followed employment, or whether employment would help to alter traditional values among wives currently nonemployed.

It is clear that the broad issue of the impact of wife employment on authority relations, and hence on conjugal cohesion, is extremely complex. We may suggest at this point that, in general, at both the behavioral and ideological levels, her employment is associated with greater actual and normative authority. Conversely, nonemployment seems to be associated with less actual and normative authority. But there are important deviations to these generalizations, and we know virtually nothing of the causal sequences involved. Neither can we say very much about the linkage of the "wife employment-authority syndrome" to feelings of solidarity and conjugal cohesion, particularly in view of the different situational definitions by sex. But given the projected long-term increases in wife employment, and also given the increasing pressures toward egalitarianism in marriage as well as in every phase of society—especially by contemporary college youth—the further analysis of this syndrome would seem to be essential for an accurate and full-orbed understanding of structure and process within the modern conjugal unit.

CONCLUSION

In this chapter, we have had two major objectives: one, to try to link theoretically the question of conjugal family authority to the opportunity system; and second, to link it to conjugal cohesion. On the basis of studies measuring the decision-making and conflict-resolution dimensions, Heer proposes that husband dominance is more prevalent in upper-status families because wives have more to respect, value, and retain in their husbands. Lower-status wives possess less of these elements, and thus are more prone to assert their will and claim greater power for themselves.

Using the more general framework of opportunity integration, an attempt was made to test this proposition in terms of conjugal conflict resolution. The results showed less articulated males to be more dominant than higher-status males, in terms of both unilateral and shared decisions. Yet a measure of the "formal authority" dimension indicated that less advantaged wives question the exercise of male power per se. Consequently, a refined proposition emerged suggesting that in spite of male propensity to resolve contested issues in their favor at all levels of opportunity integration, such resolution is deemed less legitimate by wives as level of opportunity integration decreases. With decreased economic integration, therefore, comes greater strain or tension over authority relations. With increased articulation comes a clearer definition of male authority as being legitimate, plus greater actual sharing of conflict resolution, and presumably therefore, more satisfaction in general with the processes of authority relations. In all likelihood, cohesion of the conjugal unit is thus reinforced, whereas in the former situation it is weakened.

Finally, some attention was given to the impact of the wife's employment on authority relations. In general, it appeared that her employment enhanced her authority, whereas nonemployment lessened it. However, there were significant exceptions to this generalization. In view of the long-term trends toward greater wife employment and toward greater equalitarianism in our society, extensive investigations are required into their complex interrelationships, and thus into their consequences for conjugal cohesion.

CHAPTER

SEVEN

Achievement Values for Children

WE HAVE EXAMINED, WITHIN THE CONTEXT OF THE ECONOMIC OPPORTUNITY structure, the expressive dimension of the conjugal unit, its obverse in hostility relations, and the instrumental dimension of the conjugal unit, specifically in terms of authority relations. This chapter takes up one aspect of the broad area of parent-child interaction, namely, socialization. Within this realm, which is itself exceedingly broad, we shall focus specifically on the kinds of achievement values that parents hold for—and presumably transmit to—their children.[1] In short, what are the relative consequences, for this type of socialization, of being differentially linked to the reward structure of our society? For just as it made a difference in husband-wife relations, we would expect—and of course, many other studies suggest—

---

[1] There is, of course, no guarantee that values held by parents for children will be effectively transmitted. All we intend to do in this chapter is deal with the issue of how parents believe their children ought to behave. The issue of those conditions under which children actually accept or reject certain parental values is beyond the scope of our research design. One effort to assess value transmission (as measured by value-similarity between mother and son) is in Bernard C. Rosen, "Family Structure and Value Transmission," *Merrill-Palmer Quarterly*, 10 (1964), pp. 59–76. The point that socialization covers a wide foci of interests, including preparation for occupational achievement, is made very well by John A. Clausen, *Socialization and Society*, Boston: Little, Brown and Company, 1968, p. 6.

that degree of opportunity articulation should make a difference here as well.[2]

These kinds of parent-child relations, however, should not be thought of as necessarily totally distinct from husband-wife relations. There is in fact a theoretical linkage between them. First of all, in Chapter Six, we saw that child-training in general is one area of husband-wife disagreement. How to socialize children, in other words, may be looked upon as part of the instrumental dimension of conjugal interaction. Each partner has a particular set of ideas, values, and behaviors he wishes to see communicated to and exhibited by his children. His orientations may not always mesh with those of alter. Therefore, some processes of conflict resolution might emerge to deal with these inevitable and ongoing tensions. Hence, it seems useful to subsume processes of socialization in general, and transmission of achievement values in particular, within the *W* and *X* poles of Figure 1 in Chapter One.

The utility of this type of conceptualization is that it permits us to posit a linkage between socialization for achievement and conjugal cohesion. The linkage is made through authority relations in general. We have already suggested how authority relations are related to conjugal cohesion. Consensus-conflict by husbands and wives over socialization for achievement is one facet of this larger and more comprehensive instrumental dimension. Presumably, therefore, the greater the consensus over these kinds of values, the greater the probability of conjugal cohesion. In this fashion, we are able to examine not only the relationships of economic articulation and socialization for achievement, we are able also to say something about the broader objective of this study, cohesion of the conjugal unit in modern society. The remainder of the chapter therfore will be hinged to these several interrelated notions: economic articulation and child-achievement values held by parents, husband-wife consensus over child-achievement values and the connection of this with authority relations in general, and finally implications for conjugal cohesion.

To begin to examine these complex questions, we shall utilize a series of items used by Cox in an earlier study to ascertain achievement values that mothers feel they could teach to their children.[3] This same series of

[2] A review of some of these studies appears in William H. Sewell, "Some Recent Developments in Socialization Theory and Research," reprinted in Marvin B. Sussman, ed., *Sourcebook in Marriage and the Family,* Boston: Houghton Mifflin Company, 1968 (rev.), pp. 325–26.

[3] Henrietta Cox, "Study of Social Class Variations in Value Orientations in Selected Areas of Mother-Child Behavior," unpublished doctoral dissertation, Washington University, St. Louis, 1964. Cited in Joseph A. Kahl, "Some Measurements of Achievement Orientation," *American Journal of Sociology,* 70 (May 1965), pp. 674 ff.

The respondent was asked to agree or disagree with each item. After the factor analysis described below, an "agree" response was weighted as 2, a "disagree"

items was administered to respondents in our sample. Each respondent was first asked to give his own orientations. Then the items were read again, and this time the respondent was asked to tell how he thought his own (husband-wife) felt about each particular question. For each respondent, therefore, we have his own norms about training for child-achievement, plus his perceptions of his spouse's norms. Responses pertaining to his own norms were factor-analyzed to see if more than one distinct dimension would emerge, as was the case for Cox. Two factors or dimensions emerged, the first consisting of the following items and labeled *child-passivity*. This dimension describes an orientation in which the child is taught to conform to, to be passive toward, or to simply accept conditions as he finds them within the opportunity-success system.

Passivity Dimension

1. Children should learn early there isn't much you can do about the way things are going to turn out in life. (.66)
2. Children should learn that planning only makes a person unhappy since your plans hardly ever work out anyway. (.67)
3. Nowadays the wise parent will teach the child to live for today and let tomorrow take care of itself. (.52)
4. Children should be taught that these days a person doesn't really know whom he can count on. (.68)
5. Children should be taught not to expect too much out of life so that they won't be disappointed. (.63)
6. Children should be taught that when a man is born the success he's going

response as zero. This holds for all items in both scales except #7, passivity, where a reverse procedure was followed. Thus, the more agreement, the higher the score in each scale; the less the agreement, the lower the score in each scale. Higher scores indicate greater passivity and mastery; lower scores, just the opposite.

In the procedure used for these factor analyses (available in standard package form), one is free to set in advance the number of factors he wishes to rotate. We began by rotating four, then three, factors. The resulting dimensions seemed to overlap substantively, so finally only two factors were rotated. The rotation of only two factors produced the dimensions described in the text. (The "passivity" factor explained 32 percent of the total variance; mastery, 20 percent.) These two orientations appear to be distinct postures vis-à-vis the opportunity system. Items 2 and 5 in the mastery dimension, it will be noted, show somewhat lower factor loadings than items 1, 3, and 4. This may be because 2 and 5 tend to emphasize primarily the intrinsic worth of and dedication to a task. Yet an emphasis of this sort both implies and indeed leads to mastery of most tasks. Specifically for the child, this begins first with challenges in school which, if actually met in such careful and ascetic fashion, certainly contribute to "academic mastery." In addition, both the emphasis per se plus satisfactory school experiences then contribute in turn to later "occupational mastery." Therefore, it seems clear that these items—although stressing a particular nuance of mastery—certainly "belong" in the dimension taken as a whole.

to have is already in the cards, so he might as well accept it and not fight against it. (.55)

7. Children should learn early that most people can be trusted. (–.40)

The second dimension consists of the following items and is labeled *child-mastery*. This term describes an orientation in which the child is taught to be active in relation to the economic opportunity system, to seek to manipulate it and master it in as rational a fashion as possible.

Mastery Dimension

1. Above all, parents should try to help their children get further ahead than they were able to get. (.50)
2. A child should be taught from infancy to take the greatest pride in doing things well. (.33)
3. Children ought to learn to try hard to come out on top in games and sports. (.60)
4. A mother ought to teach her child to do everything he does better than anyone else. (.49)
5. Children should be taught the job comes first, even if it means giving up most of the fun. (.26)

In sum, the passivity dimension taps parental norms that underscore adjustment to, and acceptance of the opportunity-success system, *i.e.*, how the child can "make the best of it" as it stands. On the other side, the mastery dimension emphasizes norms regarding activity toward, use of, this same system in order to gain individual attainments and rewards. When perceptions of spouse orientations were factor-analyzed, similar results emerged: two dimensions, with the same items loading together as above, and with approximately the same amount of total variance explained in each case. Hence, we have a measure of each respondent's own child-mastery norms, and a separate measure of his perception of his spouse's child-mastery norms, based on an identical scale. The same two types of measures apply to each respondent in terms of child passivity norms.[4] Our expectation is that as the level of opportunity integration increases, there should be greater emphasis on child-mastery norms and less emphasis on child-passivity norms, and conversely. This expectation should hold not only for the objective criteria, but also for the several dimensions of alienation and anomie.

[4] The correlation of the passivity and mastery dimensions (respondent's *own* values) is $r=.19$. Between respondent passivity and perception of spouse passivity, $r=.84$. Between respondent passivity and perception of spouse mastery, $r=.23$. Between respondent mastery and spouse passivity, $r=.21$; and between respondent mastery and spouse mastery, $r=.79$.

Pearlin and Kohn provide a rationale for this kind of expectation, at least in terms of the criterion of occupation.[5] They wanted to explain why cross-national data showed that middle-class fathers (and mothers) hold self-control or self-direction values for children, whereas working-class parents hold to values of obedience. To account for these differences, they argue that lower-status occupations require closer supervision, less self-reliance, and more contact with things rather than with people or ideas, when compared to higher-status occupations. These three characteristics lead to lesser flexibility and independence among lower-status jobs, which in turn "spills over" onto the kinds of values both husbands and wives hold for children. Rigidity and conformity on the job lead parents to value and to try to instill these kinds of values (obedience, conformity) in their children. Flexibility and independence on the middle-class job (less supervision, more self-reliance, and contact with ideas and people), on the other hand, lead parents to value and strive for these different kinds of behavior (self-control, independence, initiative) in their children.

There is a close similarity between their conception of self-control or self-direction and the formulation here of mastery. There is likewise an analogy between obedience and passivity. The basic assumption is that the structure and interaction inherent in certain occupational positions are linked with the kinds of values parents hold for their children. Where the job position is relatively "expansive," it permits "maximization of the individual" in terms of "personal fulfillment" and achievement. This expansiveness is in turn reflected in the values (self-direction, mastery) held for children. Whereas when the job is "narrow and constricted" in terms of fulfillment and/or achievement, this too is reflected in particular socialization values (obedience, passivity).

If we continue this attempt to make more general the explanation offered by Pearlin and Kohn, we may account not only for the effects of occupation, but also for the consequences of income and education as well, plus alienation and anomie. Specifically, we might say that the greater the integration with the economic opportunity structure, the greater the rewards possessed by parents, and the greater is the tendency therefore to feel confident that their children can and should also attain these same kinds of rewards. It is somewhat difficult to apply the exchange model used for husband-wife relations to our indices of parental orientations toward children, because we are dealing only with parental attitudes and have no measures at all of child responses. Yet the exchange model applies in one sense in terms of the broader question of husband-wife authority relations.

[5] Leonard I. Pearlin and Melvin L. Kohn, "Social Class, Occupation, and Parental Values: A Cross-National Study," *American Sociological Review*, 31 (August 1966), pp. 466–79. See also Melvin L. Kohn, "Social Class and Parent-Child Relationships: An Interpretation," *American Journal of Sociology*, 68 (January 1963), pp. 471–80.

Furthermore, McKinley has suggested that the exchange model does help to explain parent-child socialization regarding achievement values:

Social life is an exchange of . . . emotional sanctions, and a position of high status means the receipt of large positive resources. The person of high status enjoys or has accumulated emotional "profit" which can be reinvested in the child to bring about socialization (or seduction) into the mode of life of the adult.[6]

His argument is that the greater the level of rewards the parent provides the child, the more the child reciprocates by willing conformity to parents' wishes. Richer makes precisely the same point when he argues that greater rewards produce, in exchange, greater "compliance" to parents' expectations.[7] Winch too asserts that the more the rewards parents provide to children, the more strongly the child identifies with (is influenced by) them.[8] Unfortunately, our data do not permit a direct test of what appears to be a striking theoretical convergence regarding the applicability of reciprocity theory to parent-child relations. Such a test would seem imperative eventually to ascertain whether exchange theory is sufficiently broad to explain these kinds of relations, as well as those between husbands and wives, plus —as Sussman notes—those between kin and conjugal unit. [9]

Nevertheless, using reward levels as an explanatory variable, we can at least begin to move in the direction of establishing some preliminary notions regarding the potential utility of exchange theory in parent-child relations. For instance, we might posit that varying reward levels tend to generate degrees of passivity and/or mastery on the part of parents toward children. Consider the father who has mastered or is mastering the opportunity structure. He has taken the risks necessary to attain, and they have "paid off." Because he has been "active" vis-à-vis the opportunity structure, we may fully expect that he will encourage activity in his children. And his encouragement will carry the ring of authenticity both to himself and his children. For, in addition to his verbally stated values, he is an actual role-model—an "active" figure with whom the child (in exchange) may identify and thus reinforce his own movement toward mastery of the opportunity system, and away from mere "acceptance" or adjustment to it or to contingent circumstances. In short, a sense of self-confidence based on attainments deemed of great value in our society should lead parents to seek to

6 Donald G. McKinley, *Social Class and Family Life*, New York: The Free Press, 1964, pp. 251–52.

7 Stephen Richer, "The Economics of Child Rearing," *Journal of Marriage and the Family*, 30 (August 1968), pp. 462–66.

8 Robert F. Winch, *Identification and Its Familial Determinants*, Indianapolis: The Bobbs-Merrill Co., Inc., 1962.

9 See our Chap. One.

instill the same kinds of mastery-type values in their children. Since they have attained, they feel there is every reason to think their children can and will attain too.

Conversley, with less economic integration comes less of a sense of confidence with regard to the opportunity structure. This attitude too should spill over onto achievement values transmitted to children. Because the father has mastered the success system less skillfully, he may stress less positively the need for mastery in his children. He may encourage passivity, *i.e.*, caution, less risk-taking, and a tendency to "make the best of things as they are," rather than to seek to manipulate them to advantage. Here, too, he is an "effective" role model of a sort to his children. Since he has not mastered the opportunity system, it becomes more difficult for parents and children alike to believe that the children could actually do it. Thus, these kinds of children are influenced more strongly by passivity-type values rather than by those emphasizing mastery. Lack of confidence among these parents might lead them to stress adjustment, acceptance, and conformity, instead of activism, initiative, and mastery.

In this connection, an important question for further research might be the family conditions under which so-called "new left" college students develop. The literature suggests that many of these students come from homes "strongly articulated" into the economic system, and yet they tend to reject their parents' "success" values.[10] It may be that this "wholesale" rejection is a temporary phenomenon and that when they finally leave school, they may slowly gravitate into the more advantaged segments of the economic opportunity structure—although they may perhaps move toward those occupations that are more person-oriented rather than money-oriented.

Tables 7-1, 7-2, and 7-3 present the mean scores of both the passivity and the mastery scales, for both husbands and wives in terms of the several dimensions of economic integration. The higher the score on the passivity scale, the more passive the parent believes his child ought to be. A high score reflects orientations on the part of parents that children ought to be "accepting of" and "relatively inactive toward" the economic opportunity structure. (See items listed earlier, with weights, footnote 3.) Conversely, the lower the score, the less passive, accepting, and inactive the parent believes his child ought to be toward the means and ends inherent in achievement and success.

Looking first at the passivity columns, we find that without exception, at the lower levels of integration, both sexes score considerably higher (*i.e.*, more passive and inactive) than those with greater integration. It is clear therefore that *the greater the integration into the opportunity structure,*

---

[10] Seymour Martin Lipset, "Students and Politics in Comparative Perspective," in Stephen R. Granbard, ed., *Daedalus,* 97 (Winter 1968), p. 4.

the less strongly do parents hold passivity-type achievement values for their children, and conversely, the lesser their own integration, the more strongly they hold passivity-type achievement values for their children. As integration into the opportunity system *decreases,* parents are more likely to stress caution, deemphasize risk-taking, and encourage adjustment to, rather than manipulation of, that same system. As articulation increases, parents tend to deemphasize caution and seldom give the impression to children that risk-taking is undesirable or that manipulation of the opportunity structure is beyond one's grasp. Hence, using this dimension of achievement values, our earlier theoretical expectations are confirmed.

But when we examine the mastery dimension, a somewhat different picture emerges, and our earlier conceptual model stands in need of partial revision. A high mastery score implies that the parent believes his child ought to strive, work hard, and attain all that his capabilities will permit. (See items and weights listed under "Mastery Dimension.") A lower score would indicate that parents hold these kinds of values less strongly than parents with a higher score. In a very real sense the mastery dimension is a genuine part of the American Dream syndrome. The child works hard and well and ultimately exceeds the social level of his parents. On the other hand, the passivity dimension "tells it the way it is" as far as a large proportion of Americans are concerned—those who participate less fully in rewards inherent in the opportunity structure. In their case, in spite of probable verbal assent to The American Dream, they are also painfully aware of the difficulty of actually fulfilling it.

Tables 7-1, 7-2, and 7-3 reveal that the less the articulation into the economic opportunity structure, the stronger is the commitment to mastery type values. In other words, more advantaged parents seem to hold to mastery values for their children somewhat less strongly than do less advantaged parents. Several points, however, need to be made in this connection. One, the range or spread of mean mastery scores is considerably more narrow here than is the spread of mean passivity scores.

Using SEI in Table 7-1 as representative of the other dimensions, we see that males in the high rank SEI category (80–96) have a mastery score of 7.0, whereas the greatest mastery score is reported by husbands in a low rank SEI. ($\bar{x} = 8.33$), or a difference of 1.33. In contrast to this relative similarity of scores, on the passivity dimension we find that the difference between lowest and highest husband mean scores by SEI is 4.18 (5.22 *vs.* 1.04). The figure of "one point something" (here 1.04 highest SEI), which appears so consistently among those with most articulation, reflects little or almost no passivity orientations at all. Moreover, this same type of pattern (wider disparities in passivity than in mastery scores) is repeated for both sexes throughout all the dimensions.

The point is that economic articulation distinguishes much wider divergences in terms of passivity values than it does for mastery values. The great and consistent differences in the size of the F ratios (*e.g.*, male SEI, passivity=24.44; mastery=7.57) serve to underscore this point. In fact, over both anomie dimensions, and two of the three alienation dimensions, differences between husbands over mastery values are not significant at all. It would thus appear that as we drop down the various rungs of the ladder of achievement and success, we discover great disparity in passivity orientations toward children. Lower-status husbands and wives, in short, are considerably more passive than are higher-status parents.

At the same time, lower-status parents are only somewhat more oriented toward mastery values for children than are higher-status parents. Relatively speaking, all parents in the sample are much closer to each other in terms of their mastery (or American Dream) orientations toward children than they are in their passivity orientations. In this regard, it should be recalled that our sample excludes most of the so-called "lower-lower class," *i.e.*, persons virtually outside the opportunity structure. Perhaps they would not score high on the mastery dimension; perhaps they would give hardly any assent at all to the American Dream syndrome. But among those who are in some sense part of the economic opportunity system—even minimally—one of the elements that appears to bind them together is strong commitment to mastery-type values.

Some of the implications of this pattern may be considered in the following fashion. Less articulated husbands and wives communicate to their children, on the one side, that there is very little one can do to manipulate the opportunity structure. It is "bigger" than they are, more threatening, less amenable to rational efforts to wrest benefits from it. Therefore, all one can do is accept it as it is, be passive toward it. One is "better off" adjusting to it than "fighting it." Yet, on the other side, they are keenly aware of the traditional American stress on rational mastery, hard work, diligent effort, and constant striving to "make something of oneself." Like almost all American parents, they do want their children to fulfill the "American Dream" and to "succeed in life." And since they themselves are relatively disadvantaged, they sincerely want their children to "have more" than they do. Not incidentally, the first item in the mastery scale taps precisely this desire of parents to have their children surpass their own status.

This paradox, among the less articulated, of holding both passivity and mastery-type values simultaneously, has been noted elsewhere in the literature. Merton, for example, concludes that less advantaged parents often have job aspirations for their children that are as high or even higher than those of more advantaged parents.[11] (Our data on mastery-type values

---

[11] Robert K. Merton, "Social Structure and Anomie: Revisions and Extensions,"

tend to bear out this kind of theoretical expectation.) But such aspirations are unrealistic, he contends, because the means to achieve these goals tend not to be effectively transmitted by disadvantaged parents. Chinoy provides additional empirical support that less advantaged workers possess "an almost universally expressed desire that their sons not go into the factory, that they do 'better than that.' " [12]

Purcell also found that most blue-collar workers (foremen, in particular) do not want their children to "follow in their footsteps," but instead, to rise above the blue-collar level.

> The future of the workingman's son or daughter touches upon an important, personal area of his life ; his aspirations and ideals. . . . "The American Dream" of anybody's son rising to any height [leads] Americans commonly [to] hope that their children will "do better" than they did. Considering the prestige our culture attaches to white-collar jobs and to the professions, it is not surprising that many working people wish their children to achieve such jobs and professions.[13]

Likewise, in a fashion similar to our findings regarding mastery, Mizruchi reports that "getting ahead in life" is "slightly more important" to lower-class respondents than to respondents with higher status. This is true at the same time that he found that the lower the social class, the more limited were perceived chances for success.[14] Turner has conceptualized this same kind of paradox in terms of what he calls "value relevancy." He says:

> Social classes differ not so much in the values which they endorse in general as in the extent to which they regard these values as applicable to themselves as goals for their own striving. . . . Admiration for the risk-taker, for the expert on serious topics, and for the person who excels his friends is uniformly shared by men from high and low backgrounds. The latter, however, are unwilling to make these values their own personal goals, probably because the working-class situation does not reward them as the middle-class situation does.[15]

in Ruth Nanda Anshen, ed., *The Family: Its Function and Destiny*, New York: Harper and Row, Publishers, 1959 (rev.), pp. 309–12.

[12] Ely Chinoy, *Automobile Workers and the American Dream*, Garden City, N.Y.: Doubleday and Company, Inc., 1955, p. 127.

[13] Theodore V. Purcell, *Blue Collar Man*, Cambridge, Mass.: Harvard University Press, 1960, p. 161.

[14] Ephraim H. Mizruchi, *Success and Opportunity*, New York: The Free Press, 1964, pp. 70 and 84.

[15] Ralph H. Turner, *The Social Context of Ambition*, San Francisco: Chandler Publishing Co., 1964, pp. 80 and 85. See also Hyman Rodman, "The Lower-class Value Stretch," *Social Forces*, December 1963, pp. 205–15.

Applying Turner's reasoning to our findings, we may say that although mastery of the opportunity structure is uniformly shared by most segments of the population, its relevancy for some is diminished by a feeling of passivity, a feeling that "no matter how good it is, it really can't be for me (or for my children)." Less advantaged parents evidently tend to focus their own aspirations and ambitions for status on their children. Since their offspring are currently "number two," they actually do want them to "try harder" and become "number one." And if we examine closely the items that loaded together on the mastery dimension, we find in fact these do emphasize "trying harder."

But to husbands and wives who see themselves and their children as already "number one" (relatively speaking) or close to it, these kinds of notions have somewhat less meaning. There is therefore less reason for them to communicate values of this type as strongly to their children. Children from these kinds of families are already relatively "advantaged" in terms of where they start out in relation to the opportunity structure. But while it becomes less important to stress mastery, it is extremely crucial for these parents to convey to their children that they need not (or must not) be passive or docile toward the opportunity-success system. For in spite of the position accorded them by their parents, there is no ironclad guarantee, in a fluid society such as ours, that their children will maintain this position. And if perchance their children should take a fatalistic and passive attitude toward the opportunity structure, then they could very well become downwardly mobile.

In short, the scores of the more integrated parents suggest that they transmit to their children the notion of mastery at a moderate level. The notion of passivity is conveyed weakly or hardly at all. The self-confidence, prestige, and status of these parents based on attained rewards, enables them to rule out any ideas that their children need "accept" a set of conditions that overwhelm efforts at success. Consequently, their children tend to get an image of the opportunity structure as something that they are already part of and that can be rationally manipulated. Likewise, the image of themselves that they receive, with respect to the opportunity structure, is that they must not be passive toward it, but instead be reasonably active in seeking to obtain its rewards. Finally, the total picture carries with it a high probability that their efforts will actually be rewarded, and this in turn provides strong motivation to be active—to seek to "master" the opportunity structure. These children are socialized then to perceive a "fit" between the American Dream and what is reasonable for them. And the fit would appear to include the notion that there is no reason whatsoever why they cannot expect to share bountifully in that Dream. One consequence of this expectation is that more advantaged children usually tend to maintain the general status levels of their parents.

But less advantaged children find themselves in an ambiguous situation of conflicting orientations. They find their parents conveying basically contradictory notions, *i.e.*, they are supposed to master something that "cannot" be mastered, to manipulate the nonmanipulable. In their desire to have their children become socially mobile, these kinds of parents put substantial pressures on them to try very hard (perhaps even "too hard"). Yet in curious and paradoxical fashion, with perhaps both parents and children being unaware of it, they paint a bleak picture of the child's actual chances to "make it" as an individual.

Lower-status persons appear to be just as oriented as those with higher status to the American Dream, to the idea that hard work and diligent effort will "surely" eventuate in success; and yet they are less likely to achieve the same occupational levels as those with higher status.[16] They have been socialized to believe that "there isn't much you can do about the way things turn out," or that "plans don't work out anyway," or that "success is ultimately in the cards"—in the hands of a capricious fate or random forces of chance. Believing this, they often set their realistic expectations for type of job, advancement, and social status relatively low. They do this at the same time that they might possess high aspirations, because they are unwilling and/or unable to bestir themselves to take the risks inherent in actually gaining these high aspirations.

And they shy from the risks, as Turner notes, because it appears to them that the chances for failure far outweigh those for rewards. This tendency is due, in part at least, to the capricious image of the opportunity-success structure conveyed to them by their parents. Having internalized passivity orientations throughout their childhood, it is extremely difficult to slough them off—even if they wished to do so—as adults. As a result, the data require us to modify somewhat our conceptual schema. As is often the case, the realities in the "real world" are more complex than was expected.

It had been thought that with limited economic articulation would come less stress on mastery. It was felt that minimal achievement and success would *both* accentuate passivity *and* attenuate mastery. We find instead that it does only the former. Traditional beliefs regarding hard work, striving, and so on, are just as strong—even somewhat stronger—among the less advantaged than they are among the more advantaged. Limited material and status rewards do not easily shake one's faith in the American Dream. Perhaps the somewhat greater stress on mastery on the part of the less advantaged is a "mechanism of overcompensation." As adults, the parents

16 Obviously, this is not to say that there is not substantial mobility in American society by lower status individuals. At the same time, however, some 63 percent of working-class sons remain at that same level; only some 37 percent move into the white collar ranks. Peter M. Blau and Otis Dudley Duncan, *The American Occupational Structure*, New York: John Wiley and Sons, Inc., 1967, p. 433.

find it difficult to face the possibility that their "faith" in the Dream might be misplaced. Consequently, they cling to it more tenaciously and seek to pass it on with greater diligence than would otherwise be required. There may even be a kind of "true believer" mentality here that operates to accentuate mastery values.

In passing, it should be noted that to the extent such generalizations are valid, they tend to cast further doubt on the thinking of some that the American Dream–protestant ethic syndrome is expiring in our society. In Chapter One, Wilensky's arguments to the contrary were cited; and throughout the entire volume up to this point, the weight of evidence suggests that traditional achievement and success orientations still prevail in our society and continue to have definite consequences for behavior. For example, the failure of the SEI index to distinguish between levels of occupational or of success aspirations for respondents themselves as adults, tends to corroborate the pattern here. On the one hand, lower-status adults do not differ from higher status adults regarding aspirations for themselves; on the other hand they tend to exceed those with higher status in the levels of success values they hold for their children.

Regardless of degree of articulation into the opportunity structure, therefore, it would appear that there is a more or less equal distribution of commitment to traditional achievement-success orientations held by adults for this generation and for the next. There simply is no "hard evidence" that these kinds of traditional values are fading. If they were, we might expect them to begin to fade first among the more disadvantaged, those who possess fewer economic or status rewards. The less the rewards, one might presume, the less the willingness to believe in or to maintain the old patterns. But instead, there is a strong desire by almost all parents to see them maintained and to see their children participate in them.[17]

Therefore, we must conclude that with decreased articulation into the economic opportunity structure comes increased emphasis on passivity combined with a strong emphasis on mastery. With decreased articulation, in short, there emerges a set of basically contradictory and incompatible value orientations toward achievement and success. Conversely, with increased articulation there emerges a decreased emphasis on passivity (as expected), combined with moderate emphasis on mastery. The child exposed to these kinds of value orientations finds them to be essentially compatible and complementary.

Moreover, in Table 7-4 (using education as representative), we find that parents who perceive their milieu (including the opportunity structure) as disorderly or unmanageable in general (high anomy) show increases

[17] Currently, for example, one of the aims stated by many Negro leaders as extremely crucial is that the children of lower-class blacks will, as adults, participate fully in the affluence now denied to their elders.

(cf. Table 7-1) in passivity scores and also in mastery scores. Those who possess a *low* sense of anomy (orderly milieu) show a drop (cf. Table 7-1) in both types of orientations. These changes occur at all articulation levels under both high and low anomy, but systematic differences in mastery and passivity between levels continue to remain strongly significant in all eight instances.

Therefore, at the same status level, parents who perceive their immediate world in general as chaotic are more likely to encourage their children to be *passive* toward the opportunity structure than parents who see it as ordered. At the same time, those parents who perceive their milieu as chaotic are also more prone (than parents who perceive it as orderly) to stress the American Dream—hard work, diligent effort, *i.e.*, mastery. Hence, a strong sense of anomy exacerbates the situation described above, particularly among the less advantaged. On the one hand, it stimulates greater transmission of passivity type values because it creates an even more dismal and capricious picture of the "world out there"—the world that presumably is to be manipulated, but yet cannot be. Yet evidently it also heightens the perceived need or pressure for even greater mastery.

Perhaps the attitude develops that if "things are so bad out there, then you [the child] are going to have to work that much harder to overcome them." But this curious paradox is futile, for high parental anomy only widens the gap between what the child is told he should do and what he is told he can do. The pressure to strive is substantially increased in a situation where the possibilities of the striving's "paying off" are severely minimized. For the less advantaged child who faces numerous other factors deleterious to achievement and success, the heightened tension in this type of situation is simply an additional onerous burden.

By the same token, low anomy makes even more favorable the outlook for achievement and success (particularly among the more disadvantaged), for it reduces transmission of passivity values—an obvious benefit. Moreover, by reducing the level of stress on mastery, it tends perhaps to relieve undue tensions and anxieties so that in combination with lowered passivity, a certain level of success might appear more attainable than would otherwise be the case. For example, it has often been noted that lower-status children tend to have totally unrealistic job aspirations (lawyer, physician, and so on,) and as a result never give serious thought to the *attainable*, thus "settling down" to the *comfortable*, near the job level of their parents. But a child from a blue-collar home characterized by low anomy (and thus less passivity and more moderate mastery) might feel that he could actually become, for instance, a school teacher, and thus move deliberately and effectively in that direction. In short, a situation of low anomy could help to close the gap between what the child is told he should do and what he feels he actually can do.

It seems clear that the issue of achievement values that parents believe ought to be transmitted to children (plus the broader issue of child-achievement in general) is an extremely complex one. There are obviously many factors other than those discussed here that enter in at both the sociological and psychological levels.[18] Parental orientations toward passivity and mastery are only one part of the total picture. There is urgent need for a research design that will incorporate as many facets of the whole as possible. But in so far as these particular dimensions are effectively transmitted, they help shape the child's sense of orientation toward the opportunity structure. Perhaps another way to put it is to think of passivity as a negative orientation and mastery as a positive orientation. It may be that in lower-status homes, the presence of the negative tends to cancel out the potentially beneficial consequences of the positive—the American Dream syndrome shared by most Americans. Yet, in higher status homes, the relative absence of the negative enables the positive to operate; it is not canceled out, and thus participation in the Dream becomes more of a reality.

In sum, we are forced to modify our original theoretical expectations to state that the greater the integration of parents into the opportunity structure, the more weakly will they convey passivity-type achievement values to their children, and the more moderate will become their stress on mastery. The less the integration into this same structure, the more strongly will parents transmit passivity-type values, and the more strongly will they convey mastery-type values as well. Finally, a positive perception of one's milieu reduces the strength of transmission of both types of orientations, whereas a negative perception increases the strength of their transmission. As far as the actual attainment of achievement and success is concerned, it would appear that the former combination of moderate mastery and low passivity is more optimal. High stress on mastery combined with great emphasis on passivity would seem to be more intrinsically contradictory, with the result being relative inertia with respect to the opportunity structure.

Concomitantly, we would therefore suggest that, in terms of social mobility, passivity-type values are more crucial than mastery values. To the extent they are found strongly among more advantaged children, we might expect downward mobility. To the extent that they are absent among certain less advantaged children, we might expect upward mobility. It is well known, of course, that relative status maintenance (rather than mobility) characterizes the majority of our male population. This fact suggests that less advantaged parents—who themselves have not found the opportunity structure manipulable—tend, in the majority of families, to pass this passivity orientation on to their children. Likewise, most advantaged families

---

[18] See, for example, Sewell, *op. cit.*, and also Rosen, *op. cit.*

apparently tend to convey effectively the notion of a rationally manipulable opportunity structure.

The discussion so far completes one objective of this chapter, viz., to examine the linkage between the opportunity structure and socialization for achievement values. The remaining goal is to see if this dimension of family structure and interaction is linked in any way to conjugal cohesion. To accomplish this, of course, we need to determine if certain categories of husbands and wives show any consistent differences in the strength with which they hold either the orientations of passivity or of mastery.

For example, one plausible hypothesis might be that the less the articulation with the economic opportunity system, the less the value consensus between spouses over child-achievement values. It may be that less advantaged husbands, because they are more involved in the production sector than wives, are perhaps more anxious than wives that their children "get ahead" in life. Therefore, they may seek to put more pressure on their children to do so. This may be true of husbands at the same time that they feel more frustrated, and thus passive toward the opportunity structure and strongly communicate this kind of orientation as well.

Yet an alternative hypothesis might be that lower-status wives are more frustrated and anxious than husbands about child-achievement, and thus stress mastery even more strongly than they do. Such wives may, for instance, be even more likely than males to try to "live out" their lives and their success aspirations through their children. But they might also put less stress on passivity than their husbands, sensing perhaps more keenly the inherent contradiction with mastery. To examine issues of these kinds, we have made a comparison of the mastery and passivity orientations of each respondent with his perceptions of his own spouse's orientations.

In Table 7-5, the dimensions of education and success expectations are representative of the objective and subjective dimensions of articulation with the economic system. With respect to the passivity orientation, it appears that neither husbands nor wives perceive themselves as differing greatly from their own spouses. Wives, however, consistently perceive their husbands to be more passive than they, whereas husbands *sometimes* see their wives as being more passive. Except for wives with "fair" success expectations, differences between spouses are not significant, although in general wives perceive larger differences than husbands do, and consequently the F ratios for wives generally tend to be somewhat greater than they are for husbands. Moreover, there seems to be no discernible pattern by degree of opportunity articulation, either in terms of differences in mean scores or in strength of the correlations. In other words, there seems to be general consensus between husbands and wives at each status level over the passivity orientation, with some indication that wives perceive their husbands to be somewhat more passive than they themselves are.

In Table 7-6, respondents and their own spouses are compared over the mastery dimension. As with passivity, it appears that husbands and wives generally see their spouses as being in agreement with themselves over this orientation. But, as before, wives see greater divergence than do husbands. They tend consistently to perceive their husbands as holding mastery values more strongly than they themselves do, although these differences are never significant.

Comparing across lines of economic articulation, an interesting pattern emerges with regard to the correlation between wife's own mastery orientations and her perceptions of her husband's. Both in the objective and subjective dimensions, the greater the level of articulation, the stronger the correlation between wife's mastery values and her perceptions of her husband's. This at least suggests that at lower status levels wives perceive less strength of agreement between themselves and their husbands over mastery values than do wives at higher status levels. Basically, then, it would seem that in spite of the general consensus between spouses over mastery as well as over passivity, there is some evidence that wives (especially those with less opportunity articulation) see more of a gap with their husbands in terms of mastery than they do for passivity.

In the overall picture, as a special case of husband-wife conflict resolution, child-achievement values do not appear to pose much of a threat to husband-wife consensus at any level of economic integration. Therefore, the kinds of child-achievement orientations held by parents, and conceptualized as an important subdimension of the instrumental sector of the conjugal unit, do not appear to pose a significant threat to conjugal cohesion per se. The fact that wives perceive their husbands to be both somewhat more passive and especially more mastery-oriented than they deserves, of course, further investigation.

The major point seems to be that *the level of opportunity integration at which husbands and wives find and/or define themselves accounts for similar kinds of child-achievement values between spouses.* There do not seem to be any systematic and/or significant differences that are a function of sex role occupancy. Neither do there appear to be major meaningful divergences by sex when comparing across articulation levels. Within the same level, there is no clear evidence that husbands are more "frustrated" or "anxious" about child achievement than wives, or that wives are more concerned than husbands about "living out" their lives through their children.

Instead, the generalizations explored earlier receive additional validation, viz., that spouses are perceived to demonstrate the same general kinds of articulation-achievement value relationships as do respondents themselves. Therefore, although the opportunity structure influences the strength of these values in both sexes, it tends to do so fairly equally so that they do

179

not appear to constitute much of a potentially divisive issue, and thus a possible threat to conjugal cohesion. This does not mean that husbands and wives may not differ—perhaps even substantially—about other areas of socialization. There is some evidence that they do, particularly in terms of discipline, of degree of nurture and control.[19] But this is a different facet of socialization and is beyond the scope of our data. Further research is needed into husband-wife consensus-conflict, not only over child-achievement values, but over other significant and problematic dimensions of socialization as well.

CONCLUSION

Two questions were examined in this chapter: the relationships between the opportunity structure and child-achievement values, and what linkage (if any) exists between these kinds of orientations and conjugal cohesion. With respect to the first general question, we saw that as opportunity integration increases, orientations toward passivity and mastery are combined in such a way as to minimize substantially any emphasis on the former, and to stress the latter in moderate fashion. As the level of integration decreases, there is greater stress on both types of orientations, and particularly on passivity.

It was suggested that the optimal combination for achievement or maintenance of status in our society is that found in more advantaged families, chiefly because risks become defined as reasonable and attainable in terms of projected rewards. More advantaged parents communicate the positive (*i.e.*, in terms of attainment) orientations they do because of the sense of worth and confidence they themselves have gained through taking risks, and thus successfully attaining the rewards and status they hold. Less advantaged parents communicate greater caution and docility toward achievement because they themselves have not gained as great a sense of excellence and confidence, having participated less fully and successfully in the processes of rewarded risk-taking.

The second issue was whether these kinds of parental orientations are potentially a special form of husband-wife conflict resolution. The evidence showed that within the same status levels, husbands and wives perceive their own spouses to share pretty much the same level of orientation over both passivity and mastery that they themselves do. Therefore, whereas theoretically, dissensus over these kinds of values (a particular type of conjugal conflict-resolution) could potentially threaten conjugal cohesion, it does not appear to do so in the modern conjugal unit. Instead, the evident

---

[19] For example, see Melvin L. Kohn and Eleanor E. Carroll, "Social Class and the Allocation of Parental Responsibilities," *Sociometry*, 23 (1960), pp. 372–92.

consensus over these values could perhaps be construed as one element contributing to the solidarity and cohesion of those units in the sample— even among those with relatively less economic articulation.

Lastly, because the transmission of these kinds of values probably rarely becomes an issue to be decided by either husband or wife, the exchange model discussed in Chapter Six (the exchange of status for legitimate authority) apparently has limited application in this regard. When both partners agree on what is normative, the notion of bargaining becomes less potent as an explanatory tool. Perhaps future research could consider what processes between husbands and wives lead to the relatively strong consensus shown in the data.

Nevertheless, given the fact that of late there has been increasing interest in exchange theory as a tool to explain certain types of parent-child interchange, this chapter serves as a further step in the direction of its use in this way. That is, after showing that parental achievement attitudes vary systematically by status, the next steps would be, (1) to see if children's attitudes vary with those of their parents, and (2) to seek to demonstrate if processes of exchange and reciprocity account best for these similarities.

CHAPTER

EIGHT

·

Toward
a Theory of
Conjugal
Cohesion
in Modern
Society

THE PURPOSE OF THIS LAST CHAPTER IS NOT TO RECAPITULATE IN DETAIL the specific findings of earlier chapters; that is done in the Conclusion of each chapter. Instead, there are three objectives: The major one is to attempt to tie together theoretically the several generalizations that have gone before. Second, and part of this, is to try to identify some of the more pertinent questions that were not answered in earlier chapters, and at the same time, to suggest guideliness for future research to attempt to deal with these questions. Finally, also stemming from our theoretical bases, brief comments are made regarding some practical implications of this study.

First then, a theoretical overview. Certain general theoretical notions that cover a wide range of substantive areas in sociology—subsuming numerous empirical generalizations—were employed to examine the modern conjugal family. For example, there is the broad question of the conditions of order-disorder, of cohesion. Also included were those orientations known as reciprocity and exchange—the interdependence to which they give rise—and the subsequent linkage to cohesion. A major concern is the interrelationship of systems in modern society—in this case, the economic and the kinship systems. Also raised were the questions of alienation and anomie: What conditions give rise to them, what are their consequences, how are they linked to the matter of cohesion? Of great import is the issue of the internal role structure of social systems, and the related question of norms that are differentiated into rights, duties, and options. Underlying the entire discussion were the dominant values of achievement and success—themes that probably lie at the core of American culture. Moreover, also central in the discussion and strongly related to cohesion are matters invoking *the definition of the situation, i.e.,* how do the various persons or parts in any system view and evaluate the cultural, structural, and interactional forces impinging on them? Finally, and intrinsic to this latter question, is the issue of system values and goals, *i.e.,* what are the desired ends sought by persons or parts in any collectivity?

We shall now try and move down from these rather abstract levels to the conjugal family to see how they help us understand it. But in so doing, we should always be prepared to move back up to the more general level and down again to other substantive areas where these general notions might also have explanatory power. In this fashion is systematic social theory developed. We begin at the cultural level with the dominant values of occupational achievement and material success. For good or ill, these values pervade every segment of our social structure—obviously the economic system, but also the kinship system. It so happens that the conjugal family in our society is the social unit in which achievement and success are displayed and thus "proved."

Efforts to "prove" success do not reflect a Marxian proclivity for gain, but instead the traditional ascetic Protestant notion of worth and respect based on material success. The upshot is that material success, suitably displayed, becomes a major goal of this particular social unit. But in order to consume, resources must be available; and in modern society these are most generally gained via the economic system. It is here that Parsons and others have described the role differentiation that occurs between parts of the conjugal unit. The male assumes the role of chief resource provider, and it is his occupation that provides the most significant linkage of the economic and conjugal systems.

But if one major goal of the modern conjugal unit is the display and proof of success, the other equally important goal is expressive satisfactions. To the degree that both major goals are met, the system will be that much more cohesive. In this regard and in terms of role differentiation, the wife assumes the position of "expressive hub" of the conjugal family. It should be noted that this type of role differentiation and these dual goals apply chiefly to those families located in the lower-working class and above. Within the lower or "lower-lower" class, the extent of the relevancy and pertinence of these types of role expectations and system goals becomes more problematic.[1]

In the role of provider, the husband's duties to his wife include objective rewards of status, prestige, and income, but also subjective rewards in the form of certain powerful feelings toward the economic opportunity system. These consist of allayed feelings of alienation and anomie. Alienation here refers to the feeling that one is currently "cut off" from achievement and success—one is powerless to use means deemed necessary for success, discontent with job rewards, and relatively estranged from the status system. *Anomie* here refers to the feeling that one's future chances for achievement-success are blocked. The husband, in short, is obligated to provide his wife with the feeling that she and the family are not currently "cut off" from the opportunity structure, plus the feeling that she (and her children) are not "blocked" from attainment of *future* success goals as well. At several points we saw that these "subjective" rewards are often more potent in terms of husband-wife interaction than are "objective" rewards.

The duty of the husband to provide objective and subjective rewards corresponds to the wife's right to receive these rewards from him. But as she does receive rewards, this puts her in his debt—she must now reciprocate, she must express her gratitude and show rectitude. She now has a duty to meet her husband's rights. But it is not a duty of unwilling constraint. She is now highly motivated to reciprocate positively. To do so, she fulfills certain expressive duties (primary relations) to meet his expressive rights. Likewise, she has certain instrumental household duties to fulfill that meet his rights in this particular sector as well. But as she performs both kinds of duties, he is then bound to reciprocate in the performance of his expressive duties that correspond to her expressive rights. Concomitantly, he is also bound to continue fulfillment of his economic duties.

The consequences of these ongoing processes are evident on both the structural and social psychological levels. First is the structural effect of interdependence: where there is a high degree of mutual interdependence, there is cohesion—there is order. Chapter One presents a detailed discus-

---

[1] On the other hand at least two reports found that lower-class Negroes do in fact share dominant values regarding both economic and conjugal roles. But because Negroes at this status level are frustrated in attaining these goals, other kinds of patterns emerge out of the exigencies of their white-dominated situations. See Elliot Liebow, *Tally's Corner,* Boston: Little, Brown and Company, 1967; also Lee Rainwater, "Crucible of Identity: The Negro Lower-class Family," in Gerald Handel, ed., *The Psychosocial Interior of the Family,* Chicago: Aldine Publishing Company, 1967, p. 371.

sion drawn from Gouldner on the linkage of exchange theory to the phenomenon of interdependence and the persistence of social systems. Second is the definition of the situation as "satisfactory" by the principal actors involved. Where economic and expressive goals are being met, and the issue of authority regarding internal tensions is being resolved in legitimate fashion, there also we find cohesion and order. Thus persistence of any social system, including the conjugal unit, is not based solely on either structural or processual elements operating independently of one another. Cohesion is dependent on both structure and process. The assumption made by some that structural interdependence is missing from the modern conjugal unit simply because spouses do not physically labor together on the family farm is misleading. Interdependence based on economic-status factors persists in spite of role differentiation. Role differentiation has made husband-wife interdependence more complex and subtle, but no less present or potent.

Before moving to a consideration of problems for future investigation, it is useful to form our conclusions into a set of propositions. These propositions link the entire study together and provide a springboard for ongoing research. In the interests of parsimony, these propositions are stated in general form. Some of them contain specific modifications that yet do not alter their general sense. These modifications can be noted by consulting the earlier chapters. Moreover, in considering the following generalizations, the reader should recall that our sample tended to exclude those who, for practical purposes, are outside the opportunity structure. Thus, these generalizations apply chiefly to what may be termed the "lower reaches" of the "stable" working class and above.

1. The greater the articulation or integration (at the objective level: systematic increases in occupational prestige, education, income; on the subjective level: systematic reductions in the several dimensions of alienation and anomie) of the conjugal unit into the economic opportunity structure, and thus the greater the level of rewards provided by the husband, the greater the perceived satisfaction with the three major dimensions of husband-wife primary relations, and conversely.

   a. For affiliativeness, generally true for both sexes.

   b. For physical affect, generally true for both sexes, except less so for males in terms of objective indices of economic integration.

   c. For empathy, strongly true for both sexes.

   d. The consequences of perceiving oneself, one's general milieu, the spouse's view of a particular primary relation, and the family life style in positive terms is generally an increase in one's own evaluation of a particular primary relation, in comparison to the consequences of perceiving these four mediating dimensions in negative terms, which generally results in a decrease in one's own evaluation of primary relations.

e. The longer the marriage, the more negative, in general, is the evaluation of affiliativeness and physical affect.

f. The longer the marriage, the more positive is the evaluation of empathy.

2. The less the degree of economic opportunity integration, the greater the degree of hostility between husbands and wives, and conversely.

   a. The consequence of a positive self-esteem is to reduce levels of perceived hostility; the consequence of a negative perception of oneself is to increase levels of perceived hostility.

3. a. Among employed wives, the higher the status of her job and the higher the status of her husband, the more positively she evaluates primary relations when compared to nonemployed wives with same husband status.

   b. Among employed wives, the lower the status of her job and the lower the status of her husband, the less positively she evaluates primary relations when compared to nonemployed wives with same husband status.

   c. Among husbands of employed wives, there is less satisfaction with primary relations than among husbands of comparable economic integration with nonemployed wives.

      (1) The major exceptions are husbands with least integration who have employed wives and who show greater satisfaction than comparable husbands with nonemployed wives.

4. a. The less the economic opportunity integration (objective and subjective), the more frequent is the dominance of husbands in conflict resolution.

   b. The greater the economic opportunity integration, the greater the probability of shared authority between spouses in conflict resolution.

   c. The less the economic articulation, the less traditional and the more modern are wives in their beliefs regarding male authority, and conversely.

   d. The less the integration, the less legitimate to wives is the dominance of husbands in the resolution of conjugal conflict, and conversely.

   e. From the perspective of the wife, employment increases her participation in conflict resolution. From the perspective of the husband, the less his education the more likely he is to perceive wife employment as increasing her participation in conflict resolution, and nonemployment as decreasing it; whereas the greater his education the more likely he is to perceive wife employment as decreasing her participation and nonemployment as increasing it.

   f. If the wife is employed, then both husbands and wives from these households generally appear less traditional and more modern in their beliefs regarding male authority. If the wife is not employed, then there is more of a tendency for both sexes to be traditional in outlook.

5. *a.* The lower the level of economic opportunity integration, the more strongly do parents hold (and presumably try to transmit) for their children passivity values vis-à-vis the opportunity structure, and conversely.

   b. The lower the integration, the more strongly do parents hold (and presumably try to transmit) for their children mastery values vis-à-vis the opportunity structure, and conversely.

   c. Combining these propositions (5a and 5b), we may say that the lower the level of articulation, the greater is the dissonance or conflict in achievement orientations to which the child is exposed. The higher the articulation, the greater or more consistent is the "fit" experienced by the child in terms of achievement orientations.

   d. The more orderly the milieu is perceived to be by the parent, the less strongly he tends to hold both passivity and mastery-type values, and conversely.

   e. There tends to be general perceived consensus between husbands and wives over child-passivity and child-mastery values at each level of economic articulation.

6. Summary

   a. Therefore, the greater the degree of material-status rewards provided by the husband, the greater is the degree of perceived satisfaction with primary relations (valued goals) and with authority relations, and thus:
   (1) The greater is the degree of husband-wife interdependence.
   (2) The greater are the degree of husband-wife feelings of cohesion and solidarity.

   b. The greater is the interdependence, and the greater the feelings of cohesion and solidarity, the greater is the probability of system-maintenance, of stability, of order, and the more is dissolution unlikely.

   c. Conversely, the less the degree of material-status rewards provided by the husband, the less the degree of perceived satisfaction with primary relations and with authority relations. Therefore:
   (1) The less is the degree of husband-wife interdependence.
   (2) The less is the degree of feelings of solidarity and cohesion.
   (3) The less is the probability of system-maintenance.

Among questions that arise out of these propositions, and one that certainly needs future examination, is the place of psychological variables in husband-wife interaction. For other than self-esteem and anomy, we have not dealt with important psychological factors such as personality needs or personality characteristics, and so on. What we have attempted is a structural combined with with a social-psychological analysis of the conjugal family. Principles of reciprocity and exchange between duties and rights of positions and roles provide the vehicle for this "synthesized approach" toward an explanation of conjugal cohesion.

But by no means would this model explain all the variance in husband-wife interaction. Personality factors must account for some of it, and help explain continued attraction for each other and for a desire to maintain the marriage relationship.[2] Future investigation, therefore, should address itself to the systematic isolation of some of these factors. There should also then be an attempt to integrate these psychological variables with the sociological model presented here. Until that time, we lack a full-orbed theory of conjugal cohesion. Specifically, psychological variables would seem excellently suited and perhaps requisite to deviant case analysis. These would include, for instance, dissolution among those with relatively high economic integration, and maintenance of the marriage among the relatively disadvantaged. But deviant case analysis alone is not the only function of psychological variables. We would expect that in all marriages certain personality configurations in their own right play a major role in husband-wife interaction, and thus ultimately in conjugal cohesion.

Some other instances of marriages that deviate from the general model might be due to three variations on the theme of rejection of the "success ethos" and its implications for definitions of personal excellence. First, on religious grounds, a strong case can be made for the deprecation of material gain and status based on the biblical warnings against covetousness. Hence the Catholic stress on the virtue of poverty, and the ascetic Protestant suspicion of conspicuous consumption. Weber notes that John Wesley, for example, advised eighteenth-century Christians to give away most of their newly got gain in order to avoid the inevitable perils that attend thereto.[3]

Therefore, those who today are strongly committed to these kinds of values, and who are perhaps only relatively or even less advantaged, are probably willing to overlook limited economic rewards. Limited means are deemed a "test of faith sent by God." Because the whole economic issue is therefore ultimately in Beneficient Hands, marital primary relations do not have the same relationship to economic rewards that they do in

---

[2] Winch notes that "very little has been found in the way of personality traits that are consistent predictors of marital felicity or stability." But he also points out that to conclude that "personality makes no difference in the marriage relationship . . . seems contrary to common sense." Robert F. Winch, *The Modern Family,* New York: Holt, Rinehart and Winston, Inc., 1963 (rev.), p. 712. Useful steps toward identifying important psychological elements have been taken, for instance, by Susan R. Orden and Norman B. Bradburn, "Dimensions of Marriage Happiness," *American Journal of Sociology,* 73 (May 1968), especially pp. 730–31. See also Gerald Handel, *The Psychological Interior of the Family,* Chicago: Aldine Publishing Company, 1967, especially Chaps. 1 and 23.

[3] Max Weber, *The Protestant Ethic and the Spirit of Capitalism,* New York: Charles Scribner's Sons, 1958 edition, pp. 175–76.

other families. In addition, wives in these kinds of situations are also likely to be very traditional regarding male authority, and thus to grant their husbands genuine deference regardless of the reward levels they may provide.

Then, too, a highly rationalized, intellectual Humanism could have the same consequences. Although Humanists are not often likely to be found among the ranks of the disadvantaged, and thus not put to the "acid test," some of them might hold a "contempt" for the materialism of our society. They might define it as crude, vulgar, and demeaning, and not "worthy" to be linked with interpersonal relations. This type of strong commitment therefore could distinguish these kinds of persons, in terms of actual conjugal behavior, from the masses who may simply hold to vague and general notions of romantic love. For the latter, simply holding to romantic love does not negate the systematic effects of varying levels of economic rewards. But for strongly committed Humanists, such negation might indeed occur. More will be said later regarding romantic love—for now, it suffices to distinguish its consequences from those of a highly refined Humanist philosophy.

Finally, there is that third minority of the population that has "turned off and dropped out." Whether among "hippies" or the "extreme new left," or some lower-class families, or whatever, there may not be clearly stated religious or Humanist values, but simply a feeling that the modern "rat race to success" is absurd. Since for them it lacks meaning, they refuse to be a part of it. This third category may, in some cases, represent the activist extension among the young of Humanist orientations. Theoretically, it is significant to note that in the past there has been an association between rejection of individualistic occupational success and attempts at revisions of conjugal family structure.[4] This was true of the Oneida Community, Communist family experiments, the kibbutzim, and now of certain "Hip communes."

To borrow Goode's terminology, there is a "fit" between the conjugal family form and the modern technological system.[5] As applied here, those people who reject one part of the fit seem to reject the other as well; those who accept one part tend to accept the other also. To the extent that individual occupational achievements are minimized, it seems more possible to experiment with variations in family form. To the extent individual achievement is central, as it is currently in our society, the less possible it seems to be to deviate greatly from the dominant family form. What the actual causal chain may be awaits further investigation, but the

---

[4] Gerald R. Leslie, *The Family in Social Context,* New York: Oxford University Press, 1967, p. 150. See also Peter M. Blau and Otis Dudley Duncan, *The American Occupational Structure,* New York: John Wiley and Sons, Inc., 1967, p. 205.

[5] William J. Goode, *World Revolution and Family Patterns,* New York: The Free Press, 1963, pp. 13 ff.

fact of this kind of association underlies once again the intrinsic linkage of the economic and kinship systems.

Aside from psychological variables and deviant case analysis, there is the question of limits or threshholds. We have assumed that cohesion varies with degree of interdependence and situational satisfaction, and that dissolution of the conjugal unit takes place when feelings of cohesion and solidarity are diminished beyond a certain point. But when does that point occur? What may be tolerable levels of interdependence and satisfaction for certain couples may be far too low for others. It is at this crucial point that the insights of Thibaut and Kelley can be fruitfully applied. The twin notions of *comparison level* (CL) and particularly *comparison level for alternatives* (CL alt) speak to the question of threshholds. (See footnote 2, Chapter Two.) CL refers to the "standard by which the person evaluates the rewards and costs of a given relationship in terms of what he feels he 'deserves.' " [6] CL alt is the reference point to decide whether or not to remain in the relationship. "It can be looked at as the lowest level of reward which the individual will accept in order to continue in the relationship." [7]

Thus, future research into the limits of situational satisfaction and interdependence—limits beyond which cohesion and solidarity are quite seriously undermined—ought probably to be conceptualized in terms of CL and especially CL alt. Special attention might be given to those situational and psychological conditions that give rise to varying degrees of CL alt within the framework of similar levels of economic inputs. We have noted again and again the complexity of analyzing the cohesion of any social system, including the conjugal family. The complexity is nowhere more evident than when we attempt to investigate the host of intricate and interrelated factors that might influence CL alt. Yet it would seem that such efforts are called for if progress is to be made in grasping more fully the complex phenomenon of cohesion. Ideally, a longitudinal study in which families are followed over a period of several years would be best suited to determine this kind of issue. The sample might be heavily weighted with those in the blue-collar ranges of the economic structure, in order to gain maximum cases of actual dissolution, and also to take particular note of units that remain intact.

Part of this threshholds question hangs on the relative importance to husbands and wives of the three levels of primary interaction plus legitimate authority. We have inferred a priority of primary relations—especially as the length of the marriage increases. But this priority may vary by

6 John W. Thibaut and Harold H. Kelley, *The Social Psychology of Groups,* New York: John Wiley and Sons, Inc., 1959,pp. 21–24. See also Edwin P. Hollander, *Principles and Methods of Social Psychology,* New York: Oxford University Press, 1967, p. 205.

7 Thibaut and Kelley, *op. cit.*

factors such as class or education. Likewise, degree of acceptance of an unsatisfactory authority or power situation may vary by certain kinds of variables, perhaps personality factors. At the same time, there may also exist a priority of objective and subjective economic-status rewards. Thus, certain combinations of instrumental factors and expressive elements may link together. First, evidence for such priorities needs to be established. If this is possible, then perhaps a rank ordering of these combinations could be discovered and showed to be related to varying degrees of conjugal cohesion. To carry out such intricate objectives, certain powerful statistical techniques would be useful if the data deserve them. Such techniques are currently available to sociologists, and provided certain assumptions can be met, they could help to attain the objectives just noted and thus enhance considerably our knowledge of structure and process within the conjugal unit.

An enormously complex issue hinges around wife employment. We have assumed that the money she brings into the household is not generally defined by the husband as a reward to which he is indebted to reciprocate either expressively or in terms of authority. Instead, he seems to view it as either a threat (moderate to low status) or as an incursion (higher status). Only do the lowest-status males seem to view it as a reward to which they are motivated to respond positively on the expressive plane. Yet employed higher-status wives evidently do see it as some form of benefit or resource they bring into the family, as a result of which they perceive their husbands "as if" they respond more positively.

As suggested in the text, women are probably increasingly coming to view employment behaviors as a right inherent in the role of wife. Husbands, on the other side, still regard such behaviors more as an option. The actual existence and extent of this strain requires considerable examination. For if over the next generation a growing proportion of wives come to define employment strongly as a right, then it is possible that current established role differentiation could be undercut. Wives of this kind might be less likely to define their husbands as the chief provider on whom their status, prestige, self-worth, and material well-being depend. The long-term consequences for conjugal cohesion of such a major shift in definitions of rights, duties, and options are difficult to foresee without further research. A crucial factor to consider is the degree to which male expectations change in the same direction and at the same pace as those of females. If our data are any indication, the "ancient war between the sexes" promises to be waged in this sector for some time to come.

Not unrelated to this larger theoretical issue is the question of potentially different "definitions of the situation" by sex. Many studies of the family have relied solely on wives' perceptions. By using both sexes, we have been able to isolate important differences between them in both the instrumental and the expressive dimensions. Research carried out on groups larger than a dyad should not ordinarily overlook sampling the perspectives and interests of distinctive, and perhaps competing, subparts. Whenever possible, therefore, it would seem that the additional richness provided through the perspectives of males, as well as females, is a highly useful and perhaps even necessary element in family research.

Whether or not, however, both spouses from the same household are required (instead of the procedure followed herein) is not certain. Which of these alternatives is chosen would depend ultimately on the nature of the theoretical problem that informs the research design. The major point is that generalizations based on data from only one sex should not be applied to the conjugal family qua unit. They should be labeled as the perceptions of one sex and regarded as tentative until they are also tested on the opposite sex.

Interviewing both spouses from the same household could become quite expensive, particularly if repeated call-backs are necessary to find them both at home together. Unless they are interviewed simultaneously (and presumably separately), or else one immediately after the other, we run a serious risk of collusion over interview items. The whole question is further complicated by the greater likelihood of refusals when the couple is asked to "give up so much family time" to the interviewer. Additional research is needed to determine both the problems and advantages of this type of design in comparison with the one used for this study.[8]

Another important question centers around the relevance of the classic notions of alienation and anomie for understanding of the conjugal unit. They have been defined here in specific and somewhat rigorous fashion to denote feeling states of husband and wife toward the economic opportunity structure. There is no reason why these pregnant constructs that carry so many subtle nuances and rich overtones should not be used to illuminate and to sensitize us to processes of great significance. For in view of the American Dream they apprehend something that is very real indeed to members of the conjugal unit. What, for example, is more threatening in

[8] Immediately after leaving the respondent's home, the interviewer completed a series of evaluation questions, one of which asked if anyone other than the respondent was present during the interview (including near enough to eavesdrop, as far as the interviewer could tell). In 59 percent of the households, no one at all was present at any time during the interview. In the remaining 41 percent of the households, someone else was present for some part of the interview. Of this number, about half were spouses, the remainder children, friends, or other relatives. But in the overwhelming majority of the households included in this 41 percent, the "intruder" was there for only part of the interview, *e.g.*, 10 questions or so. The interviewers reported that the usual pattern in such households was for the extra party to sit in on the beginning of the interview, while relatively innocuous fact questions were asked. Once initial curiosity was satisfied, the party would generally leave the room to do something else. Presumably, therefore, bias in the data as a result of spouse presence and silent pressure was relatively minimal.

our society than to feel cut off from its opportunity system? And perhaps even worse is the feeling that, in our future-oriented society, the future is, after all, not so golden but actually quite bleak.

The data of earlier chapters made it quite clear that these kinds of feeling states play a significant role in conjugal interaction. In many instances, they appeared to be more consistent and more powerful than so-called "objective" elements. The immediate need, however, is for research to validate or else to modify the findings here regarding their relationships to family structure. In addition, the long-range need is to try to develop further the more general theoretical linkage between their utility in explaining kinship patterns and their utility elsewhere. For in spite of the fact that there is no coherent "alienation theory" or "anomie theory," and although some are thus suggesting a moratorium on these notions, their usefulness here indicates this suggestion may be premature. It is likely that the feeling states represented by these constructs do pervade most elements of our social structure in varying degrees. That they exist within the conjugal family seems evident. It is therefore necessary not only to elaborate their existence there, but also to trace these orientations to other segments of society, to define and measure them in appropriate fashion, and then to compare and contrast them with the conditions and consequences of their existence within these several subparts, including the family system.

Discussion about the subjective feeling states provides a bridge into the core question of exchange theory and its application to the conjugal family. As Buckley points out, Homans' views of exchange are deficient in that they fail to deal explicitly with social-psychological notions of self-identities, self-rewards, self-respect.[9] Throughout this volume, we have attempted to couch notions of reciprocity and exchange in this fashion—in terms of what Buckley calls "G. H. Mead's behaviorism rather than with Skinner's variety." At this social-psychological level, it is little wonder that dimensions of alienation and anomie figured strongly both in terms of expressive satisfactions and the question of conjugal authority. But the major point here is that exchange theory should not be thought of as foreign to conjugal dyadic interaction. The exchange of "sentiments of liking" for attainment of system goals is a generalized principle that applies within the bounds of the conjugal unit, as well as in many other types of social structures.

In his recent discussion of exchange theory, Blau refers to relationships "that are considered ends in themselves" as "intrinsic relations." In "intrinsic relations," he claims, "sacrifices are made without any apparent thought of return." Blau argues that it is not the purpose of "contribu-

[9] Walter Buckley, *Sociology and Modern Systems Theory*, Englewood Cliffs, N.J.: Prentice-Hall, Inc., 1967, p. 112.

tions to a loved one" to "elicit specific returns. . . ." *Yet he does not rule out reciprocity in intrinsic relations.* Rewards by person to other, he states, are "inducements for the other to make a corresponding commitment and continue the association." Although rejecting any *"quid pro quo* of explicit services in these intimate relations of extrinsic significance," he admits that if person does not feel requited by other, "serious strain is introduced into the relationship." He also notes that the definitions of rectitude and gratification depend on the actor's subjective evaluation of same.[10]

In that context, Blau makes only oblique references to the conjugal unit per se. He seems to imply, for instance, that "love relations" between a man and woman (interestingly, the husband and wife roles are not mentioned) or between mother and child are intrinsic-type relations. Yet he nowhere states that exchange theory is not applicable to analysis of the conjugal family. This fact plus his assertion of reciprocity even within intrinsic relations suggests some ambiguity on his part regarding its applicability. Now it seems clear that in nonfamilial intrinsic relations (where formalized economic and "extrinsic" elements enter in remotely, if at all) Blau's comments regarding altruism have particular force.

Moreover, in future research on the applicability of exchange theory to the conjugal unit, he implicitly poses an important issue, *i.e.*, those conditions that determine the degree to which, in particular interaction dimensions, reciprocity is expected merely in terms of generalized commitment to the total relationship, or else expected in terms of more specific reward elements. The key point, however, is that in addition to being a center of "significant intrinsic relationships," the conjugal unit is equally a center of significant "extrinsic" relations, in terms of economic production and consumption behaviors. Hence, the modern conjugal family cannot be treated solely in its intrinsic or expressive sense, and does not therefore fall totally under the rubric of Blau's discussion. In short, while his insights regarding intrinsic attachments cannot be overlooked, his arguments in no way undermine the potential utility and fruitfulness of explaining certain aspects of conjugal structure and interaction through use of exchange theory.

The thesis of Buckley's volume on the scope and direction of current systems theory in sociology is that notions such as bargain, exchange, reciprocity, game theory, and so on, represent a significant trend away from consensus theory per se. The latter often conveys a static picture of social structure, and does not conveniently deal with social process. Specifically in the family, role consensus (or value or normative consensus) is necessary but not sufficient to explain the processes of cohesion, or lack of it. As Buckley puts it, "This *transactional process* of exchange, negotiation or bar-

10 Peter M. Blau, *Exchange and Power in Social Life,* New York: John Wiley and Sons, Inc., 1964, p. 36. See Stephen Richer, "The Economics of Child Rearing," *Journal of Marriage and the Family,* 30 (August 1968), p. 462, for a brief criticism of Blau for allegedly excluding the family from the scope of exchange theory.

gaining is thus inherently a morphogenic process out of which emerge relatively stable social and cultural structures." [11] That role recilprocity goes beyond role complementarity in explaining cohesion is also precisely Gouldner's point.[12] This point stands in contrast to Spiegel's analysis of the family when he argues that "complementarity is of the greatest significance because it is chiefly responsible for that degree of harmony and stability which occurs in interpersonal relations." [13]

If Buckley's assessment is correct regarding the increasing utilization of exchange theory as over against consensus theory, then it makes great sense to seek to expand its potential application within the conjugal unit. The efforts herein represent only an initial phase. Further research might well address itself to at least two related questions: (1) the appropriateness of the basic exchange model posited here, viz., attainment of goals at the task-oriented level (economic-status rewards) generates sentiments of solidarity at the expressive and instrumental-authority levels. Second, we need to know much more about the specific nature of those processes, and indeed we need to know where and how principles of reciprocity, bargaining, and exchange apply throughout all phases of conjugal relationships. It should not be assumed, in short, that exchange theory in conjugal setting is limited to the situations or in the ways suggested in the text.

More specifically, one of the chief strengths of exchange theory is its capability to cope with ongoing process. The conjugal family seems ideally suited for studies of bargaining and exchange in response, for instance, to clashes or tensions of expectations and behaviors.[14] The projected long-term changes in women's role rights are an excellent example of one particularly significant issue that is amenable to this approach. Consensus theory alone is obviously not capable of handling it in satisfactory fashion. In the past, family investigations have been accused of theoretical sterility.[15] The seeming convergence in modern sociology on theories of process and exchange provides an ideal opportunity for family studies to shake this opprobrium and join the mainstream of sociological theory. The opportunity should not be lost.

Finally, in view of the growing concern among some sociologists that

[11] *Op. cit.*, p. 160.

[12] Alvin W. Gouldner, "The Norm of Reciprocity: A Preliminary Statement," *American Sociological Review*, 25 (April 1960), pp. 173–75.

[13] John P. Spiegel, "The Resolution of Role Conflict within the Family," in Norman W. Bell and Ezra F. Vogel, eds., *A Modern Introduction to the Family,* New York: The Free Press, 1960, p. 364.

[14] Richer, *op. cit.*, points out that at least one effort has been made in this direction by Jessie Bernard, "The Adjustment of Married Mates," in H. T. Christensen, ed., *Handbook of Marriage and the Family,* Chicago: Rand McNally and Co., 1964, pp. 675–739.

[15] Although, as Stryker notes, "Family sociologists are by no means peculiar in this respect." Sheldon Stryker, "The Interactional and Situational Approaches," in Christensen, *ibid.*, p. 126.

our studies at least point to some practical implications for public policy, we shall consider this question briefly. We must be extremely cautious here, for, as Bell notes, since World War II, "the study of the family came increasingly to be identified with various moralistic 'how-to-do-it' approaches. These approaches, frequently presented under the guise of being authentic social science, were often primarily value prescriptions. . . . This group often passed off under the label of 'sociology' such cliches as . . . 'husbands and wives can resolve their problems by being honest and talking them out. . . .' " [16] His telling point is that there has been an unfortunate and incompatible admixture of social science and value-judgments that has been to the detriment of both.

There is no doubt that the pervasiveness of the romantic love complex, as discussed in Chapter One, is largely responsible for the value-prescriptions that have influenced family studies. Married persons are "supposed" to maintain maximum expressive satisfactions chiefly on the basis of their "personality strengths." They are not "supposed" to allow crass materialistic factors to enter into their relationship. Now it is the case that our society has a value-commitment to "satisfactory" and "meaningful" marriage in the same sense that it does to "good schools" or "good mental health" or "full voter participation" in the electoral process, and so on. To the extent that this is true, then this study has certain practical implications.

In terms of single young people within our society, many myths surrounding the romantic love complex need to be discarded. Through various means, such as pamphlets, books, high school and college courses, and so on, youth could be made aware of some of the realities of an acquisitive society in so far as these realities will impinge on later marital interaction. Presumably such awareness might lead to added discretion—especially among the working class, and perhaps for girls in particular—with regard to mate selection.

Recent years have seen increased efforts by certain educators to get courses on "sex education" into the elementary and secondary schools. For the most part, these attempts have not met with much success, largely because most parents are "afraid" of "exposing" their children to "too much sex too soon." Granted that such fears are naïve (given sex exposure through the media), there may be some validity in arguing that a program of courses that implies that sex education is the prime way to prepare children for courtship and marriage is far too narrow a perspective. Parents would be much less opposed and the children would profit considerably more if such programs were broadened to include a greater range of issues which are part of courtship and marriage patterns. This would involve not

[16] Robert R. Bell, *Studies in Marriage and the Family*, New York: Thomas Y. Crowell Company, 1968, pp. v–vi.

merely a renaming of the courses from "sex" to "family-life education" (as they are already called in some high schools). It would also mean primarily that such courses would set these behavior patterns explicitly within the context of the larger society. In this framework the student would come to see that marriage is not withdrawn from the fabric of the larger social structure; it is not the asocial thing that some make it out to be. Instead, they would come to perceive that much of what will occur in their later marital situations is inevitably related to certain bonds with the society at large.

Some social philosophers have defended "romantic love" against certain misgivings on the grounds that it provides relative freedom of mate selection, and of course no one would wish to abridge this freedom. But greater knowledge regarding the realities of economic factors, which might in turn lead to a "wiser" choice of one's mate, is not at all incompatible with freedom in mate selection. One could argue, in fact, that this knowledge ultimately provides greater freedom, because it perhaps reduces the likelihood that one will be embarrasingly "caught" in a marital situation that is significantly less than one might wish it to be. No one, of course, is arguing for an extreme emphasis on a premarital calculus of the projected partner's net "worth" or "achievement potential." The only point is that, given our society's current values regarding marriage, all the knowledge that might aid in the attainment of these values should be brought into focus. And, therefore, knowledge regarding economic-status factors cannot be overlooked.

APPENDIX A

DATA GATHERING AND SAMPLING PROCEDURES. THROUGHOUT THIS VOLUME, but particularly in the Preface and in Chapters One and Two, we have alluded briefly to some of the methods used to gather the data for this study. This section expands and systematizes additional pertinent methodological information. The study was carried out in the city of Indianapolis from late January through March, 1967, under the sponsorship and direction of the Institute of Social Research, Department of Sociology, Indiana University. It was the second in a series of ongoing annual studies, sponsored by the Institute, known as the Indianapolis Area Project (IAP). Face-to-face interviews, in the homes of the respondents, were conducted by skilled interviewers, both from the *National Opinion Research Center* (400 cases) and by specially trained graduate students (516 cases). The latter carried out their tasks as one segment of their year-long involvement in the IAP. Skill and diligence in student interviewing, as well as in their other efforts in the IAP, are reasonably assured, because the student interviewers were being graded for their efforts in several required courses throughout the year.

Moreover, as further incentive for careful work, the awarding of the M.A. degree, as well as admission to the doctoral program, is largely contingent on their efforts in the whole of the IAP project. In comparing student and NORC interviews in terms of the distributions of the variables used for analysis in the study, no statistically significant differences emerged. Furthermore, one of the students in the project, for his thesis paper, carried out an intensive analysis of certain conditions of interview bias. One of his findings was that there were no significant differences between students and NORC personnel in terms of communication with respondents or in any type of systematic interview bias per se. Hence, the fact that two different sets of interviewers were used to gather the data does not appear to introduce systematic bias that might have a negative effect on their analysis or interpretation.

Every sample survey faces particular problems in its execution, and none is ever carried out to the complete satisfaction of those involved.

As background to some of the problems encountered by this survey, we shall present first a summary of the actual technical procedures followed in drawing the sample. The following is taken from a detailed report prepared by Robert Wait, who was responsible for IAP sampling requirements in 1967 (as he had been in 1966). A much more comprehensive elaboration of the details involved in drawing the sample is available on request from the Institute of Social Research, Indiana University.

The 1966–67 Indianapolis Area Project used a multi-stage cluster sample [1] which was designed to give all currently married persons in the Indianapolis area a known and equal probability of selection. In the *first* stage, blocks were systematically selected within an area which included the city of Indianapolis and the built-up residential areas lying outside but adjacent to the city limits. Excluded from the sampled area were central-city census tracts which had median family income below $4,000, according to the 1960 census.[2]

In the *second* stage of the sampling process, dwelling units were systematically sampled from within the selected blocks. A dwelling unit was defined—following Census Bureau practice—as a group of rooms (or a single room) occupied as separate living quarters by a family, by a group of persons living together, or by a single individual. Excluded from consideration at this point were institutionalized living quarters, such as fraternities, hotels, hospitals, and homes for the aged. The sample was clustered so that, on the average, four dwelling units per block were selected.

The *final* stage of the sampling process provided for the random selection of a single married respondent from each selected dwelling unit. Only persons who were currently married and who were living with their spouses at the time of the study were selected to be interviewed. Persons who were single, widowed, divorced, or married but not living with their spouse at the time of the study were not selected.

To summarize Wait's description and to take up from there, the sample was basically a two-stage area probability sample. The first stage consisted of a systematic sampling of blocks, the second of a systematic sampling of dwelling units within these blocks, and finally a sampling of only one married person (sex predesignated to interviewer) from each dwelling unit. The sample therefore was a highly specialized one. To be included, the respondent had to be married, currently living with his spouse (wives whose husbands were on overseas duty in the armed forces, for instance, were screened out of the sample), and meet the predesignated sex requirement.

Whenever a sample becomes this specialized, we may expect greater

[1] See Leslie Kish, "A Two-stage Sample of a City," *American Sociological Review,* 17 (1952), pp. 761–69.

[2] The excluded tracts were numbers 518, 529, 531, 535, 540, and 563. Five of these tracts had populations that were more than 95 percent nonwhite, whereas the population of the sixth was more than 75 percent nonwhite.

difficulties in attaining maximum completion rates than we would otherwise. We began the study with a total pool of 2,111 addresses. This was twice as large a sample as we felt we would eventually obtain (the final sample size was 916), but was necessary because of the attenuation that would inevitably occur.

Our interviewers discovered that there were 149 vacant dwelling units, and thus these addresses were out of the sample. Likewise, they found that there were 167 nondwelling units (businesses, stores, and so on), and these too were out of the sample. The interviewers contacted 568 addresses in which there were no married couples (rather, the single, widowed, divorced, separated) living there *at that time*. These three situations reduced our sample by 884, to a figure of 1,227 households.

Moreover, at 64 addresses—although the interviewers made at least two, three, and often more call-backs—no one was ever found at home. In these cases, it was often difficult, if not impossible, to know for sure if the dwelling unit was actually occupied by a married couple who were currently living together. This information could only be obtained if perchance a neighbor was nearby, claimed that he knew the information, was willing to render it, and—most vital of all—was accurate in the assessment. Because it was essential for inclusion in our sample that a household actually contain a married couple, and that they be currently living together, it was decided to consider these "doubtful" households as out of the sample, much as we had done when it was actually verified that the dwelling unit was occupied by a nonmarried couple. The rationale was that inasmuch as neighbors were often unavailable, or else refused the required information, or might have been incorrect, it was less risky to consider these households as out of sample than to retain them.

Their exclusion left the total pool of addresses where respondents were actually contacted at 1,163. From these 1,163 households, 916 completed interviews were obtained, resulting in a completion rate of 78.7 percent. Of the remaining proportion of 21.3 percent, 17.2 percent represented what Goode calls "genuine" refusals—individuals who told the interviewer in person they did not wish to participate (including some break-offs).[3] The remaining 4.1 percent consisted chiefly of people who said they wanted to participate, but who, owing to serious illness or to out-of-town commitments (in the case of several business executives) were forced to postpone their appointments until after our field work was scheduled to end. These cloudy participants contribute to what Goode calls a "gross" refusal rate.

There are several points to be made about these refusal rates. First, as Goode points out, "any researcher is troubled by losses beyond 8–10 percent." His own study had a "gross" refusal rate of 19 percent, and a

[3] William J. Goode, *After Divorce,* New York: The Free Press, 1956, p. 352.

"genuine" refusal rate of 15–17 percent.[4] A "modal figure," he suggests, "for refusals in public opinion polling might fall between 10–14 percent, [and] even established polling organizations have at times suffered losses as high as 17–18 percent," and he notes that some studies have had refusal rates as high as 45 percent. He concludes therefore that his "losses were not overly high," that is, they were approximately near what other sample surveys generally tend to experience. Given the fact that ours was also a highly specialized sample, and given the additional consideration that we included males (something that many surveys do not precisely because of the greater tendency of males to be unavailable and to refuse), it may be said that our "genuine" and "gross" refusal rates are not unreasonable.

But, as Goode notes, a second and ultimately much more significant question is this: "Whether the losses are high or low, the crucial empirical question is whether they make any difference." [5] That is, does a certain level of refusals bias the sample to such a degree that the relationships that emerge are unreliable, and thus of uncertain validity? If those who refused could have been included in the sample, would their responses produce significant changes in the patterns of responses within the data?

To try to deal with this question, Chart A presents a comparison of certain 1960 census data for the Indianapolis Standard Metropolitan Statistical Area (SMSA) with certain of our sample data.[6] The comparison is of proportions of households, with husband and wife present (excluding single people and the female heads of households, as well as "other male head") in each of the major occupational categories (in terms of occupation of male head) used by the Census Bureau. "Households with husband-wife present," conforms, of course, to one of our prime sampling criteria. Respondents in our sample are placed in the various occupational categories through a transformation routine on the Duncan SEI, available in Standard Package Form.[7]

Chart A reveals a strong correspondence between the two sets of data with regard to proportions of households (husband-wife present) in the various occupational groupings. These data provide evidence that our sample is adequately representative of the occupational distribution of the Indianapolis SMSA. In terms of the central theoretical issue of the study, this is extremely vital. Occupational position is a major indicant of what we have called "articulation with the economic opportunity system." Therefore, if certain occupational categories were severely underrepresented, and

---

[4] *Ibid.*

[5] *Ibid.*

[6] U.S. Bureau of the Census, *U.S. Census of Population: 1960.* Detailed *Characteristics. Indiana.* Final Report P (1)–16 D. U.S. Government Printing Office, Washington, D.C., p. 382.

[7] Contact the Institute for Social Research, Indiana University, Bloomington, 47401.

Chart A. Proportions of Households, by Male Head (both spouses present) in Major Occupation Categories, Indianapolis SMSA—1960 Census and 1967 IAP Sample

Year	Number of Households, Husband and Wife Present	Professional, Technical, and Kindred	Managers, Officials and Proprietors	Clerical, Sales, and Kindred	Craftsmen, Foremen and Kindred	Operatives and Kindred	Service Workers, Including Private Household Helpers	Laborers, Excluding Farm and Mine	Farmers and Farm Managers	Farm Laborers and Foremen	Occupation Not Reported
1960 Census	140,042 100.0%	(17,313) 12.3%	(17,939) 12.8%	(22,893) 16.3%	(31,327) 22.3%	(29,031) 20.7%	(7,688) 5.4%	(6,915) 4.9%	(580) 0.4%	(221) 0.1%	(6,135) 4.3%
1967 Sample	916 100.0%	(109) 11.9%	(167) 18.2%	(122) 13.3%	(227) 24.8%	(175) 19.1%	(63) 6.9%	(38) 4.1%	(4) 0.4%	(4) 0.4%	(7) 0.8%
		1	2	3	4	5	6	7	8	9	10

others grossly overrepresented at the expense of the former, then we would face serious additional problems in data analysis and interpretation. This would be especially true if there were these great inequalities in representation vis-à-vis the upper and lower levels of the opportunity structure—for instance, between the traditional white-collar and blue-collar or non-manual and manual groupings.

But such undue skewing does not appear to occur. Take, for example, categories 1, 2, and 3: the white-collar categories. In Category 1, the professional grouping, we have undersampled by only .4 percent. Whereas in Category 2 (managers) there is an oversampling of 5.4 percent, this white-collar "advantage" is balanced by an undersampling in Category 3 (clerical) of 3.0 percent. If we add the 3.0 and .4 percent from Categories 1 and 3 and subtract 3.4 from 5.4 percent (Category 2), the total proportion of white-collar respondents in our sample is only 2 percent greater than that recorded in the 1960 census. Moreover, this overall increase may simply reflect the general "upgrading" of occupational levels during the period 1960–67. That is, the actual proportion of white-collar workers in Indianapolis—particularly managers and officials—was very likely greater in 1967 than it was in 1960. And our data may simply reflect this "upgrading" rather than systematic bias in sampling.

The "upgrading" argument may help to explain the 2.5 percent oversampling in Category 4 (craftsmen, foremen), technically a blue-collar category, though sometimes referred to as "marginal" between middle and working classes. There were probably more of these kinds of workers in Indianapolis in 1967 than there were in 1960. Furthermore, the 2.5 percent oversampling in this blue-collar grouping may tend to balance the analogous 2 per cent oversampling figure in the white-collar grouping. The 1.6 percent underrepresentation in Category 5 (operatives) is likewise probably balanced by the 1.5 percent overrepresentation among service workers (Category 6).

Categories 7, 8, and 9 are remarkably similar in reported proportions. The figures among laborers (Category 7) are particularly significant because they indicate that we have represented adequately in the sample those blue-collar households near the bottom of the opportunity structure. (This is so in spite of our exclusion of the lowest income census tracts.[8]) Many

---

[8] As indicated in Chap. One, males are often not present among households within these tracts. Hence, such households would not have fitted our sampling requirements. And even when males are present, they may be unemployed or only spasmodically employed. Therefore, exclusion of these tracts does not reduce very much one's chances of getting a distribution that is fairly representative of occupations of married males in households where both spouses are present. Note from Chart A that in roughly 6100 households, the Census Bureau indicates that occupation of male head was not reported. It is very likely that the great majority of these households are located in tracts such as those excluded here, i.e., those that the Bureau finds perennially difficult to enumerate accurately. If all employed males (in these tracts) with spouse present were actually enumerated, it is not probable that

studies report that refusal rates are highest among these kinds of households, and therefore they often tend to be seriously underrepresented, especially in studies of the family. But this does not appear to be so here. The .8 percent difference may be due simply to a decrease in these kinds of jobs during the years 1960–67. The 4.3 percent figure under census data in Category 10 probably reflects, in large measure, efforts of the Census Bureau to sample those census tracts purposely excluded from our sample, *i.e.*, those households pretty much outside the opportunity structure. The .8 percent figure for our data is due to failure of the interviewer to get information adequate enough for coding requirements. Hence, Category 10 does not indicate any systematic bias in our sample data.

Therefore, taken as a whole, the comparisons in Chart A suggest that in spite of problems with refusals, the 1967 IAP sample appears to be representative of the occupational structure (above the lower-lower class) of the greater Indianapolis area at that period. The refusals do not seem to be systematically associated with any particular occupational grouping. The refusals thus appear to have been more or less randomly distributed over the occupational (or social class) structure. If this is indeed the case, the probability of severe and serious systematic bias in the data owing to refusals is thereby lessened.

The natural question that then arises is what accounts for these particular refusal rates, and concomitantly, for their relatively uniform distribution. Many factors were undoubtedly at work, some of which appear in every sample survey (sensitive questions, and so on), and others that are not now known. But there was one over factor for a goodly number of refusals—a reason stated again and again by many potential respondents who declined cooperation. It was based on the fact that the Indiana State Legislature commenced its biennial session in the same month as our project began in the capital city of Indianapolis. As is true of most state universities, in the minds of conservative citizens and state legislators, Indiana University has the undeserved reputation of being a hotbed of "agitators, demonstrators, communists, sex deviants and perverts, hippies, rebels, and anarchists." At the time of the interviewing, several "scandals of sorts" were brewing on the main campus (as is perennially the case), and these received generous coverage from the two hyperconservative Indianapolis newspapers. (These, incidentally are the only ones in the city and are owned by the same firm. They have the dubious distinction of being severely castigated by the late Senator Robert F. Kennedy for gross unfairness and inequities in reporting his 1968 primary campaign in the state.)

Moreover, the campus scandal during our interviewing period was par-

---

much of a change in the overall SMSA occupational distribution would emerge, except possibly at the unskilled levels.

ticularly "juicy." Some twenty students (out of 26,000) had publicly announced the establishment on campus of "The Sexual Freedom League." The Indianapolis newspapers never bothered to stress the numerical insignificance of the group, nor its basic aims, which were essentially philosophical rather that behavioral. It was enough to imply that IU was "permitting sexual orgies" at the taxpayers' expense. Concurrently, the university was presenting large budget requests to the legislature, and the two newspapers portrayed vividly the "irony" of great sums of the taxpayers' dollars going to support the "corruption" extant at IU.

The upshot of these interrelated elements, as far as our potential respondents (at all class levels) were concerned, was that they plainly—and often emphatically—told our interviewers that they would "have nothing to do" with Indiana University. They "certainly did not wish to cooperate *in any way* with such a wicked place." Thus certain news coverage, combining certain student activities with large budget requests, created for a period of weeks a climate highly unfavorable to *anything* connected to Indiana University. Unfortunately, this span of time was just that in which we were going out to citizens excited by distorted publicity. The result was an attitude of noncooperation much stronger than usual toward sample surveys—and particularly so for Indianapolis, as noted by NORC personnel who work there permanently.

But the fortunate thing is that this resistance appears to have been randomly distributed throughout the occupational (or class) structure of the SMSA. Noncooperation did not appear to be systematically linked to any particular social stratum or strata. Furthermore, refusals for the above complex of reasons (whether stated overtly or not) are not likely to be connected in either theoretical or substantive fashion to the kinds of issues being explored in our study. Had we been investigating political, educational, or social welfare questions, for instance, the issue of refusals for the above reasons would probably be more pertinent. Given the evident randomness of the refusals, and the apparent reasons for a large portion of them (those above the "modal" figure), it can be suggested that the refusals do not appear to bias seriously the patterning of relationships that emerged from the data.

Moreover, as Lenski notes in the Appendix to his Detroit Area Study, it is the patterning of relationships, within a large and meaningful theoretical context, that should command the major attention of social scientists.[9] For the fact is that in the foreseeable future we are going to have to live with less than ideal data-gathering and sampling techniques. Conditions beyond our control (such as those just described) will tend to affect us adversely. Given these inevitable drawbacks, we should nonetheless seek for "relationships among a goodly number of variables with comparable

[9] Gerhard Lenski, *The Religious Factor*, Garden City, New York: Doubleday Anchor Books, 1963, p. 369.

theoretical significance." [10] This has been the overriding "technique" followed throughout this study. Whatever weaknesses there are in any sample can at least begin to be compensated for by this kind of procedure. For example, our constant comparison of findings by *sex* constitutes an important check on the reliability of data in the particular substantive area in view. Likewise, our use of numerous indicants of economic articulation provided a further reliability check on emergent associations. Similarly, repetition of certain independent and intervening variables in connection with different dependent variables can be counted as additional evidence of reliability.

Furthermore, in this same vein, a word should be said regarding our use of significance tests. We wholly concur with Lenski:

> Tests of significance should be recognized for what they are: merely one of the tools available to social scientists to aid in the formation of judgments concerning the validity and generalizability of findings based on observations of samples. At best, tests of significance are a poor substitute for the test of *replication*.[11]

In short, we have sought to use the significance test simply as one additional tool (albeit a useful one) to assess our sample data with respect to its internal validity (relationships being other than chance), and also its external validity or generalizability.

In this latter connection, Lenski makes the point that comparison with the findings of other studies is crucial in determining the generalizability of one's own findings. This is, of course, a foundation stone of theory building. In this book, we have first built on the work that has gone before in order to construct an initial theoretical frame; and second, we have carried out constant comparison with other studies, in order to confirm generalizations, modify and/or extend them, and to indicate hypotheses for further exploration. Tests of significance, in short, were only one device or technique among many to aid in the attainment of the prime goal of this volume as stated in the preface, viz., to contribute to the development of systematic social theory.

10 *Ibid.*

11 *Ibid.*, p. 368. The significance test used most frequently throughout the study was the one-way analysis of variance. Its chief advantage over the *t* test for our purposes is, as Blalock notes, that "a single test may be used in place of many." Because of so many of the variables used in the analysis contained more than two categories, a series of *t* tests comparing several pairs at a time make meaningful interpretation extremely difficult. The *anova*, through comparisons of several categories simultaneously, overcomes this problem. See Hubert M. Blalock, Jr., *Social Statistics*, New York: McGraw-Hill Book Company, 1960, p. 252. Occasionally in the text, frequency tables were used when our interest was in proportions rather than in mean scores. In those instances, the χ^2 test was used.

Kish has argued that failure to have a simple random sample should make one extremely cautious in his use of the traditional types of significance tests.[12] Part of the problem, he argues, is that probability statements at the .05 or .10 level, for example, may actually reflect .10 or .20 situations or worse. It becomes especially acute if one's conclusions must rest on only one or two .05 statements. In this study, there are numerous relationships to support the basic theory, many of which attain the .01 level, and some go beyond to .001. The fact of numerous relationships that are significant at the .01 level and beyond at least begins to speak to the problem raised by Kish. By means of a kind of "internal replication" in which many relationships are (strongly) statistically significant, there is reasonable evidence that the findings are reliable, that they are other than random occurrences.

At the same time, however, Gold makes the telling point that even simple "random sampling is by no means a necessary criterion for establishing the validity of a proposition statistically expressed." Instead, he argues: "The validity we seek in social science research can come only from repeated observation under varying conditions of population." Of what use then is a significance test? It is "an index of reliability. . . . a preliminary screening that any hypothesis must pass to merit further investigation." Gold continues:

. . . A meaningful and useful interpretation can be given to a test of significance applied to any set of data, without regard to sampling considerations. A test of significance can be viewed as an attempt to fit observed data to a model. The model is that of a random process which, for a given set of data, can generate a sampling distribution of a statistic whose characteristics are known. A decision about the substantive significance or importance, *not statistical significance*, of an observed relationship can be made on the basis of the degree to which the model provides a good fit. In the absence of other explicit criteria, the degree of fit can be taken as an explicit minimum criterion which any relationship taken to be important must meet and which is superior to subjective variable judgments of importance." [13]

Therefore, as a "minimum criterion," the significance test becomes one means toward the goal of establishing a meaningful susbstantive and theoretical framework. It was in this sense that it was utilized here.

---

[12] Leslie Kish, "Confidence Intervals for Clustered Samples," *American Sociological Review*, 22 (April 1957), pp. 154–65.

[13] David Gold, "Statistical Tests and Substantive Significance," *The American Sociologist*, 4 (February 1969), p. 43.

Table 2-1

Objective Economic-Opportunity Integration and Companionship

Companionship Evaluation (Mean Scores)

SEI Ranking	HUSBANDS	WIVES
00–19	2.55 (109)	2.33 (116)
20–39	2.59 (112)	2.44 (125)
40–59	2.85 (83)	2.44 (100)
60–79	2.86 (88)	2.74 (114)
80–96	3.04 (23)	2.82 (39)
	df between groups = 4	df = 4 & 489
	df within groups = 410	$F = 2.92$ ($p < .05$)
	$F = 2.71$ ($p < .05$)	

Years of Education		
0–8	2.54 (83)	2.13 (68)
9–11	2.48 (86)	2.43 (115)
12	2.74 (133)	2.53 (200)
13–15	2.92 (54)	2.70 (64)
16+	3.04 (61)	2.89 (49)
	df = 4 & 412	df = 4 & 491
	$F = 4.35$ ($p < .01$)	$F = 4.03$ ($p < .01$)

Annual Income		
Poor	2.72 (86)	2.37 (135)
Fair	2.73 (115)	2.49 (120)
Good	2.68 (96)	2.59 (113)
High	2.72 (103)	2.55 (108)
	df = 3 & 396	df = 3 & 472
	$F = .04$ (n.s.)	$F = .92$ (n.s.)

Table 2-2

Wife Employment and Companionship

Companionship Evaluation (Mean Scores)

Is Wife Employed?	HUSBANDS	WIVES
Yes	2.64 (176)	2.45 (184)
No	2.75 (240)	2.54 (312)
	df = 1 & 414	df = 1 & 414
	$F = 1.23$ (n.s.)	$F = .70$ (n.s.)

208

Table 2-3

Wife's Occupational Level and Companionship

Companionship Evaluation (Mean Scores)

Wife's SEI	HUSBANDS	WIVES
Low	2.39 (81)	2.08 (80)
High	2.75 (89)	2.76 (100)
	df = 1 & 168	df = 1 & 178
	F = 6.70 (p < .01)	F = 16.67
		(p < .001)

Table 2-4

Alienation and Companionship

Companionship Evaluation (Mean Scores)

Degree of Perceived Powerlessness	HUSBANDS	WIVES
Low	2.80 (158)	2.67 (119)
Average	2.71 (221)	2.50 (296)
High	2.41 (34)	2.27 (76)
	df = 2 & 410	df = 2 & 488
	F = 2.27 (n.s.)	F = 2.86 (n.s.)
Degree of Discontent with Husband's Full-time Job		
Very discontent	2.37 (40)	2.02 (47)
Discontent	2.59 (134)	2.35 (151)
Content	2.76 (194)	2.60 (240)
Very Content	3.13 (51)	2.93 (59)
	df = 3 & 415	df = 3 & 493
	F = 5.80 (p < .001)	F = 7.41
		(p < .001)
Degree of Status Estrangement		
Low	2.88 (162)	2.65 (212)
Medium	2.73 (78)	2.52 (109)
High	2.56 (179)	2.34 (175)
	df = 2 & 416	df = 2 & 493
	F = 4.42 (p < .05)	F = 3.47 (p < .05)

Table 2-5

Anomie and Companionship

Companionship Evaluation (Mean Scores)

	HUSBANDS	WIVES
Level of Occupational Achievement Expectations for Husband		
Poor	2.21 (37)	2.10 (30)
Fair	2.57 (100)	2.36 (119)
Good	2.94 (143)	2.63 (172)
	df = 2 & 277	df = 2 & 318
	$F = 11.61$ $(p < .001)$	$F = 3.75$ $(p < .05)$
Level of Success Expectations		
Excellent	2.81 (108)	2.82 (131)
Fair	2.65 (189)	2.46 (234)
Somewhat limited	2.77 (68)	2.35 (79)
Very poor	2.50 (18)	1.68 (25)
	df = 3 & 379	df = 3 & 465
	$F = 1.05$ (n.s.)	$F = 9.52$ $(p < .001)$

Table 2-6

Occupational Status and Self-esteem

SEI Ranking	SELF-ESTEEM IN HUSBANDS				SELF-ESTEEM IN WIVES			
	Low	High	T	N	Low	High	T	N
00–19	64.2	35.8	100%	(109)	63.8	36.2	100%	(116)
20–39	54.5	45.5	100%	(112)	64.0	36.0	100%	(125)
40–59	49.4	50.6	100%	(83)	68.0	32.0	100%	(100)
60–79	39.8	60.2	100%	(88)	59.6	40.4	100%	(114)
80–96	52.2	47.8	100%	(23)	64.1	35.9	100%	(39)
	$\chi^2 = 12.2$ $(p < .05)$				$\chi^2 = 1.6$ (n.s.)			

Table 2-7

Economic Integration, Self-esteem, and Companionship

Companionship Evaluation (Mean Scores)

Years of Education	SELF-ESTEEM IN HUSBANDS		SELF-ESTEEM IN WIVES	
	Low	High	Low	High
0–8	2.50 (57)−	2.61 (26)+	1.94 (50)−	2.66 (18)+
9–11	2.28 (53)−	2.62 (32)+	2.30 (84)−	2.56 (30)+
12	2.59 (59)−	2.86 (74)+	2.33 (127)−	2.77 (72)+
13–15	2.81 (27)−	3.03 (27)+	2.73 (34)+	2.66 (30)−
16+	2.77 (22)−	3.05 (38)+	2.42 (21)−	3.25 (28)+
	df = 4 & 213	df = 4 & 192	df = 4 & 311	df = 4 & 173
	$F = 2.18$	$F = 2.07$	$F = 2.86$	$F = 2.52$
	(n.s.)	(n.s.)	($p < .05$)	($p < .05$)

Degree of Discontent with Husband's Full-time Job				
Very discontent	2.32 (34)−	2.66 (6)+	1.68 (32)−	2.73 (15)+
Discontent	2.41 (81)−	2.75 (52)+	2.27 (107)−	2.56 (44)+
Content	2.62 (90)−	2.83 (103)+	2.39 (148)−	2.80 (90)+
Very content	3.28 (14)+	3.08 (37)−	2.76 (30)−	3.10 (29)+
	df = 3 & 215	df = 3 & 194	df = 3 & 313	df = 3 & 174
	$F = 4.84$	$F = 1.33$	$F = 5.83$	$F = 2.05$
	($p < .01$)	(n.s.)	($p < .001$)	(n.s.)

Table 2-8

Economic Integration, Anomy, and Companionship

Companionship Evaluation (Mean Scores)

Years of Education	ANOMY IN HUSBANDS		ANOMY IN WIVES	
	Low	High	Low	High
0–8	2.73 (15)+	2.50 (68)−	2.25 (8)+	2.11 (60)−
9–11	2.60 (25)+	2.33 (60)−	2.60 (28)+	2.30 (86)−
12	2.87 (71)+	2.59 (62)−	2.57 (83)+	2.43 (116)−
13–15	2.88 (34)−	3.00 (20)+	2.89 (46)+	2.22 (18)−
16+	2.97 (41)−	2.81 (11)−	2.94 (38)+	2.72 (11)−
	df = 4 & 189	df = 4 & 216	df = 4 & 198	df = 4 & 286
	$F = .87$	$F = 2.73$	$F = 1.87$	$F = 1.32$
	(n.s.)	($p < .05$)	(n.s.)	(n.s.)

Table 2-8 (continued)

Companionship Evaluation (Mean Scores)

	ANOMY IN HUSBANDS		ANOMY IN WIVES	
Degree of Discontent with Husband's Full-time Job	Low	High	Low	High
Very discontent	2.50 (10)+	2.33 (30)−	2.18 (11)+	1.97 (36)−
Discontent	2.76 (50)+	2.42 (83)−	2.61 (39)+	2.26 (112)−
Content	2.85 (100)+	2.61 (93)−	2.73 (115)+	2.37 (123)−
Very content	3.11 (36)−	3.20 (15)+	2.86 (38)−	3.04 (21)+
	df = 3 & 192		df = 3 & 199	df = 3 & 288
	$F = 1.83$	$F = 4.40$	$F = 1.56$	$F = 4.78$
	(n.s.)	($p < .01$)	(n.s.)	($p = .01$)

Table 2-9

Economic Integration, Spouse Affiliativeness, and Companionship

Companionship Evaluation (Mean Scores)

	HUSBANDS		WIVES	

Perception of Whether Spouse Ranks Affiliativeness as Low or High

Years of Education	Low	High	Low	High
0–8	2.00 (36)−	2.95 (47)+	1.58 (39)−	2.86 (29)+
9–11	1.72 (44)−	3.14 (41)+	1.56 (50)−	3.01 (64)+
12	2.01 (55)−	3.25 (78)+	1.65 (79)−	3.05 (120)+
13–15	2.30 (20)−	3.29 (34)+	1.70 (20)−	3.23 (43)+
16+	2.45 (24)−	3.27 (36)+	1.80 (10)−	3.17 (39)+
	df = 4 & 174	df = 4 & 231	df = 4 & 193	df = 4 & 290
	$F = 3.86$	$F = 3.46$	$F = .21$	$F = 1.78$
	($p < .01$)	($p < .01$)	(n.s.)	(n.s.)
Degree of Discontent with Husband's Full-time Job				
Very-discontent	1.58 (17)−	2.95 (23)+	1.26 (26)−	2.95 (21)+
Discontent	1.79 (62)−	3.21 (71)+	1.56 (73)−	3.10 (78)+
Content	2.13 (81)−	3.16 (112)+	1.75 (87)−	3.02 (150)+
Very content	2.78 (19)−	3.34 (32)+	1.91 (12)−	3.19 (47)+
	df = 3 & 175	df = 3 & 234	df = 3 & 194	df = 3 & 292
	$F = 10.60$	$F = 2.62$	$F = 2.42$	$F = 1.02$
	($p < .001$)	(n.s.)	(n.s.)	(n.s.)

Table 2-10

Economic Integration, Life-style Evaluation, and Companionship

Companionship Evaluation (Mean Scores)

	HUSBANDS		WIVES	
		Satisfaction with Family Living Standard		
Years of Education	Low	High	Low	High
0–8	2.44 (59)–	2.79 (24)+	1.91 (47)–	2.61 (21)+
9–11	2.33 (57)–	2.57 (28)+	2.26 (87)–	2.74 (27)+
12	2.57 (71)–	2.93 (62)+	2.34 (118)–	2.71 (81)+
13–15	2.67 (31)–	3.26 (23)+	2.47 (34)–	2.96 (30)+
16+	2.80 (30)–	3.10 (30)+	2.72 (11)–	2.94 (38)+
	$df = 4$ & 243	$df = 4$ & 162	$df = 4$ & 292	$df = 4$ & 192
	$F = 1.72$	$F = 3.28$	$F = 2.15$	$F = .91$
	(n.s.)	($p < .05$)	(n.s.)	(n.s.)

Degree of Discontent with Husband's Full-time Job				
Very discontent	2.37 (29)=	2.36 (11)–	1.84 (38)–	2.77 (9)+
Discontent	2.45 (90)–	2.74 (43)+	2.24 (106)–	2.62 (45)+
Content	2.52 (108)–	3.00 (85)+	2.38 (135)–	2.76 (103)+
Very content	3.04 (22)–	3.20 (29)+	2.66 (18)–	3.04 (41)+
	$df = 3$ & 245	$df = 3$ & 164	$df = 3$ & 293	$df = 3$ & 194
	$F = 2.87$	$F = 4.57$	$F = 3.26$	$F = 1.68$
	($p < .05$)	($p < .01$)	($p < .05$)	(n.s.)

Table 2-11

Economic Integration, Wife Employment, and Companionship

Companionship Evaluation (Mean Scores)

	HUSBANDS		WIVES	
		Is Wife Employed?		
Years of Education	Yes	No	Yes	No
0–8	2.62 (43)+	2.45 (40)–	1.63 (22)–	2.35 (45)+
9–11	2.17 (34)–	2.56 (51)+	2.29 (44)–	2.42 (70)–
12	2.67 (59)–	2.80 (72)+	2.48 (82)–	2.50 (117)–
13–15	2.80 (25)–	3.03 (29)+	2.94 (17)+	2.61 (47)–
16+	3.00 (13)–	3.07 (47)+	3.21 (19)+	2.70 (30)–
	$df = 4$ & 169	$df = 4$ & 234	$df = 4$ & 179	$df = 4$ & 304
	$F = 3.06$	$F = 3.39$	$F = 6.60$	$F = .77$
	($p < .05$)	($p < .05$)	($p < .001$)	(n.s.)

Table 2-11 (continued)

Companionship Evaluation (Mean Scores)

	HUSBANDS		WIVES	
	Is Wife Employed?			
Degree of Discontent with Husband's Full-time Job				
	Yes	No	Yes	No
Very discontent	2.22 (22)−	2.55 (18)+	2.04 (21)+	2.00 (26)−
Discontent	2.55 (58)−	2.54 (73)−	2.38 (73)+	2.33 (78)−
Content	2.64 (74)−	2.78 (119)+	2.62 (79)+	2.54 (158)−
Very content	3.04 (21)−	3.20 (30)+	3.00 (11)+	2.91 (48)−
	df = 3 & 171	df = 3 & 236	df = 3 & 180	df = 3 & 306
	F = 3.21	F = 4.78	F = 2.05	F = 6.04
	(p < .05)	(p < .01)	(n.s.)	(p < .001)

Table 2-12

Economic Integration, Length of Marriage, and Companionship

Companionship Evaluation (Mean Scores)

	HUSBANDS		WIVES	
	Length of Marriage			
Years of Education	Young	Mature	Young	Mature
0–8	2.61 (21)+	2.51 (62)−	1.95 (23)−	2.22 (45)+
9–11	2.36 (46)−	2.47 (38)−	2.27 (62)−	2.50 (52)+
12	2.63 (72)−	2.86 (61)+	2.48 (116)−	2.51 (83)−
13–15	2.96 (28)+	2.88 (26)−	2.71 (38)+	2.69 (26)−
16+	3.00 (31)−	2.89 (29)−	3.12 (25)+	2.66 (24)−
	df = 4 & 193	df = 4 & 211	df = 4 & 259	df = 4 & 225
	F = 2.93	F = 2.99	F = 4.75	F = 1.22
	(p < .05)	(p < .05)	(p < .001)	(n.s.)
Degree of Discontent with Husband's Full-time Job				
Very discontent	2.40 (22)+	2.35 (17)−	2.01 (27)−	2.03 (20)+
Discontent	2.55 (70)−	2.53 (63)−	2.29 (87)−	2.43 (64)+
Content	2.75 (84)−	2.72 (109)−	2.57 (119)−	2.52 (119)−
Very content	3.04 (23)−	3.21 (28)+	3.03 (32)+	2.81 (27)−
	df = 3 & 195	df = 3 & 213	df = 3 & 261	df = 3 & 226
	F = 2.35	F = 5.89	F = 5.63	F = 2.60
	(n.s.)	(p < .001)	(p < .001)	(n.s.)

Table 3-1

Objective Economic-Opportunity Integration and Physical Affect

Affect Evaluation (Mean Scores)

Husband's SEI Ranking	HUSBANDS	WIVES
00–19	2.71 (109)	2.48 (114)
20–39	2.79 (112)	2.74 (124)
40–59	2.86 (83)	2.65 (100)
60–79	2.92 (88)	3.07 (114)
80–96	3.17 (23)	2.94 (39)
	df = 4 & 410	df = 4 & 486
	$F = 1.08$ (n.s.)	$F = 5.20$
		$(p < .001)$
Years of Education		
0–8	2.59 (83)	2.31 (67)
9–11	2.63 (86)	2.58 (114)
12	2.97 (133)	2.81 (200)
13–15	2.90 (54)	3.06 (63)
16+	3.04 (51)	3.10 (49)
	df = 4 & 412	df = 4 & 488
	$F = 3.03$ $(p < .05)$	$F = 6.76$
		$(p < .001)$
Annual Income		
Poor	2.89 (86)	2.53 (135)
Fair	2.85 (115)	2.73 (119)
Good	2.71 (96)	2.91 (113)
High	2.85 (103)	2.85 (107)
	df = 3 & 396	df = 3 & 470
	$F = .50$ (n.s.)	$F = 3.33$ $(p < .05)$

Table 3-2

Wife Employment and Physical Affect

Affect Evaluation (Mean Scores)

Is Wife Employed?	HUSBANDS	WIVES
Yes	2.69 (176)	2.78 (183)
No	2.90 (240)	2.73 (310)
	df = 1 & 414	df = 1 & 491
	$F = 3.80$ (n.s.)	$F = .18$ (n.s.)

Table 3-3

Wife's Occupational Level and Physical Affect

Affect Evaluation (Mean Scores)

Wife's SEI	HUSBANDS	WIVES
Low	2.53 (81)	2.50 (78)
High	2.78 (89)	2.89 (100)
	df = 1 & 168	df = 1 & 176
	F = 2.92 (n.s.)	F = 7.36 (p < .01)

Table 3-4

Alienation and Physical Affect

Affect Evaluation (Mean Scores)

Degree of Perceived Powerlessness	HUSBANDS	WIVES
Low	2.97 (158)	2.94 (118)
Average	2.84 (221)	2.75 (294)
High	2.20 (34)	2.40 (76)
	df = 2 & 410	df = 2 & 485
	F = 7.32 (p < .001)	F = 6.18 (p < .01)
Degree of Discontent with Husband's Full-time Job		
Very discontent	2.50 (40)	2.17 (47)
Discontent	2.68 (134)	2.54 (149)
Content	2.92 (194)	2.89 (239)
Very content	3.15 (51)	3.15 (59)
	df = 3 & 415	df = 3 & 490
	F = 4.11 (p < .05)	F = 12.09 (p < .001)
Degree of Status Estrangement		
Low	3.00 (162)	2.93 (212)
Medium	2.88 (78)	2.69 (108)
High	2.65 (179)	2.57 (173)
	df = 2 & 416	df = 2 & 490
	F = 4.52 (p < .05)	F = 5.92 (p < .01)

216

Table 3-5

Anomie and Physical Affect

Affect Evaluation (Mean Scores)

Level of Occu-pational Achieve-ment Expectations for Husband	HUSBANDS	WIVES
Poor	2.27 (37)	2.03 (29)
Fair	2.60 (100)	2.66 (119)
Good	3.06 (143)	2.97 (171)
	df = 2 & 277	df = 2 & 316
	$F = 14.62$ $(p < .001)$	$F = 14.92$ $(p < .001)$

Level of Success Expectations		
Excellent	3.01 (108)	3.10 (131)
Fair	2.73 (189)	2.68 (232)
Somewhat limited	2.67 (68)	2.56 (79)
Very poor	2.61 (18)	1.72 (25)
	df = 3 & 379	df = 3 & 463
	$F = 2.75$ $(p < .05)$	$F = 15.58$ $(p < .001)$

Table 3-6

Economic Integration, Self-esteem, and Physical Affect

Affect Evaluation (Mean Scores)

Husband's SEI Ranking	SELF-ESTEEM IN HUSBANDS		SELF-ESTEEM IN WIVES	
	Low	High	Low	High
00–19	2.61 (70)−	2.73 (38)+	2.35 (74)−	2.59 (42)+
20–39	2.40 (59)−	3.00 (51)+	2.63 (80)−	2.72 (44)−
40–59	2.52 (40)−	3.04 (42)+	2.50 (68)−	2.96 (32)+
60–79	2.71 (35)−	3.05 (53)+	2.72 (68)−	3.36 (44)+
80–96	3.08 (12)−	3.27 (11)+	2.88 (25)−	3.07 (14)+
	df = 4 & 211	df = 4 & 190	df = 4 & 310	df = 4 & 171
	$F = 1.57$	$F = 1.48$	$F = 2.06$	$F = 5.52$
	(n.s.)	(n.s.)	(n.s.)	$(p < .001)$

Table 3-6 (continued)

Affect Evaluation (Mean Scores)

Degree of Status Es- trangement	SELF-ESTEEM IN HUSBANDS		SELF-ESTEEM IN WIVES	
	Low	High	Low	High
Low	2.70 (65)−	3.14 (96)+	2.74 (127)−	3.15 (84)+
Medium	2.65 (40)−	2.80 (36)−	2.63 (76)−	2.75 (33)+
High	2.47 (113)−	2.87 (65)+	2.35 (114)−	2.69 (59)+
	$df = 2$ & 215	$df = 2$ & 194	$df = 2$ & 314	$df = 2$ & 173
	$F = 1.34$	$F = 3.58$	$F = 4.54$	$F = 5.93$
	(n.s.)	($p < .05$)	($p < .05$)	($p < .01$)

Table 3-7

Economic Integration, Anomy, and Physical Affect

Affect Evaluation (Mean Scores)

Husband's SEI Ranking	ANOMY IN HUSBANDS		ANOMY IN WIVES	
	Low	High	Low	High
0–19	3.05 (34)+	2.47 (74)−	2.80 (30)+	2.31 (86)−
20–39	3.13 (37)+	2.45 (73)−	2.92 (39)+	2.55 (85)−
40–59	2.78 (31)−	2.80 (41)−	2.89 (38)+	2.50 (62)−
60–79	2.96 (41)+	2.81 (27)−	3.11 (69)+	2.74 (43)−
80–96	3.14 (21)−	3.50 (2)+	2.92 (26)−	3.00 (13)+
	$df = 4$ & 189	$df = 4$ & 212	$df = 4$ & 197	$df = 4$ & 284
	$F = 1.22$	$F = 2.15$	$F = .98$	$F = 2.17$
	(n.s.)	(n.s.)	(n.s.)	(n.s.)
Degree of Status Es- trangement				
Low	3.01 (104)+	2.87 (57)−	3.05 (115)+	2.72 (96)−
Medium	2.80 (35)−	2.65 (41)−	2.89 (47)+	2.50 (62)−
High	3.03 (57)+	2.42 (121)−	2.79 (39)+	2.38 (134)−
	$df = 2$ & 193	$df = 2$ & 216	$df = 2$ & 198	$df = 2$ & 289
	$F = 1.07$	$F = 4.77$	$F = 1.65$	$F = 3.31$
	(n.s.)	$p < .01$)	(n.s.)	($p < .05$)

Table 3-8

Economic Integration, Spouse Affect, and Respondent Affect

Affect Evaluation (Mean Scores)

	HUSBANDS		WIVES	
	Perception of Whether Spouse Ranks Physical Affect as Low or High			
Husband's SEI Ranking	Low	High	Low	High
0–19	1.97 (47)−	3.18 (61)+	1.66 (54)−	3.11 (62)+
20–39	1.93 (43)−	3.16 (67)+	1.96 (50)−	3.18 (72)+
40–59	2.00 (30)−	3.30 (50)+	2.06 (45)−	3.12 (54)+
60–79	2.33 (33)−	3.27 (55)+	2.10 (30)−	3.29 (81)+
80–96	3.00 (8)−	3.26 (15)+	2.30 (10)−	3.17 (29)+
	df = 4 & 156	df = 4 & 243	df = 4 & 184	df = 4 & 293
	$F = 3.32$	$F = .67$	$F = 1.83$	$F = 1.09$
	$(p < .05)$	(n.s.)	(n.s.)	(n.s.)
Degree of Status Estrangement				
Low	2.37 (54)−	3.28 (106)+	2.00 (65)−	3.31 (145)+
Medium	1.96 (28)−	3.16 (48)+	2.12 (48)−	3.11 (60)+
High	1.95 (81)−	3.19 (96)+	1.75 (76)−	3.05 (95)+
	df = 2 & 160	df = 2 & 247	df = 2 & 186	df = 2 & 297
	$F = 3.87$	$F = .98$	$F = 2.46$	$F = 6.39$
	$(p < .05)$	(n.s.)	(n.s.)	$(p < .01)$

Table 3-9

Economic Integration, Life-style Evaluation, and Physical Affect

Affect Evaluation (Mean Scores)

	HUSBANDS		WIVES	
	Satisfaction with Family Living Standard			
Husband's SEI Ranking	Low	High	Low	High
0–19	2.46 (81)−	3.22 (27)+	2.31 (93)−	2.95 (23)+
20–39	2.44 (65)−	3.02 (45)+	2.50 (78)−	2.95 (46)+
40–59	2.65 (43)−	2.94 (39)+	2.40 (60)−	3.02 (40)+
60–79	2.86 (46)−	2.97 (42)+	2.72 (44)−	3.13 (68)+
80–96	3.08 (12)−	3.27 (11)+	2.94 (19)=	2.95 (20)+
	df = 4 & 242	df = 4 & 159	df = 4 & 289	df = 4 & 192
	$F = 2.74$	$F = .79$	$F = 2.55$	$F = .43$
	$(p < .05)$	(n.s.)	$(p < .05)$	(n.s.)

Table 3-9 (continued)

Affect Evaluation (Mean Scores)

	HUSBANDS		*WIVES*	
	Satisfaction with Family Living Standard			
Degree of Status-Es-trangement	*Low*	*High*	*Low*	*High*
Low	2.73 (69)—	3.14 (92)+	2.60 (96)—	3.15 (115)+
Medium	2.61 (52)—	2.95 (24)+	2.52 (70)—	2.92 (39)+
High	2.50 (127)—	2.92 (51)+	2.35 (129)—	2.81 (44)+
	df = 2 & 245	df = 2 & 164	df = 2 & 292	df = 2 & 195
	F = 1.45	F = 1.45	F = 1.82	F = 3.13
	(n.s.)	(n.s.)	(n.s.)	(p < .05)

Table 3-10

Economic Integration, Wife Employment, and Physical Affect

Affect Evaluation (Mean Scores)

	HUSBANDS		*WIVES*	
	Is Wife Employed?			
Husband's SEI Ranking	*Yes*	*No*	*Yes*	*No*
00–19	2.60 (56)—	2.70 (52)—	2.50 (53)+	2.38 (63)—
20–39	2.64 (48)—	2.70 (62)—	2.78 (50)+	2.59 (74)—
40–59	2.57 (40)—	2.95 (40)+	2.68 (39)+	2.63 (61)—
60–79	2.88 (25)—	2.93 (63)+	3.08 (31)+	2.93 (81)—
80–96	3.11 (5)—	3.40 (18)+	2.92 (8)—	3.03 (30)+
	df = 4 & 169	df = 4 & 230	df = 4 & 176	df = 4 & 304
	F = 1.17	F = 1.53	F = 1.74	F = 4.28
	(n.s.)	(n.s.)	(n.s.)	(p < .01)
Degree of Status Es-trangement				
Low	2.81 (59)—	3.04 (101)+	2.98 (71)+	2.86 (139)—
Medium	2.66 (33)—	2.90 (42)+	2.67 (31)—	2.66 (78)—
High	2.55 (83)—	2.63 (95)—	2.44 (79)—	2.50 (94)—
	df = 2 & 172	df = 2 & 235	df = 2 & 178	df = 2 & 308
	F = 1.22	F = 5.27	F = 5.87	F = 4.16
	(n.s.)	(p < .01)	(p < .01)	(p < .05)

Table 3-11

Economic Integration, Length of Marriage, and Physical Affect

Affect Evaluation (Mean Scores)

	HUSBANDS		WIVES	
		Length of	Marriage	
Husband's SEI Ranking	Young	Mature	Young	Mature
00–19	2.71 (52)=	2.61 (55)−	2.55 (58)+	2.32 (58)−
20–39	2.80 (49)+	2.72 (61)−	2.76 (75)+	2.67 (49)−
40–59	3.00 (42)+	2.57 (40)−	2.60 (53)−	2.70 (47)+
60–79	2.97 (38)+	2.88 (50)−	3.11 (52)+	2.85 (60)−
80–96	3.12 (16)−	3.28 (7)+	2.96 (26)+	2.92 (13)−
	$df = 4 \& 192$	$df = 4 \& 208$	$df = 4 \& 259$	$df = 4 \& 222$
	$F = 1.96$	$F = 1.47$	$F = 3.06$	$F = 2.88$
	(n.s.)	(n.s.)	$(p < .05)$	$(p < .05)$
Degree of Status Estrangement				
Low	2.94 (76)−	2.98 (85)−	2.97 (107)+	2.83 (104)−
Medium	2.94 (34)+	2.54 (42)−	2.73 (65)+	2.56 (44)−
High	2.71 (89)+	2.53 (88)−	2.48 (93)−	2.46 (80)−
	$df = 2 \& 196$	$df = 2 \& 212$	$df = 2 \& 262$	$df = 2 \& 225$
	$F = 1.62$	$F = 6.43$	$F = 6.00$	$F = 4.04$
	(n.s.)	$(p < .01)$	$(p < .01)$	$(p < .05)$

Table 4-1

Objective Economic-Opportunity Integration and Empathy

Empathy Evaluation (Mean Scores)

SEI Ranking	HUSBANDS	WIVES
00–19	5.07 (109)	4.56 (116)
20–39	5.25 (112)	4.89 (125)
40–59	5.43 (83)	5.09 (100)
60–79	5.65 (88)	5.40 (114)
80–96	5.95 (23)	5.38 (39)
	$df = 4 \& 410$	$df = 4 \& 489$
	$F = 2.79 \ (p < .05)$	$F = 3.90 \ (p < .01)$

Table 4-1 (continued)

Empathy Evaluation (Mean Scores)

	HUSBANDS	WIVES
Years of Education		
0–8	5.02 (83)	4.22 (68)
9–11	4.84 (86)	4.73 (115)
12	5.66 (133)	5.15 (200)
13–15	5.68 (54)	5.37 (64)
16+	5.62 (51)	5.71 (49)
	df = 4 & 412	df = 4 & 491
	F = 5.90 (p < .001)	F = 7.29 (p < .001)
Annual Income		
Poor	5.10 (86)	4.60 (135)
Fair	5.44 (115)	4.97 (120)
Good	5.22 (96)	5.15 (113)
High	5.65 (103)	5.31 (108)
	df = 3 & 396	df = 3 & 472
	F = 2.28 (n.s.)	F = 3.70 (p < .05)

Table 4-2

Alienation and Empathy

Empathy Evaluation (Mean Scores)

Degree of Perceived Powerlessness	HUSBANDS	WIVES
Low	5.55 (158)	5.30 (119)
Average	5.40 (221)	5.05 (296)
High	4.35 (34)	4.30 (76)
	df = 2 & 410	df = 2 & 488
	F = 8.60 (p < .001)	F = 7.84 (p < .001)
Degree of Discontent with Husband's Full-time Job		
Very discontent	4.77 (40)	4.00 (47)
Discontent	5.11 (134)	4.66 (151)
Content	5.50 (194)	5.20 (240)
Very content	6.01 (51)	5.86 (59)

Empathy Evaluation (Mean Scores)

Degree of Discontent with Husband's Full-time Job	HUSBANDS	WIVES
	df = 3 & 415	df = 3 & 493
	F = 6.83 (p < .001)	F = 13.39
		(p < .001)

Degree of Status Estrangement		
Low	5.64 (162)	5.35 (212)
Medium	5.44 (78)	4.90 (109)
High	5.09 (179)	4.64 (175)
	df = 2 & 416	df = 2 & 493
	F = 5.60 (p < .01)	F = 810
		(p < .001)

Table 4-3

Anomie and Empathy

Empathy Evaluation (Mean Scores)

Level of Occupational Achievement Expectations for Husband	HUSBANDS	WIVES
Poor	4.54 (37)	3.53 (30)
Fair	5.14 (100)	4.66 (119)
Good	5.76 (143)	5.44 (172)
	df = 2 & 277	df = 2 & 318
	F = 11.18 (p < .001)	F = 19.43
		(p < .001)

Level of Success Expectations		
Excellent	5.97 (108)	5.72 (131)
Fair	5.23 (189)	4.83 (234)
Somewhat limited	5.01 (68)	4.44 (79)
Very poor	4.94 (18)	3.52 (25)
	df = 3 & 379	df = 3 & 465
	F = 7.63 (p < .001)	F = 17.47
		(p < .001)

223

Table 4-4

Percentage by Sex of Reported High Expressiveness

Years of Education	High Companionship			High Physical Affect			High Empathy		
	Husbands	Wives	(H>W)	Husbands	Wives	(H>W)	Husbands	Wives	(H>W)
0–8	55.4	42.6	12.8	57.8	43.9	13.9	47.7	32.8	14.9
9–11	57.9	55.3	2.6	64.3	61.9	2.4	57.1	45.6	11.5
12	71.4	62.3	9.1	79.5	72.4	7.1	59.0	49.0	10.0
13–15	73.3	69.2	4.1	85.7	85.2	0.5	64.8	56.6	8.2
16+	81.7	79.6	2.1	80.3	83.7	3.4	69.3	63.3	6.0
						W>H			

Table 4-5

Wife Employment and Empathy

	Empathy Evaluation (Mean Scores)	
Is Wife Employed?	HUSBANDS	WIVES
Yes	5.25 (176)	4.95 (184)
No	5.47 (240)	5.03 (312)
	df = 1 & 414	df = 1 & 494
	F = 2.04 (n.s.)	F = 2.77 (n.s.)

Table 4-6

Wife's Occupational Level and Empathy

	Empathy Evaluation (Mean Scores)	
Wife's SEI	HUSBANDS	WIVES
Low	5.00 (82)	4.33 (80)
High	5.37 (89)	5.50 (100)
	df = 1 & 169	df = 1 & 178
	F = 2.31 (n.s.)	F = 18.92
		(p < .001)

Table 4-7

Economic Integration, Self-esteem, and Empathy

Empathy Evaluation (Mean Scores)

	HUSBANDS		WIVES	
	Level of Self-esteem			
Years of Education	Low	High	Low	High
0–8	4.53 (57)–	5.23 (26)+	3.88 (50)–	5.16 (18)+
9–11	4.60 (54)–	5.37 (32)+	4.70 (84)–	4.80 (31)+
12	5.44 (59)–	5.85 (74)+	4.89 (128)–	5.59 (72)+
13–15	5.14 (27)–	6.22 (27)+	5.44 (34)+	5.30 (30)–
16+	5.60 (23)–	5.63 (38)+	4.90 (21)–	6.42 (28)+
	df = 4 & 215	d = 4 & 192	df = 4 & 312	df = 4 & 174
	F = 2.96	F = 2.55	F = 4.11	F = 5.76
	(p < .05)	(p < .05)	(p < .01)	(p < .001)
Level of Success Expectations				
Excellent	5.48 (35)–	6.20 (73)+	5.54 (72)–	5.94 (59)+
Fair	5.03 (103)–	5.46 (86)+	4.67 (155)–	5.13 (79)+
Somewhat limited	4.81 (43)–	5.36 (25)+	3.82 (51)–	5.57 (28)+
Very poor	4.86 (15)–	5.33 (3)+	3.36 (22)–	4.66 (3)+
	df = 3 & 192	df = 3 & 183	df = 3 & 296	df = 3 & 165
	F = 1.11	F = 4.94	F = 13.24	F = 4.11
	(n.s.)	(p < .01)	(p < .001)	(p < .01)

Table 4-8

Economic Integration, Anomy, and Empathy

Empathy Evaluation (Mean Scores)

	HUSBANDS		WIVES	
	Level of Anomy			
Years of Education	Low	High	Low	High
0–8	5.46 (15)+	4.92 (68)–	4.37 (8)+	4.20 (60)–
9–11	5.40 (25)+	4.62 (61)–	5.75 (28)+	4.40 (87)–
12	5.88 (71)+	5.41 (62)–	5.27 (83)+	5.05 (117)–
13–15	5.79 (34)+	5.50 (20)–	5.63 (46)+	4.72 (18)–
16+	5.75 (49)+	5.08 (12)–	5.97 (38)+	4.81 (11)–

Table 4-8 (continued)

Empathy Evaluation (Mean Scores)

	HUSBANDS		WIVES	
		Level of Anomy		
	Low	High	Low	High
	df = 4 & 189	df = 4 & 218	df = 4 & 198	df = 4 & 288
	$F = .75$	$F = 2.35$	$F = 2.69$	$F = 2.82$
	(n.s.)	(n.s.)	$(p < .05)$	$(p < .05)$
Level of Success Expectations				
Excellent	5.98 (74)+	5.95 (34)−	5.75 (80)+	5.68 (51)−
Fair	5.70 (90)+	4.80 (99)−	5.21 (85)+	4.61 (149)−
Somewhat limited	5.50 (20)+	4.81 (48)−	5.50 (26)+	3.92 (53)−
Very poor	5.25 (4)+	4.57 (14)−	4.00 (2)+	3.47 (23)−
	df = 3 & 184	df = 3 & 191	df = 3 & 189	df = 3 & 272
	$F = .86$	$F = 5.74$	$F = 2.26$	$F = 12.14$
	(n.s.)	$(p < .001)$	$(p < .05)$	$(p < .001)$

Table 4-9

Economic Integration, Spouse Empathy, and Respondent Empathy

Empathy Evaluation (Mean Scores)

	HUSBANDS		WIVES	
		Perception of Whether Spouse Ranks Empathy as Low or High		
Years of Education	Low	High	Low	High
0–8	4.00 (37)−	5.84 (46)+	3.42 (40)−	5.35 (28)+
9–11	3.45 (35)−	5.80 (51)+	3.62 (56)−	5.77 (59)+
12	4.26 (45)−	6.19 (88)+	3.73 (68)−	5.87 (132)+
13–15	3.92 (13)−	6.24 (41)+	4.37 (16)−	5.70 (48)+
16+	4.64 (19)−	6.23 (42)+	4.21 (14)−	6.31 (35)+
	df = 4 & 144	df = 4 & 263	df = 4 & 189	df = 4 & 297
	$F = 3.38$	$F = 2.25$	$F = 1.25$	$F = 2.42$
	$(p < .01)$	(n.s.)	(n.s.)	$(p < .05)$

Empathy Evaluation (Mean Scores)

	HUSBANDS		WIVES	

Perception of Whether Spouse Ranks Empathy as Low or High

Level of Success Expectations	Low	High	Low	High
Excellent	5.05 (34)−	6.39 (74)+	4.43 (32)−	6.14 (97)+
Fair	4.37 (80)−	5.86 (109)+	3.87 (93)−	5.51 (138)+
Somewhat limited	4.13 (30)−	5.83 (36)+	3.55 (34)−	5.09 (44)+
Very poor	3.14 (7)−	5.09 (11)+	3.11 (18)−	4.57 (7)+
	df = 3 & 147	df = 3 & 226	df = 3 & 173	df = 3 & 282
	$F = 3.81$	$F = 3.45$	$F = 2.26$	$F = 9.74$
	($p < .01$)	($p < .05$)	(n.s.)	($p < .001$)

Table 4-10

Economic Integration, Life-Style Evaluation, and Empathy

Empathy Evaluation (Mean Scores)

	HUSBANDS		WIVES	

Satisfaction with Family Living Standard

Years of Education	Low	High	Low	High
0–8	4.72 (59)−	5.75 (24)+	3.76 (47)−	5.23 (21)+
9–11	4.44 (58)−	5.67 (28)+	4.47 (87)−	5.59 (27)+
12	5.22 (71)−	6.17 (62)+	4.76 (118)−	5.70 (82)+
13–15	5.29 (31)−	6.21 (23)+	4.76 (34)−	6.06 (30)+
16+	5.12 (31)−	6.13 (30)+	5.00 (11)−	5.92 (38)+
	df = 4 & 245	df = 4 & 162	df = 4 & 292	df = 4 & 193
	$F = 2.67$	$F = 1.41$	$F = 3.18$	$F = 1.07$
	($p < .05$)	(n.s.)	($p < .05$)	(n.s.)

Level of Success Expectations				
Excellent	5.57 (54)−	6.37 (54)+	5.01 (53)−	6.20 (78)+
Fair	4.80 (119)−	5.95 (70)+	4.53 (149)−	5.35 (85)+
Somewhat limited	4.61 (44)−	5.75 (24)+	4.24 (62)−	5.17 (17)+
Very poor	4.57 (14)−	5.25 (4)+	3.39 (23)−	5.00 (2)+
	df = 3 & 227	df = 3 & 148	df = 3 & 283	df = 3 & 178
	$F = 3.88$	$F = 2.00$	$F = 5.26$	$F = 4.93$
	($p < .01$)	(n.s.)	($p < .01$)	($p < .01$)

Table 4-11

Economic Integration, Wife Employment, and Empathy

Empathy Evaluation (Mean Scores)

	HUSBANDS		WIVES	
		Is Wife Employed?		
Years of Education	Yes	No	Yes	No
0–8	5.20 (43)+	4.82 (40)−	3.77 (22)−	4.42 (45)+
9–11	4.45 (35)−	5.11 (51)+	4.56 (44)−	4.83 (71)+
12	5.61 (59)−	5.72 (72)+	5.10 (82)−	5.17 (118)+
13–15	5.40 (25)−	5.93 (29)+	5.52 (17)+	5.31 (47)−
16+	5.53 (13)−	5.68 (47)+	6.00 (19)+	5.53 (30)−
	df = 4 & 170	df = 4 & 234	df = 4 & 179	df = 4 & 306
	F = 3.18	F = 4.09	F = 4.98	F = 2.90
	(p < .05)	(p < .01)	(p < .001)	(p < .05)
Level of Success Expectations				
Excellent	5.96 (39)−	5.99 (69)+	5.89 (49)+	5.62 (82)−
Fair	5.02 (83)−	5.40 (105)+	4.87 (89)+	4.80 (145)−
Somewhat limited	5.14 (35)+	4.84 (32)−	4.41 (33)−	4.37 (45)−
Very poor	5.08 (12)+	4.66 (6)−	3.28 (7)+	3.61 (18)+
	df = 3 & 165	df = 3 & 208	df = 3 & 174	df = 3 & 286
	F = 3.39	F = 4.93	F = 7.77	F = 10.22
	(p < .05)	(p < .01)	(p < .001)	(p < .001)

Table 4-12

Economic Integration, Length of Marriage, and Empathy

Empathy Evaluation (Mean Scores)

	HUSBANDS		WIVES	
		Length of Marriage		
Years of Education	Young	Mature	Young	Mature
0–8	4.95 (21)−	5.04 (62)+	3.91 (23)−	4.37 (45)+
9–11	4.72 (47)−	5.02 (38)+	4.71 (62)−	4.77 (53)+
12	5.55 (72)−	5.80 (61)+	5.02 (117)−	5.32 (83)+
13–15	5.42 (28)−	5.96 (26)+	5.21 (38)−	5.61 (26)+
16+	5.67 (31)+	5.56 (30)−	6.00 (25)+	5.41 (24)−
	df = 4 & 194	df = 4 & 212	df = 4 & 260	df = 4 & 226
	F = 2.51	F = 4.12	F = 4.27	F = 4.25
	(p < .05)	(p < .01)	(p < .01)	(p < .01)

Empathy Evaluation (Mean Scores)

	HUSBANDS		WIVES	
		Length of Marriage		
Level of Success Expectations	*Young*	*Mature*	*Young*	*Mature*
Excellent	5.87 (64)—	6.11 (44)+	5.64 (88)—	5.88 (43)+
Fair	5.05 (107)—	5.46 (82)+	4.79 (134)—	4.88 (100)+
Somewhat limited	4.85 (21)—	5.10 (46)+	4.40 (32)—	4.46 (47)+
Very poor	4.80 (5)—	5.00 (13)+	2.66 (9)—	4.00 (16)+
	df = 3 & 193	df = 3 & 181	df = 3 & 259	df = 3 & 202
	$F = 3.99$	$F = 4.52$	$F = 10.69$	$F = 8.14$
	$(p < .01)$	$(p < .01)$	$(p < .001)$	$(p < .001)$

Table 5-1

Objective Economic-Opportunity Integration and Hostility Toward Spouse

Level of Hostility (Mean Scores)

Husband's SEI Ranking	HUSBANDS	WIVES
00–19	4.25 (109)	4.94 (116)
20–39	3.41 (112)	4.60 (125)
40–59	3.19 (83)	4.51 (100)
60–79	2.75 (88)	2.86 (114)
80–96	2.47 (23)	3.23 (39)
	df = 4 & 410	df = 4 & 489
	$F = 2.28 \ (p < .05)$	$F = 3.61 \ (p < .01)$
Years of Education		
0–8	2.83 (83)	5.50 (68)
9–11	4.76 (86)	5.15 (115)
12	3.51 (133)	3.99 (200)
13–15	2.51 (54)	3.17 (64)
16+	2.80 (61)	2.28 (49)
	df = 4 & 412	df = 4 & 491
	$F = 4.20 \ (p < .01)$	$F = 5.14$
		$(p < .001)$

Table 5-1 (continued)

Level of Hostility (Mean Scores)

Annual Income	HUSBANDS	WIVES
Poor	4.39 (86)	5.37 (135)
Fair	3.01 (115)	4.26 (120)
Good	3.60 (96)	3.41 (113)
High	2.80 (103)	3.35 (108)
	df = 3 & 396	df = 3 & 472
	F = 3.12 (p < .05)	F = 5.13 (p < .01)

Table 5-2

Alienation and Hostility Toward Spouse

Level of Hostility (Mean Scores)

Degree of Perceived Powerlessness	HUSBANDS	WIVES
Low	3.23 (158)	3.80 (119)
Average	3.41 (221)	3.85 (296)
High	4.14 (34)	6.14 (76)
	df = 2 & 410	df = 2 & 488
	F = .74 (n.s.)	F = 7.24 (p < .001)

Degree of Discontent with Husband's Full-time Job		
Very discontent	4.35 (40)	6.78 (47)
Discontent	3.61 (134)	4.94 (151)
Content	3.43 (194)	3.57 (240)
Very content	1.92 (51)	2.64 (59)
	df = 3 & 415	df = 3 & 493
	F = 3.37 (p < .01)	F = 9.30 (p < .001)

Degree of Status Estrangement		
Low	3.09 (162)	2.86 (212)
Medium	3.47 (78)	4.44 (109)
High	3.64 (179)	5.63 (175)
	df = 2 & 416	df = 2 & 493
	F = .84 (n.s.)	F = 16.51 (p < .001)

230

Table 5-3

Anomie and Hostility Toward Spouse

Level of Hostility (Mean Scores)

Level of Occupational Achievement Expectations for Husband	HUSBANDS	WIVES
Poor	4.70 (37)	7.40 (30)
Fair	3.24 (100)	4.78 (119)
Good	3.03 (143)	3.54 (172)
	df = 2 & 277	df = 2 & 318
	F = 3.46 ($p < .05$)	F = 8.42 ($p < .001$)

Level of Success Expectations		
Excellent	2.95 (108)	3.17 (131)
Fair	3.26 (189)	4.20 (234)
Somewhat limited	3.80 (68)	4.83 (79)
Very poor	4.16 (18)	8.24 (25)
	df = 3 & 379	df = 3 & 465
	F = 1.12 (n.s.)	F = 8.49 ($p < .001$)

Table 5-4

Economic-Opportunity Integration, Self-esteem, and Hostility

Hostility Levels (Mean Scores)

Years of Education	SELF-ESTEEM IN HUSBANDS		SELF-ESTEEM IN WIVES	
	Low	High	Low	High
0–8	2.93 (43)+	2.72 (40)−	7.77 (22)+	4.46 (45)−
9–11	5.14 (35)+	4.50 (51)−	5.02 (44)−	5.23 (71)+
12	3.64 (59)+	3.47 (72)−	4.41 (82)+	3.69 (118)−
13–15	2.92 (25)+	2.17 (29)−	3.29 (17)+	3.12 (47)−
16+	1.92 (13)−	2.51 (47)−	3.10 (19)+	1.76 (30)−
	df = 4 & 170	df = 4 & 234	df = 4 & 179	df = 4 & 306
	F = 3.02	F = 2.64	F = 3.03	F = 3.55
	($p < .05$)	($p < .05$)	($p < .05$)	($p < .01$)

Table 5-4 (continued)

Hostility Levels (Mean Scores)

	SELF-ESTEEM IN HUSBANDS		SELF-ESTEEM IN WIVES	
Degree of Discontent with Husband's Full-time Job	Low	High	Low	High
Very dis-content	4.91 (34)+	1.16 (6)−	7.78 (32)+	4.66 (15)−
Discontent	3.80 (82)+	3.32 (52)−	4.76 (107)−	5.38 (44)+
Content	3.70 (91)+	3.20 (103)−	3.85 (149)+	3.13 (91)−
Very content	1.71 (14)−	2.00 (37)+	2.96 (30)+	2.31 (29)−
	df = 3 & 217	df = 3 & 194	df = 3 & 314	df = 3 & 175
	$F = 2.04$	$F = 1.68$	$F = 5.83$	$F = 3.60$
	(n.s.)	(n.s.)	$(p < .001)$	$(p < .05)$

Table 6-1

Economic-Opportunity Integration and Power in Conflict Resolution

	MALE PERCEPTION				FEMALE PERCEPTION			
			Frequency of Who Decides					
Years of Education	Wife	Hus-band	Together		Wife	Hus-band	Together	
0–8	39.1	51.6	9.4 (64)	100%	32.8	60.3	6.9 (58)	100%
9–11	28.0	53.3	18.7 (75)	100%	36.9	50.9	9.4 (106)	100%
12	33.3	46.2	20.5 (117)	100%	31.2	52.9	15.9 (189)	100%
13–15	42.9	34.7	22.4 (49)	100%	24.6	57.4	18.0 (61)	100%
16+	37.0	38.9	24.1 (54)	100%	30.2	44.2	25.6 (43)	100%
	df = 8				df = 8			
	$\chi^2 = 9.9$ (n.s.)				$\chi^2 = 13.1$ (n.s.)			
Level of Success Expectations								
Excellent	32.2	46.7	21.1 (90)	100%	30.9	47.2	22.0 (123)	100%
Fair	34.9	47.7	17.4 (172)	100%	32.4	54.3	13.2 (219)	100%
Limited	32.2	45.8	22.0 (59)	100%	38.9	55.6	5.6 (72)	100%
Poor	61.5	23.1	15.4 (13)	100%	31.8	63.6	4.5 (22)	100%
	df = 6				df = 6			
	$\chi^2 = 5.3$ (n.s.)				$\chi^2 = 13.1$ $(p < .05)$			

Table 6-2

Opportunity Articulation and Male Authority Ideology

	Male Authority Idelology (Mean Scores) (High = Modern; Low = Traditional)	
Annual Income	HUSBANDS	WIVES
Poor	2.72 (86)	3.04 (135)
Fair	3.04 (115)	3.04 (120)
Good	2.98 (96)	2.99 (113)
High	2.96 (103)	2.75 (108)
	df = 3 & 396	df = 3 & 472
	F = 2.12 (n.s.)	F = 2.93 (p < .05)
Degree of Discontent with Husband's Full-time Job		
Very discontent	2.92 (40)	3.10 (47)
Discontent	2.89 (134)	3.04 (151)
Content	2.97 (194)	2.94 (240)
Very content	2.86 (51)	2.55 (59)
	df = 3 & 415	df = 3 & 493
	F = .28 (n.s.)	F = 4.93 (p < .01)
Degree of Status Estrangement		
Low	2.90 (162)	2.82 (212)
Medium	2.98 (78)	3.05 (109)
High	2.92 (179)	3.05 (175)
	df = 2 & 416	df = 2 & 493
	F = .19 (n.s.)	F = 3.36 (p < .05)
Level of Occupational Achievement Expectations for Husband		
Poor	2.86 (37)	3.23 (30)
Fair	2.83 (100)	3.06 (119)
Good	2.89 (143)	2.82 (172)
	df = 2 & 277	df = 2 & 318
	F = .14 (n.s.)	F = 4.04 (p < .05)
Level of Success Expectations		
Excellent	2.83 (108)	2.70 (131)
Fair	2.93 (189)	3.00 (234)
Somewhat limited	2.98 (68)	3.16 (79)
Very poor	2.66 (18)	3.24 (25)
	df = 3 & 379	df = 3 & 465
	F = .84 (n.s.)	F = 6.26 (p < .001)

Table 6-3

Education, Wife Employment, and Conflict Resolution

Households—Wife Employed

	MALE PERCEPTION					FEMALE PERCEPTION				
		Hus-					Hus-			
Years of Education	Wife	band	Together			Wife	band	Together		
0–8	46.9+	43.8−	9.4=	(32)	100%	36.4+	54.5−	9.1+	(22)	100%
9–11	32.4+	52.9−	14.7−	(34)	100%	45.0+	50.0−	5.0−	(40)	100%
12	30.2−	49.1+	20.8+	(53)	100%	32.5+	55.8+	11.7−	(77)	100%
13–15	34.8+	34.8+	30.4+	(23)	100%	37.5+	56.3+	6.3−	(16)	100%
16+	25.0−	41.7+	33.3+	(12)	100%	44.4+	44.4+	11.1−	(18)	100%

$df = 8$ $\qquad$ $df = 8$

$\chi^2 = 7.9$ (n.s.) $\qquad$ $\chi^2 = 3.3$ (n.s.)

Households—Wife Not Employed

Years of Education	Wife	Hus-band	Together			Wife	Hus-band	Together		
0–8	31.3−	59.4+	9.4=	(32)	100%	28.6−	65.7+	5.7−	(35)	100%
9–11	24.4−	53.7+	22.0+	(41)	100%	36.4−	51.5+	12.1+	(66)	100%
12	37.1+	41.9−	21.0−	(62)	100%	30.4−	50.9−	18.8+	(112)	100%
13–15	50.0+	34.6−	15.4−	(46)	100%	20.0−	57.8+	22.2+	(45)	100%
16+	40.5+	38.1−	21.4−	(42)	100%	20.0−	44.0−	36.0+	(25)	100%

$df = 8$ $\qquad$ $df = 8$

$\chi^2 = 8.9$ (n.s.) $\qquad$ $\chi^2 = 14.3$ (n.s.)

Table 6-4

Discontent, Wife Employment, and Male Authority Ideology

Authority Ideology (Mean Scores)

(High = Modern; Low = Traditional)

Degree of Discontent	Wife Employed		Wife Not Employed	
	Husbands	Wives	Husbands	Wives
Very dis-content	2.86 (22)−	3.28 (21)+	3.00 (18)+	2.96 (26)−
Discontent	2.94 (59)+	3.06 (73)+	2.84 (73)−	3.03 (78)−
Content	3.04 (74)+	3.01 (79)+	2.94 (119)−	2.90 (78)−
Very content	3.04 (21)+	2.36 (11)−	2.73 (30)−	2.60 (48)+

	$df = 3$ & 172	$df = 3$ & 180	$df = 3$ & 236	$df = 3$ & 308
	$F = .30$	$F = 3.43$	$F = .46$	$F = 2.64$
	(n.s.)	$(p < .05)$	(n.s.)	$(p < .05)$

Table 7-1

Objective Economic-Opportunity Integration and Child Achievement Values (Mean Scores)

Husband's	HUSBANDS			WIVES	
SEI Ranking	Passivity	Mastery*		Passivity	Mastery*
00–19	5.22 (109)	8.15		5.12 (116)	7.75
20–39	3.63 (112)	8.33		2.97 (125)	7.50
40–59	2.31 (83)	7.49		2.56 (100)	7.45
60–79	1.29 (88)	7.01		1.90 (114)	6.71
80–96	1.04 (23)	7.00		1.12 (39)	6.23
	df = 4 & 410			df = 4 & 489	
	F = 24.44	F = 7.57		F = 17.65	F = 7.03
	(p < .001)	(p < .001)		(p < .001)	(p < .001)
Years of Education					
0–8	6.39 (83)	8.38		7.00 (68)	8.41
9–11	3.98 (86)	8.19		3.76 (115)	7.86
12	2.03 (133)	7.85		2.46 (200)	7.15
13–15	1.66 (54)	7.27		1.06 (64)	6.42
16+	1.16 (61)	6.49		0.57 (49)	5.83
	df = 4 & 412			df = 4 & 491	
	F = 42.73	F = 9.99		F = 44.55	F = 18.57
	(p < .001)	(p < .001)		(p < .001)	(p < .001)
Annual Income					
Poor	5.32 (86)	8.41		5.08 (135)	8.02
Fair	3.10 (115)	7.80		2.80 (120)	7.09
Good	2.27 (96)	7.68		2.32 (113)	6.86
High	1.59 (103)	7.08		1.29 (108)	6.91
	df = 3 & 396			df = 3 & 472	
	F = 24.84	F = 6.61		F = 28.50	F = 9.19
	(p < .001)	(p < .001)		(p < .001)	(p < .001)

*The N and df are identical in each instance to those in the passivity columns.

Table 7-2

Alienation and Child Achievement Values (Mean Scores)

	HUSBANDS		WIVES	
Degree of Perceived Powerlessness	Passivity	Mastery*	Passivity	Mastery*
Low	2.68 (158)	7.69	2.31 (119)	7.36
Average	3.25 (221)	7.78	2.98 (296)	7.17
High	4.70 (34)	7.97	4.26 (76)	7.51
	df = 2 & 410		df = 2 & 488	
	$F = 5.01$	$F = .25$	$F = 6.76$	$F = .96$
	($p < .01$)	(n.s.)	($p < .01$)	(n.s.)
Degree of Discontent with Husband's Full-time Job				
Very Discontent	5.22 (40)	8.95	5.91 (47)	8.31
Discontent	4.29 (134)	8.07	3.77 (151)	7.41
Content	2.36 (194)	7.47	2.37 (240)	7.18
Very content	1.31 (51)	7.03	1.33 (59)	6.44
	df = 3 & 415		df = 3 & 493	
	$F = 20.41$	$F = 9.08$	$F = 21.09$	$F = 7.82$
	($p < .001$)	($p < .001$)	($p < .001$)	($p < .001$)
Degree of Status Estrangement				
Low	2.16 (162)	7.55	1.92 (212)	7.01
Medium	2.37 (78)	7.57	2.62 (109)	6.80
High	4.32 (179)	8.01	4.56 (175)	7.88
	df = 2 & 416		df = 2 & 493	
	$F = 20.64$	$F = 2.38$	$F = 28.91$	$F = 12.36$
	($p < .001$)	(n.s.)	($p < .001$)	($p < .001$)

*The N and df are identical in each instance to those in the passivity columns.

Table 7-3

Anomie and Child Achievement Values (Mean Scores)

Level of Occupational Achievement Expectations for Husband	HUSBANDS		WIVES	
	Passivity	Mastery*	Passivity	Mastery*
Poor	4.40 (37)	8.37	4.80 (30)	8.13
Fair	3.42 (100)	7.65	3.00 (119)	7.33
Good	1.77 (143)	7.54	2.47 (172)	7.04
	df = 2 & 277		df = 2 & 318	
	F = 14.59	F = 2.42	F = 6.12	F = 3.68
	(p < .001)	(n.s.)	(p < .01)	(p < .05)
Level of Success Expectations				
Excellent	178 (108)	7.53	1.90 (131)	6.89
Fair	3.07 (189)	7.59	2.91 (234)	7.35
Somewhat limited	4.04 (68)	8.02	3.63 (79)	7.24
Very poor	4.00 (18)	8.50	8.20 (25)	8.24
	df = 3 & 379		df = 3 & 465	
	F = 7.92	F = 1.83	F = 24.89	F = 3.41
	(p < .001)	(n.s.)	(p < .001)	(p < .05)

*The N and df are identical in each instance to those in the *passivity* columns.

Table 7-4

Education, Anomy, and Child Achievement Values (Mean Scores)

Degree of Anomy

HUSBANDS

Years of Education	Passivity		Mastery	
	Low	High	Low	High
0–8	3.60 (15)−	7.01 (68)+	8.66 (15)+	8.32 (68)−
9–11	2.36 (25)−	4.65 (61)+	7.48 (25)−	8.49 (61)+
12	1.26 (71)−	2.91 (62)+	7.74 (71)−	7.98 (62)+
13–15	1.35 (34)−	2.20 (20)+	6.73 (34)−	8.20 (20)+
16+	0.87 (49)−	2.33 (12)+	6.34 (49)−	7.08 (12)+
	df = 4 & 189	df = 4 & 218	df = 4 & 189	df = 4 & 218
	F = 7.01	F = 16.75	F = 5.30	F = 1.79
	(p < .001	(p < .001)	(p < .001)	(n.s.)

237

Table 7-4 (continued)

Degree of Anomy

WIVES

	Passivity		Mastery	
Years of Education	*Low*	*High*	*Low*	*High*
0–8	3.12 (8)−	7.51 (60)+	7.75 (8)−	8.50 (60)+
9–11	2.17 (28)−	4.27 (87)+	7.60 (28)−	7.95 (87)+
12	1.39 (83)−	3.22 (117)+	6.66 (83)−	7.50 (117)+
13–15	1.00 (46)−	1.22 (18)+	6.28 (46)−	6.77 (18)+
16+	0.42 (38)−	1.09 (11)+	5.97 (38)+	5.36 (11)−
	df = 4 & 198	df = 4 & 288	df = 4 & 198	df = 4 & 288
	$F = 5.61$	$F = 20.34$	$F = 3.18$	$F = 10.06$
	$(p < .001)$	$(p < .001)$	$(p < .05)$	$(p < .001)$

Table 7-5

Comparison of Respondent's Own Orientations and His Perception of Own Spouse with regard to Passivity Values

	(Mean Scores)				H–W	(Mean Scores)		H > W		H–W
Years of Education	Husband	Spouse	Difference	F ratio	r	Wife	Spouse	Difference	F ratio	r
0–8	6.39*	5.91	.48 H > W	n.s., .61	.88	7.00*	7.11	.11	n.s., .02	.88
9–11	3.98	3.96	.02 H > W	n.s., .00	.83	3.76	4.61	.85	n.s., 2.93	.77
12	2.03	2.16	.13 W > H	n.s., .19	.68	2.46	3.02	.56	n.s., 3.14	.77
13–15	1.66	1.64	.02 H > W	n.s., .00	.77	1.06	1.79	.73	n.s., 3.62	.42
16+	1.16	1.44	.28 W > H	n.s., .67	.82	0.57	0.71	.14	n.s., .37	.80
Level of Success Ex-pectations										
Excellent	1.78†	1.92	.14 W > H	n.s., .16	.68	1.90†	2.21	.31	n.s., .73	.82
Fair	3.07	3.20	.13 W > H	n.s., .16	.91	2.91	3.58	.67	$p < .05$; 4.06	.79
Limited	4.04	3.61	.43 H > W	n.s., .37	.84	3.63	4.27	.64	n.s., 1.22	.81
Poor	4.00	3.77	.23 H > W	n.s., .02	.94	8.20	8.68	.48	n.s., .12	.80

*For N here, see Table 7-1.
†For N here, see Table 7-3.

Table 7-6

Comparison of Respondent's Own Orientations and His Perceptions of Own Spouse with regard to Mastery Values

	(Mean Scores)			H–W		(Mean Scores)		H > W	H–W	
	Husband	Spouse	Difference	F ratio	r	Wife	Spouse	Difference	F ratio	r
Years of Education										
0–8	8.38*	8.42	.04 W > H	n.s., .01	.72	8.41*	8.54	.13	n.s., .20	.61
9–11	8.19	8.15	.04 W > H	n.s., .02	.80	7.86	8.12	.26	n.s., 1.13	.62
12	7.85	7.61	.24 H > W	n.s., .82	.80	7.15	7.45	.30	n.s., 2.48	.69
13–15	7.27	7.09	.08 H > W	n.s., .18	.84	6.42	6.75	.33	n.s., .70	.75
16+	6.49	6.36	.13 H > W	n.s., .11	.72	5.83	6.36	.53	n.s., 1.34	.87
Level of Success Expectations										
Excellent	7.53†	7.14	.39 H > W	n.s., 1.50	.84	6.89†	7.16	.27	n.s., 1.07	.78
Fair	7.59	7.57	.02 H > W	n.s., .01	.78	7.35	7.65	.30	n.s., 2.54	.76
Limited	8.02	8.07	.05 W > H	n.s., .01	.75	7.24	7.48	.24	n.s., .64	.64
Poor	8.50	8.22	.28 H > W	n.s., .28	.81	8.24	8.40	.16	n.s., .08	.57

*For N here, see Table 7-1.
†For N here, see Table 7-3.

Bibliography

Bert N. Adams, *Kinship in an Urban Setting,* Chicago: Markham, 1968.

Norman W. Bell and Ezra F. Vogel, "Toward a Framework for Functional Analysis of Family Behavior," in Norman W. Bell and Ezra F. Vogel, *A Modern Introduction to the Family,* New York: The Free Press, 1960.

Robert R. Bell, *Premarital Sex in a Changing Society,* Englewood Cliffs, N.J.: Prentice-Hall, 1966.

Robert R. Bell, *Studies in Marriage and the Family,* New York: Thomas R. Crowell Co., 1968.

Jessie Bernard, "Developmental Tasks of the NCFR-1963–1988," *Journal of Marriage & the Family,* 26 (February, 1964).

Bruce J. Biddle and Edwin J. Thomas, *Role Theory: Concepts & Research,* New York: John Wiley & Sons, 1966.

Hubert M. Blalock, Jr., *Social Statistics,* New York: McGraw-Hill Book Co., 1960.

Peter M. Blau, *Exchange and Power in Social Life,* New York: John Wiley & Sons, 1964.

Peter M. Blau and Otis Dudley Duncan, *The American Occupational Structure,* New York: John Wiley & Sons, 1967.

Robert O. Blood Jr., *Love Match & Arranged Marriage,* New York: The Free Press, 1967.

Robert O. Blood, Jr., "The Measurement and Bases of Family Power: A Rejoinder," *Marriage & Family Living,* 25 (November, 1963).

Robert O. Blood, Jr., and Donald M. Wolfe, *Husbands and Wives,* New York: The Free Press, 1960.

Walter Buckley, *Sociology and Modern Systems Theory,* Englewood Cliffs, N.J.: Prentice-Hall, 1967.

Lee G. Burchinal, "The Premarital Dyad and Love Involvement," in Harold T. Christensen, ed., *Handbook of Marriage and the Family,* Chicago: Rand McNally, 1964.

Ernest W. Burgess, Harvey J. Locke, and Mary Margaret Thomes, *The Family,* New York: American Book Co., 1963 (Third Edition).

Glen G. Cain, *Married Women in the Labor Force,* Chicago: University of Chicago Press, 1966.

W. F. Calverton, *The Bankruptcy of Marriage,* New York: The Macaulay Co., 1928.

Ely Chinoy, *Automobile Workers and the American Dream,* Garden City, N.Y.: Doubleday & Co., 1955.

John P. Clark, "Measuring Alienation Within a Social System," *American Sociological Review,* 24 (December, 1959).

John A. Clausen, *Socialization and Society,* Boston: Little, Brown & Co., 1968.

Marshall B. Clinard, ed., *Anomie & Deviant Behavior,* The Free Press, New York, 1964.

Richard A. Cloward and Lloyd E. Ohlin, *Delinquency & Opportunity,* New York: The Free Press, 1960.

Stanley Coopersmith, *The Antecedents of Self-Esteem,* San Francisco: W. H. Freeman Co., 1967.

241

Bibliography

Ruth Laub Coser, ed., *The Family: Its Structure and Functions,* New York: St. Martin's Press, 1964.

Henrietta Cox, "Study of Social Class Variations in Value Orientations in Selected Areas of Mother-Child Behavior" (unpublished doctoral dissertation, Washington University, St. Louis, 1964).

Dwight G. Dean, "Alienation and Marital Adjustment" (unpublished paper, Dennison University, 1965).

Robert Dubin, *The World of Work,* Englewood Cliffs, N.J.: Prentice-Hall, 1958.

John N. Edwards, "The Future of the Family Revisited," *Journal of Marriage & the Family,* 29 (August, 1967).

Nelson N. Foote, "Sex as Play," *Social Problems,* (April, 1954).

H. Kent Geiger, ed., *Comparative Perspectives on Marriage & the Family,* Boston: Little, Brown & Co., 1968.

David Gold, "Statistical Tests and Substantive Significance," *The American Sociologist,* 4 (February, 1969).

William J. Goode, *After Divorce,* New York: The Free Press, 1956.

William J. Goode, "Family Disorganization," *Contemporary Social Problems,* Robert K. Merton and Robert A. Nisbet, eds., New York: Harcourt, Brace & World, 1966 (rev.).

William J. Goode, "The Theoretical Importance of Love," *American Sociological Review,* 24 (February, 1959).

William J. Goode, *World Revolution and Family Patterns,* New York: The Free Press, 1963.

Milton M. Gordon, *Social Class in American Sociology,* Durham, N.C.: Duke University Press, 1958.

Alvin W. Gouldner, "The Norm of Reciprocity: A Preliminary Statement," *American Sociological Review,* 25 (April, 1960).

Sidney M. Greenfield, *English Rustics in Black Skin,* New Haven, Conn.: College & University Press, 1966.

H. Theodore Groat and Arthur G. Neal, "Social Psychological Correlates of Urban Fertility," *American Sociological Review,* 32 (December, 1967).

David M. Heer, "Dominance & the Working Wife," *Social Forces,* 36 (May, 1958).

David M. Heer, "The Measurement & Bases of Family Power: An Overview," *Marriage & Family Living,* 25 (May, 1963).

Reuben Hill, "Contemporary Developments in Family Theory," *Journal of Marriage & the Family,* 28 (February, 1966).

Reuben Hill and Donald A. Hansen, "The Identification of Conceptual Frameworks Utilized in Family Study," *Marriage and Family Living,* 22 (November, 1960).

Lois Wladis Hoffman, "The Decision to Work," in Lois W. Hoffman and F. Ivan Nye, eds., *The Employed Mother in America,* Chicago: Rand McNally, 1963.

Edwin P. Hollander, *Principles and Methods of Social Psychology,* New York: Oxford University Press, 1967.

George C. Homans, *Social Behavior: Its Elementary Forms,* New York: Harcourt, Brace & World, 1961.

Joseph A. Kahl, "Some Measurements of Achievement Orientation," *American Journal of Sociology,* 70 (May, 1965).

Leslie Kish, "Confidence Intervals for Clustered Samples," *American Sociological Review,* 22 (April, 1957).

Leslie Kish, "A Two-Stage Sample of a City," *American Sociological Review,* 17 (1952).

Melvin L. Kohn, "Social Class and Parental Relationships: An Interpretation," *American Journal of Sociology,* 68 (January, 1963).

Melvin L. Kohn and Eleanor E. Carroll, "Social Class and the Allocation of Parental Responsibilities," *Sociometry,* 23 (1960).

Mirra Komarovoky, *Blue-Collar Marriage,* New York: Random House, 1962.

Gerhard Lenski, *The Religious Factor,* Garden City, N.Y.: Doubleday Anchor Books, 1963.

242

Bibliography

Gerald R. Leslie, *The Family in Social Context,* New York: Oxford University Press, 1967.

George Levinger, "Marital Cohesiveness and Dissolution: An Integrative Review," *Journal of Marriage & the Family,* 27 (February, 1965).

Elliot Liebow, *Tally's Corner,* Boston: Little-Brown & Co., 1967.

Seymour Martin Lipset, "Students & Politics in Comparative Perspective," *Daedalus,* 97 (Winter, 1968).

David C. McClelland, *The Achieving Society,* New York: The Free Press, 1967 (paperback).

Herbert McClosky and John N. Schaar, "Psychological Dimensions of Anomy," *American Sociological Review,* 30 (February, 1965).

Donald G. McKinley, *Social Class & Family Life,* New York: The Free Press, 1964.

Robert K. Merton, "Anomie, Anomia and Social Interaction" in Clinard, *op. cit.*

Robert K. Merton, "Intermarriage and the Social Structure: Fact & Theory," *Psychiatry,* August, 1941.

Robert K. Merton, "Social Structure & Anomie: Revisions and Extensions," in Ruth Nanda Anshen, ed., *The Family: Its Function & Destiny,* New York: Harper & Row, 1959 (rev.).

Robert K. Merton, *Social Theory and Social Structure,* New York: The Free Press, 1957 (rev.).

Ephraim Harold Mizruchi, *Success & Opportunity,* New York: The Free Press, 1964.

John Mogey, "Contemporary Developments in Family Theory: A Discussion," *Journal of Marriage and the Family,* 28 (February, 1966).

George Peter Murdock, *Social Structure,* New York: The Free Press, 1949.

Arthur G. Neal and Salomon Rettig, "On the Multidimensionality of Alienation," *American Sociological Review,* 32 (February, 1967).

Susan R. Orden and Norman B. Bradburn, "Dimensions of Marriage Happiness," *American Journal of Sociology,* 73 (May, 1968).

Talcott Parsons, "The American Family: Its Relations to Personality and to the Social Structure," in Talcott Parsons and Robert F. Bales, *Family, Socialization and Interaction Process,* New York: The Free Press, 1955, pp. 3–33.

Talcott Parsons, *The Social System,* New York: The Free Press, 1951.

Leonard Pearlin, "Alienation from Work: A Study of Nursing Personnel," *American Sociological Review,* 27 (June, 1962).

Leonard I. Pearlin and Melvin L. Kohn, "Social Class, Occupation, and Parental Values: A Cross-National Study," *American Sociological Review,* 36 (August, 1966).

Peter Pineo, "Disenchantment in the Later Years of Marriage," *Marriage & Family Living,* 23 (February, 1961).

Theodore V. Purcell, *Blue Collar Man,* Cambridge, Mass.: Harvard University Press, 1960.

Lee Rainwater, *And the Poor Get Children,* Chicago: Quadrangle Books, 1960.

Lee Rainwater, "Crucible of Identity: The Negro Lower-Class Family," in Gerald Handel, *The Psychosocial Interior of the Family,* Chicago: Aldine Publishing Co., 1967.

Lee Rainwater, "Marital Sexuality in Four Cultures of Poverty," *Journal of Marriage & the Family,* 26 (November, 1964).

Stephen Richer, "The Economics of Child Rearing," *Journal of Marriage and the Family,* 30 (August, 1968).

Hyman Rodman, "Marital Power in France, Greece, Yugoslavia, and the United States: A Cross-National Discussion," *Journal of Marriage & the Family,* 29 (May, 1967).

Bernard C. Rosen, "Family Structure and Value-Transmission," *Merrill-Palmer Quarterly,* 1964.

Morris Rosenberg, *Society and the Adolescent Self-Image,* Princeton, N.J.: Princeton University Press, 1965.

Alice S. Rossi, "Barriers to the Career Choice of Engineering, Medicine or Science

Among American Women," in J. A. Mattfeld and C. G. Van Aken, *Women and the Scientific Professions,* Cambridge, Mass.: The M.I.T. Press, 1965.

John Scanzoni, "Resolution of Occupational-Conjugal Role Conflict in Clergy Marriages," *Journal of Marriage & the Family,* 27 (August, 1965).

John R. Seeley, R. Alexander Sim, and Elizabeth W. Loosley, *Crestwood Heights,* N.Y.: John Wiley & Sons, 1963 edition.

Melvin Seeman, "On the Meaning of Alienation," *American Sociological Review,* 24 (December, 1959).

Melvin Seeman, "On the Personal Consequences of Alienation in Work," *American Sociological Review,* 32 (April, 1967).

William H. Sewell, "Some Recent Developments in Socialization Theory and Research," in M. B. Sussman, ed., *Source book in Marriage and the Family,* Boston: Houghton-Mifflin Co., 1968.

Tamotsu Shibutani, *Society and Personality,* Englewood Cliffs, N.J.: Prentice-Hall, 1961.

Raymond T. Smith, *The Negro Family in British Guiana,* London: Routledge & Kegan Paul, 1956.

John P. Spiegel, "The Resolution of Role Conflict Within the Family," in Norman W. Bell and Ezra F. Vogel, eds., *A Modern Introduction to the Family,* N.Y.: The Free Press, 1960.

Sheldon Stryker, "The Interactional and Situational Approaches," in Harold T. Christensen, ed., *Handbook of Marriage & the Family,* Chicago: Rand McNally, 1964.

Sheldon Stryker, "Role Taking: Accuracy & Adjustment," *Sociometry,* 20 (1957).

Marvin B. Sussman, "Theoretical Bases for an Urban Kinship Network System" (unpublished paper, Case-Western Reserve University, Cleveland, 1966).

Irving Tallman, "Residential Differences in Marital Interaction and Anomia Among Working-Class Families" (unpublished paper, University of Minnesota, 1967).

John W. Thibaut and Harold H. Kelley, *The Social Psychology of Groups,* N.Y.. John Wiley & Sons, 1959.

Ralph H. Turner, *The Social Context of Ambition,* San Francisco: Chandler Publishing Co., 1964.

Ezra Vogel, *Japan's New Middle Class,* Berkeley, California: University of California Press, 1963.

Max Weber, *The Protestant Ethic and the Spirit of Capitalism,* N.Y.: Charles Scribner's Sons, 1958.

Harold L. Wilensky, "Work as a Social Problem," in Howard S. Becker, ed., *Social Problems: A Modern Approach,* N.Y.: John Wiley & Sons, 1966.

Robin M. Williams, Jr., *American Society,* N.Y.: Alfred A. Knopf, 1960 edition.

Robert C. Williamson, "Economic Factors in Marital Adjustment," *Marriage & Family Living,* 14 (1952), pp. 298–301; and "Socio-Economic Factors & Marital Adjustment in an Urban Setting," *American Sociological Review,* 19 (1954), pp. 213–216.

Robert F. Winch, *The Modern Family,* N.Y.: Holt, Rinehart & Winston, 1963 (rev.).

Index